how to build
BOOKCASES and STEREO CABINETS

Wall to Wall • Built-in • Free Standing
Sectional • Lo Boy • High Boy • Record Cabinet

Donald R. Brann

REVISED EDITION — 1980

Published by

EASI-BILD DIRECTIONS SIMPLIFIED, INC.
BRIARCLIFF MANOR, NY 10510

Library of Congress Catalog No. 79-56769

Allow Fate to Lend a Helping Hand

Ever notice what strange ways some people "strike it rich?" A destitute miner drops off a slow moving freight and discovers a gold mine. Treasure hunters locate a sunken ship containing millions of dollars worth of Spanish bullion because a storm and a drunken navigator miscalculated a previously scheduled exploration site. Because I couldn't afford to make a wrong cut, luck smiled when I applied the concept of a dress pattern to lumber. And so it goes, everyone is given great opportunities if they allow fate to lend a hand.

While no one really knows what the future holds, most good luck stems from one single source — problems. These are fate's hand maidens. Every problem you solve creates stimuli that power forward movement. Every step forward creates new and larger problems. Accept each as a step up the stairs to good fortune, and you soon sit in the sunshine of success.

The biography of every important person is woven with the same golden thread. Each continually attempted doing something they had never done before. Without fully recognizing the process, each lived comparable lives filled with doing.

When you realize a minute today is worth an hour tomorrow, and invest these precious minutes in constructive effort, fate does lend a hand.

TABLE OF CONTENTS

BUILT-INS ARE EASY TO BUILD

Learning to build one bookcase, or a wall to wall built-in, provides a fun and profitable way to invest spare time. Everyone who has learned to drive a car, cook, sew or saw can build handsome cabinets wall to wall or floor to ceiling, to fill whatever space is available. Those living in an apartment or in a rented house should build free standing cabinets. Getting on site job experience building what you need helps amateurs make like pros. Those wanting to start a part or full time business should take a picture of each project and show it to those most likely to buy. Homeowners and professionals, doctors, lawyers and most commercial business need office furniture. Those offered in this book can fill a big market.

This free standing bookcase measures 11¼ x 35½ x 6'6¾''. Solid doors in base and glass doors in top cabinet provide excellent display and storage for books, china, glassware, etc. Professionals are prime customers for this size cabinet. Directions for building begin on page 36.

(3)

Framing a door with one or more units adds a "built-in" quality with no need to drive nails or brackets into a wall or floor.

This handsome unit can frame a window, mirror or door. The base cabinet provides considerable storage space. Simplified directions permit building to size specified or to size desired. Directions begin on page 52.

(5)

Hinged cabinet doors and sliding drawers in this free standing or wall to wall unit have great appeal to apartment dwellers. See page 63 for step-by-step directions.

Since a bookcase and bar cabinet, Illus. 6, and room dividers, Illus. 7, are in popular demand, those interested in starting a part or full time business will find these projects easy to build and easy to sell. All can be built to size specified or to size needed to fill space available.

Youngsters taking vocational training find building these room dividers, Illus. 7, and sectional bookcases, Illus. 8, a profitable way to learn woodworking.

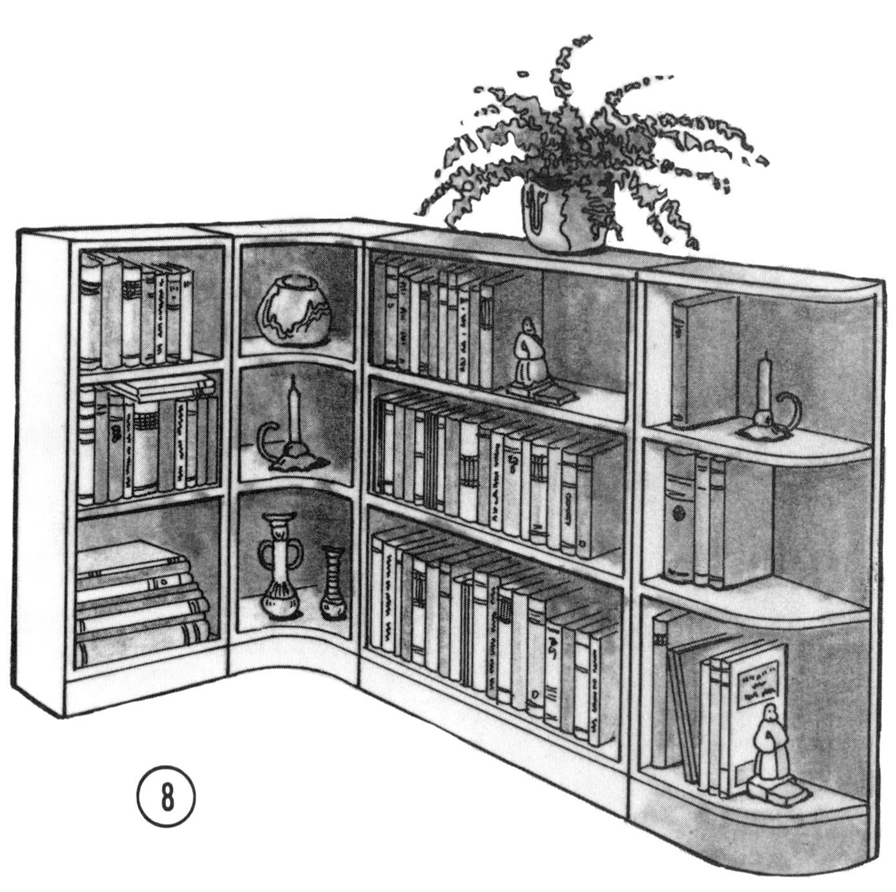

This sectional bookcase contains matching units. The corner and end cases should be built to size directions specify, while the bookcase can be built any length space permits. Directions starting on page 95 simplify building.

（9）

Stereo and speaker cabinets can be built as a free standing unit, or built-in. Directions specify and simplify use of acoustic fabric for speaker cabinet and for facing matching storage cabinets. Directions for building begin on page 111.

To fully appreciate how a professional makes each installation, read directions through completely before purchasing any material. Always apply glue where directions suggest. Dip screws in glue before driving.

Check end of each piece of lumber with a square before measuring length required. Always use a square when drawing each line, Illus. 10.

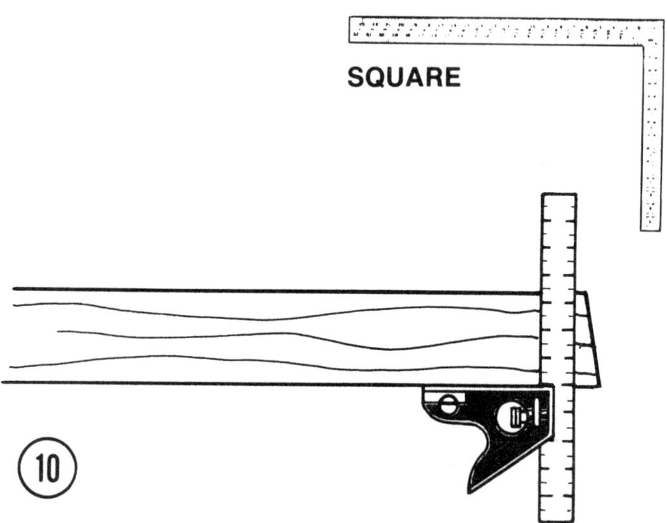

Those living in an apartment or rented house can build the wall to wall units, Illus. 1, 2, without nailing to wall, floor or ceiling. If the unit is free standing, it's yours. Nail it in and it belongs to the landlord. You could also be liable for damage if you drive nails into the floor or wall.

Transforming a blank wall into a handsome bookcase is a fun and constructive way to use time, one that can prove to be a richly rewarding and relaxing experience. The physical and mental effort pays instant dividends in providing hours of complete escape.

16

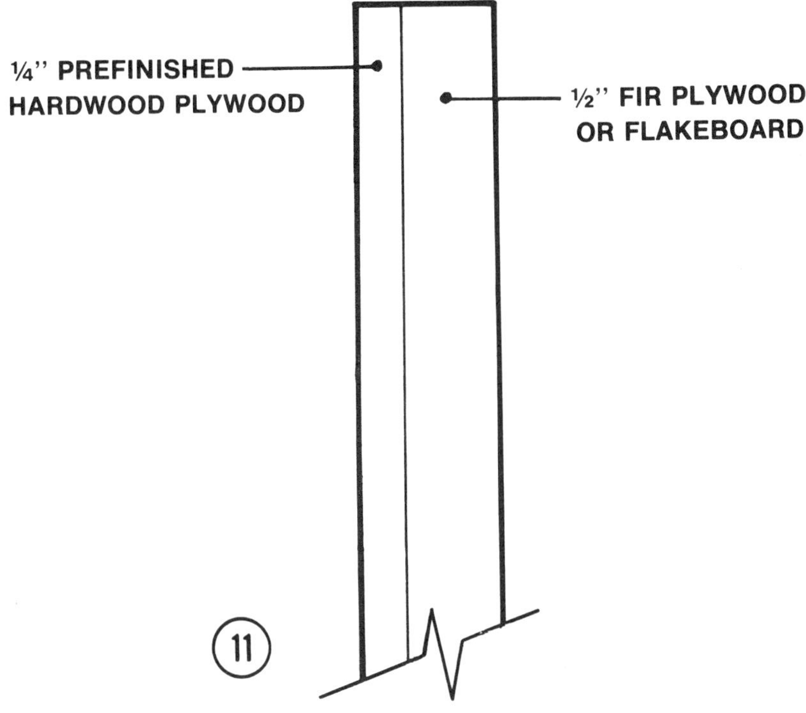

The list of material permits building the project to size noted. If you alter any dimension, buy material to length required. Those building in a paneled room should use matching plywood. While ¾" hardwood veneered plywood is available on special order, it's expensive. You can achieve the same effect, at considerably less cost, by gluing ¼" hardwood plywood to ½" fir plywood or flakeboard, Illus. 11. Edges can be finished by applying paper thin matching veneer available from your plywood dealer.

Doors can be made in the same way. The inside flakeboard face can be stained or painted.

WALL TO WALL BOOKCASE

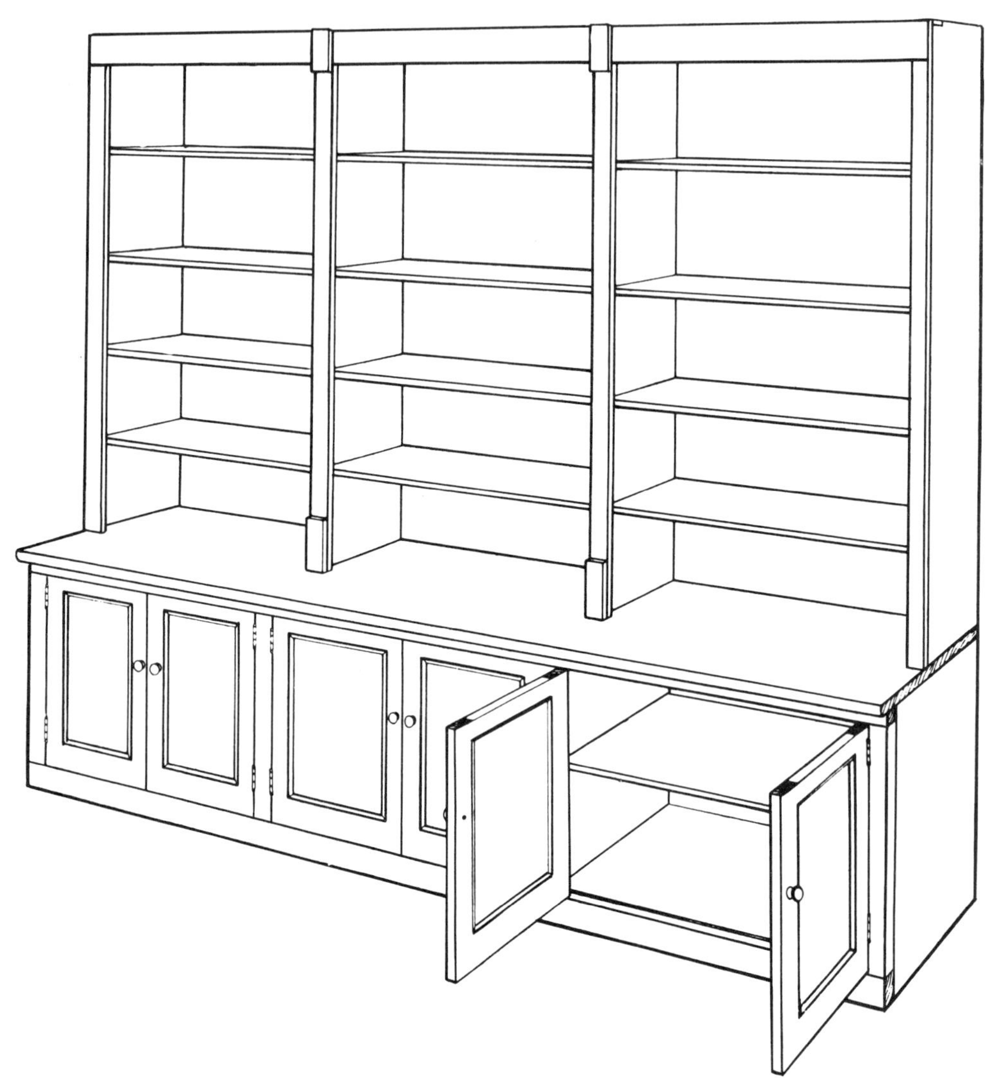

To build a wall to wall bookcase, Illus. 1, to cover a 12'0'' wall, 8'0'' high, you will need the following. If you order lumber as listed, it makes the retailer very happy. 1 x 2 — 4/12, 2/8 means four pieces 1 x 2 x 12', two pieces 1 x 2 x 8'.

LIST OF MATERIAL

1 x 2 — 4/12,2/8
1 x 3 — 4/12,1/8
1 x 6 — 1/12,1/14
1 x 8 — 5/12,1/8 or use ¾ x 4 x 8 plywood good two sides
1 x 10 — 6/12
1 x 12 — 1/14
5/4 x 3 — 3/12,1/10,1/8
5/4 x 4 — 1/12,1/10
1 — ⅜ x 4 x 6
36 lineal ft. ¼" quarter round
36 lineal ft. ⅜ x ½" stile or glass bead
14 lineal ft. 1¾ x 2" crown molding
10 lineal ft. ¾ x 2¼" pilaster molding
12 lineal ft. ¾" molding

1 box 1" brads
1 box ⅜" corrugated fasteners
1 lb. 4 penny finishing nails
1 lb. 6 penny finishing nails
1 doz. 2" No. 12 screws
9 doz. 1¼" No. 9 screws
50 lineal ft. of metal shelf standard
6 pairs 2½ x 1 11/16" loose pin butt hinges
6 bullet type cabinet door catches
6 — 1 or 1¼" door knobs or pulls

Consider stock lumber as measuring:

1 x 2 — ¾ x 1½"
1 x 6 — ¾ x 5½"
1 x 8 — ¾ x 7¼"
1 x 10 — ¾ x 9¼"
1 x 12 — ¾ x 11¼"
5/4 x 3 — 1-1/16 x 2½"
5/4 x 4 — 1-1/16 x 3½"

5/4" stock surfaced four sides (S4S) measures between 1 1/16 to 1⅛". Plywood and flakeboard measures full thickness specified.

If bookcase is to be painted, use ¾" flakeboard or fir plywood good two sides (both faces sanded).

TOOLS NEEDED

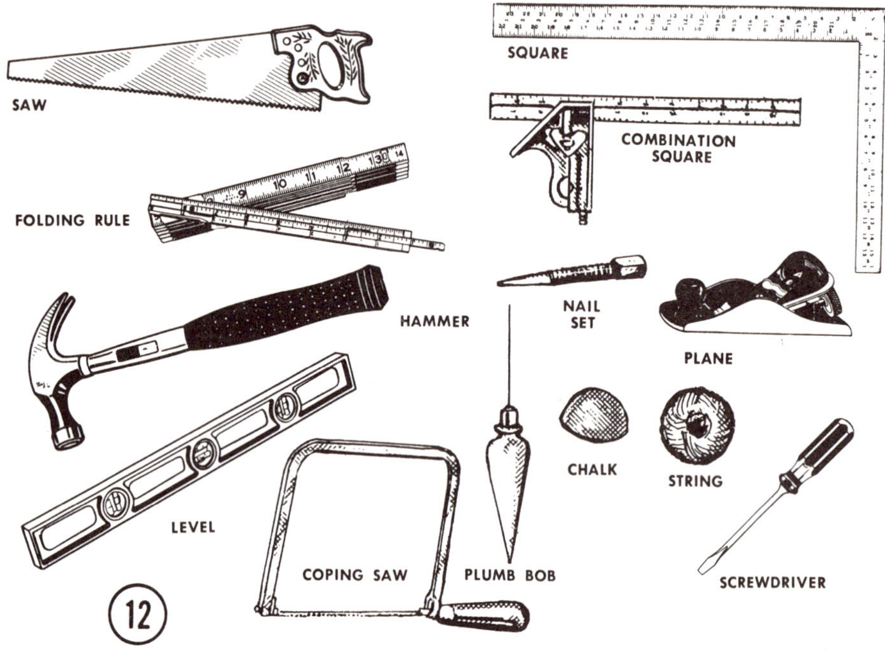

You will need a hammer, cross cut, rip and coping saw, plane, carpenter's square, combination square, chalk line, plumb bob, level, nailset, folding rule and screwdriver, Illus. 12. A chalk line simplifies marking straight lines on floor, wall or ceiling. You merely apply chalk to a line, stretch it between two points, hold taut against surface, snap, and you have a straight line.

20

To simplify construction and to build like a "pro," remove the shoe, baseboard and ceiling molding within area of bookcase, Illus. 13. Those who rent should not remove shoe or baseboard. It will be necessary to notch sides to receive shoe and base.

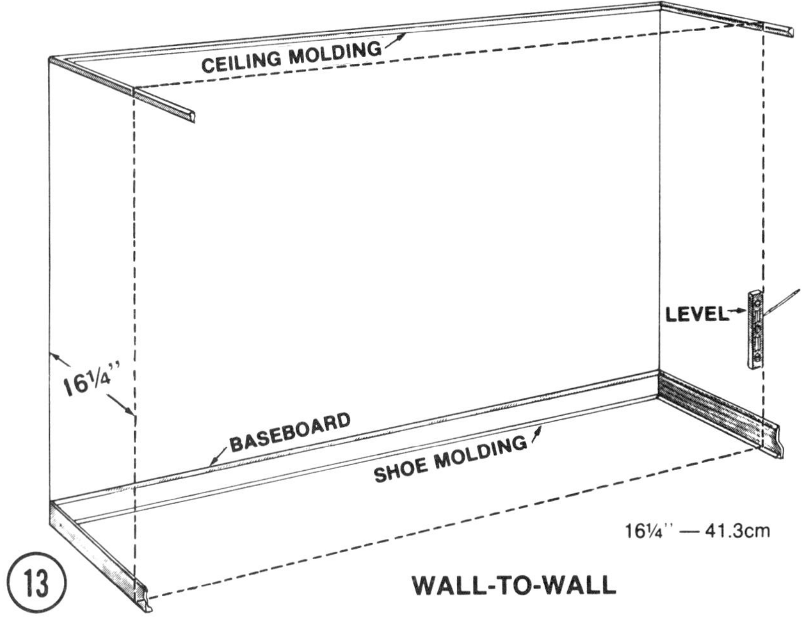

Measure 16¼" from back wall. Snap a chalk line on ceiling. Drop a plumb bob from ceiling line to floor. Snap a chalk line on floor. Now measure distance from line on floor to wall. If it measures 16¼" or more, it's OK. If it measures less than 16¼", move floor line to 16¼", snap a new line. Using plumb bob to guide you, snap a line on ceiling plumb with new line on floor.

As Illus. 14 indicates, a wall to wall bookcase consists of two ends A, and as many partitions as space requires. Space partitions three to four feet apart. If space necessitates placing a partition less than three feet, it's entirely satisfactory. We do not recommend partitions more than four feet apart.

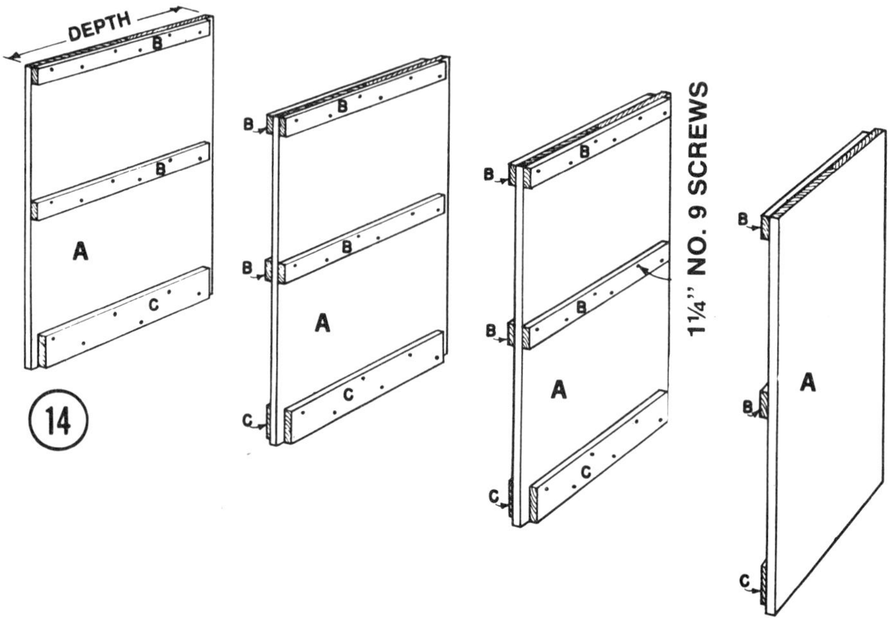

Illus. 15 shows a base cabinet as a separate unit. Building a base cabinet, then a bookcase on top, simplifies handling.

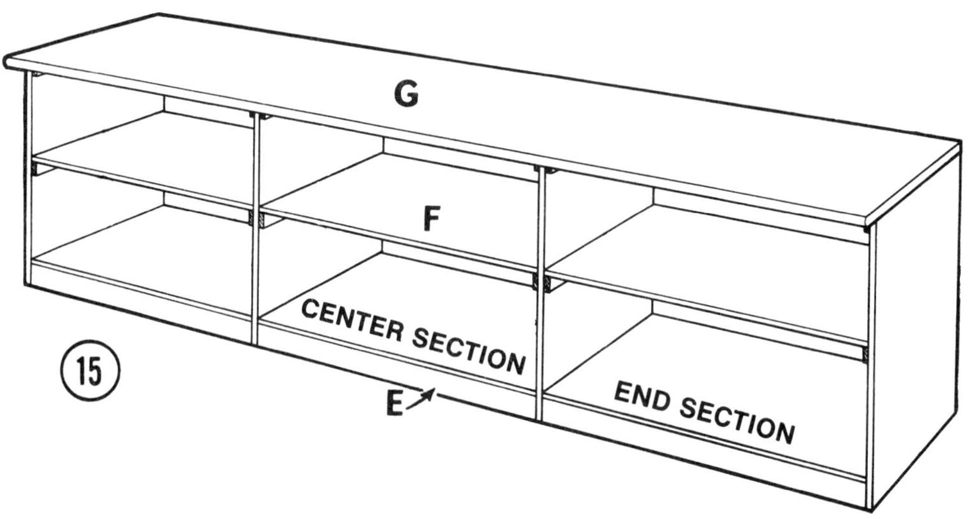

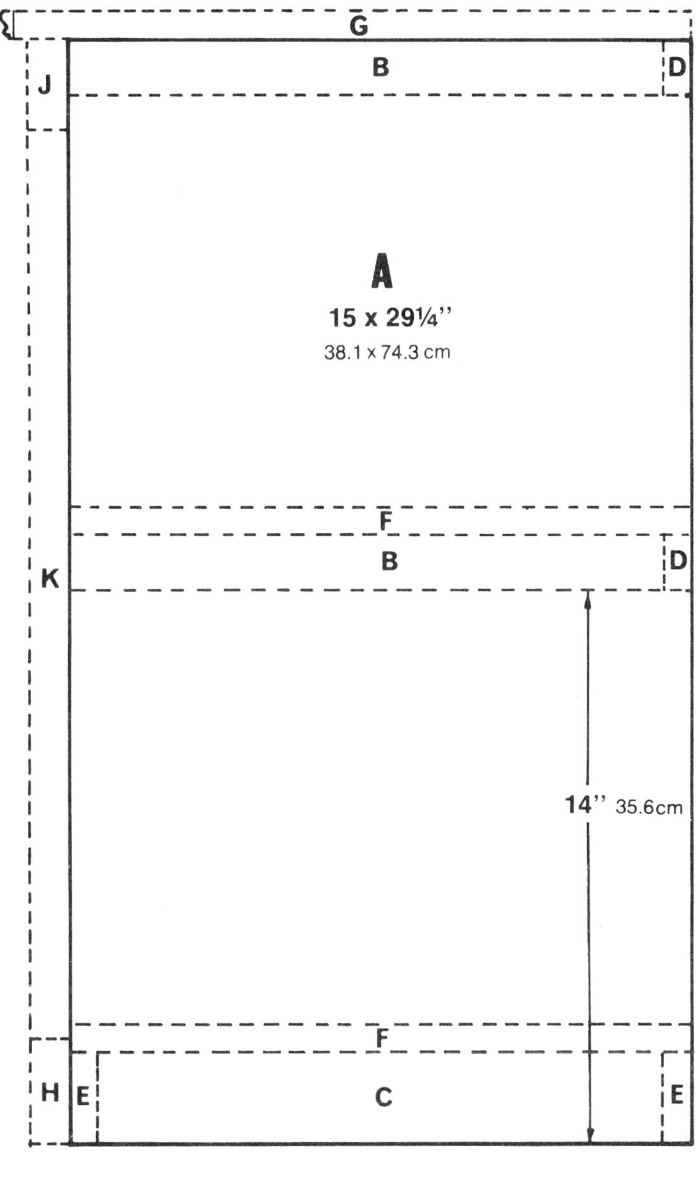

Step-by-step directions cover construction of a 12' built-in bookcase. Alter length to fit any other space.

Cut two ends A - 15 x 29¼", Illus. 14,16. Use ¾" plywood or flakeboard. Cut twelve 1 x 2 x 14¼" for B. Cut six 1 x 3 x 13½" for C. (B and C can also be cut from ¾" plywood.)

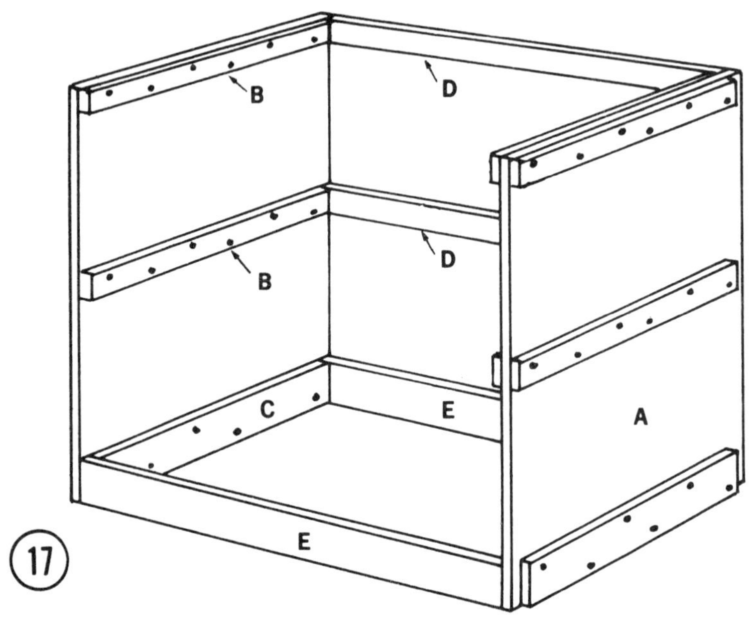

LUMBER SIZES

D — 1 x 2" S4S to ¾ x 1½"

E — 1 x 3" S4S to ¾ x 2½"

Apply glue and fasten B to inside of A, in position indicated, Illus. 16. Fasten C to A, ¾" from front and back edge of A to allow for E, using 1¼" No. 9 flathead screws.

Apply glue and fasten B and C in position shown, Illus. 14,16, to both sides of each partition. B is fastened flush at front and ¾" from back edge. C sets back ¾" from front and back edge on each partition.

Measure space where bookcase is to be installed. Divide into three equal parts, or build two equal end sections, Illus. 17. The center section can be equal in size to end section, smaller or larger, as space dictates.

24

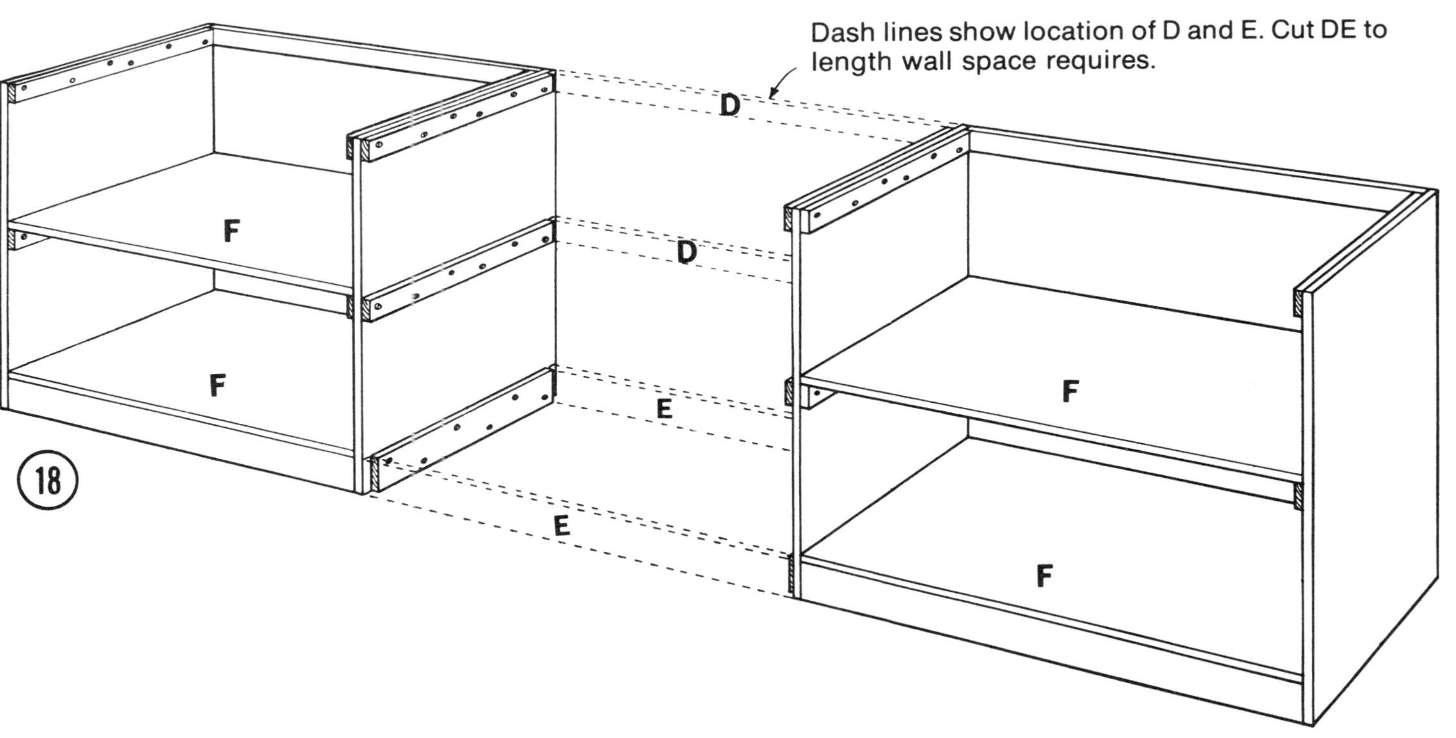

Dash lines show location of D and E. Cut DE to length wall space requires.
D
D
E
E
F
F
F
F
18

Cut four equal lengths of 1 x 2 for D, and four lengths of 1 x 3 for E, Illus. 18. Apply glue and nail A to E and D, D to B, E to C with 6 penny finishing nails.

Place assembly in position. Check with level. Using a piece of wood shingle, shim assembly level and plumb. Fasten end sections to wall using 2'' No. 12 screws or toenail to floor. In rented space, just shim in level and plumb position. Do not fasten to floor or wall.

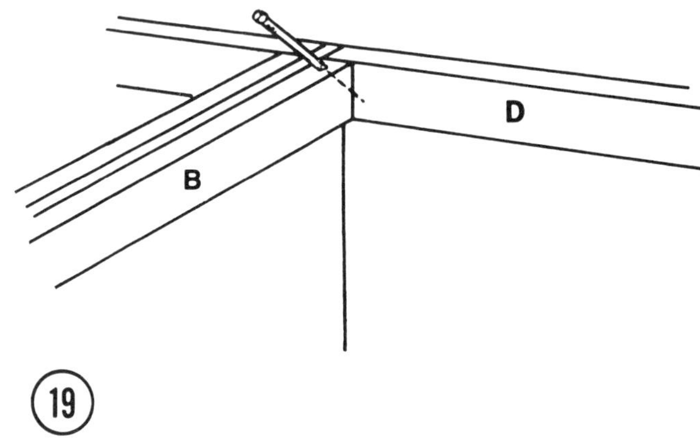

19

Cut shelves F to size required. Nail into position. Nail F to CE, BD, Illus. 18.

Cut top G, Illus. 20, from clear lumber, no knots. Glue up 1 x 12 and 1 x 6. Use clamps. You can drive ⅜'' corrugated fasteners into bottom face. Cut to width required to maintain overall width of 16⅞''. Place 1 x 12 out front. Nail G to ends and partitions with 6 penny finishing nails, Illus. 15. G can also be cut from ¾'' plywood or flakeboard.

26

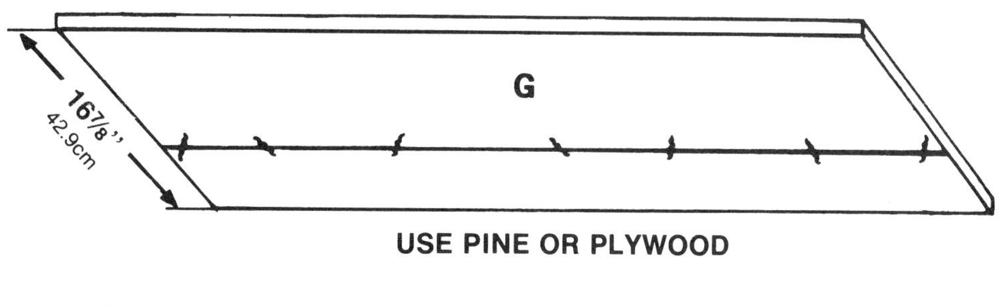

(20)

Countersink heads. Fill holes with wood filler for painting; use matching Putty Stik for hardwood.

Cut 5/4 x 4 to 3" width, by length required for H, Illus. 21. Nail 5/4 x 3 (2½" wide) in position shown for J. Cut four stiles K, use 5/4 x 3 by length required. Nail in position shown. Center K over edge of partitions.

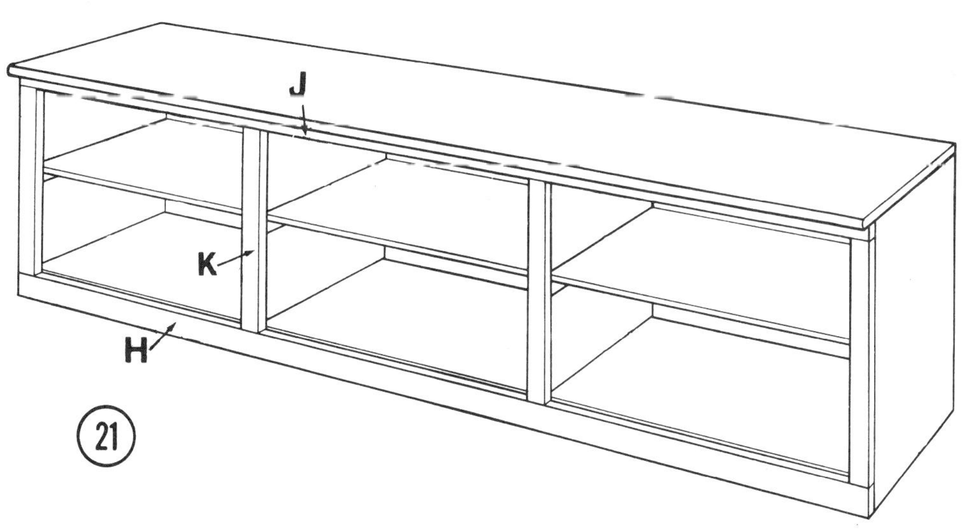

(21)

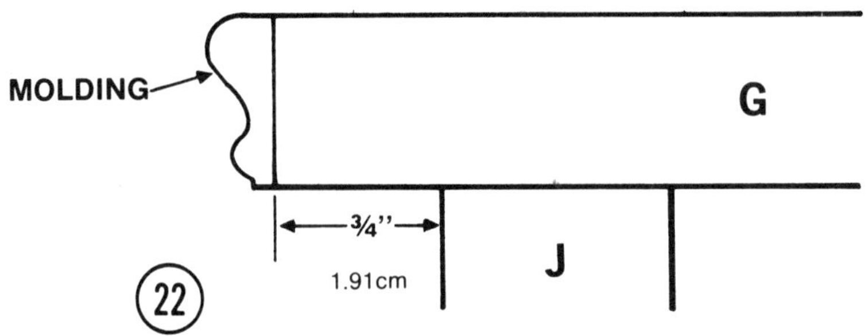

Apply molding to finish edge of G, Illus. 22.

Make doors, Illus. 23. Build door to height of opening less thickness of a 6 penny finishing nail. Test size required by cutting one stile.

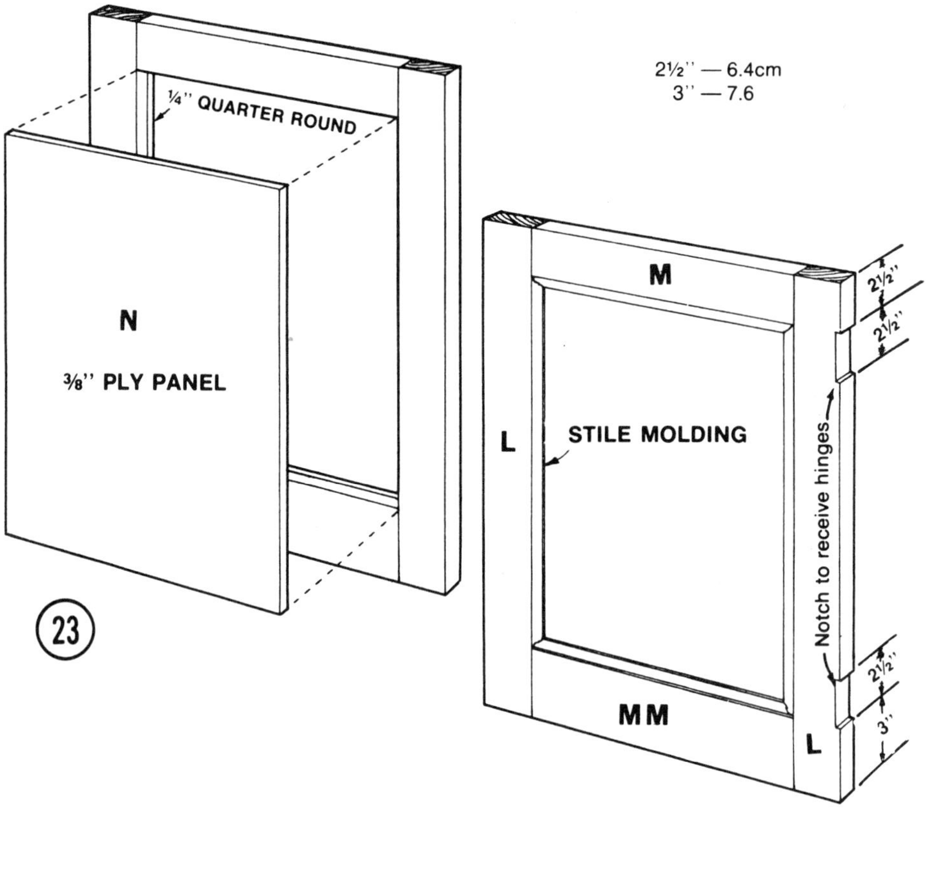

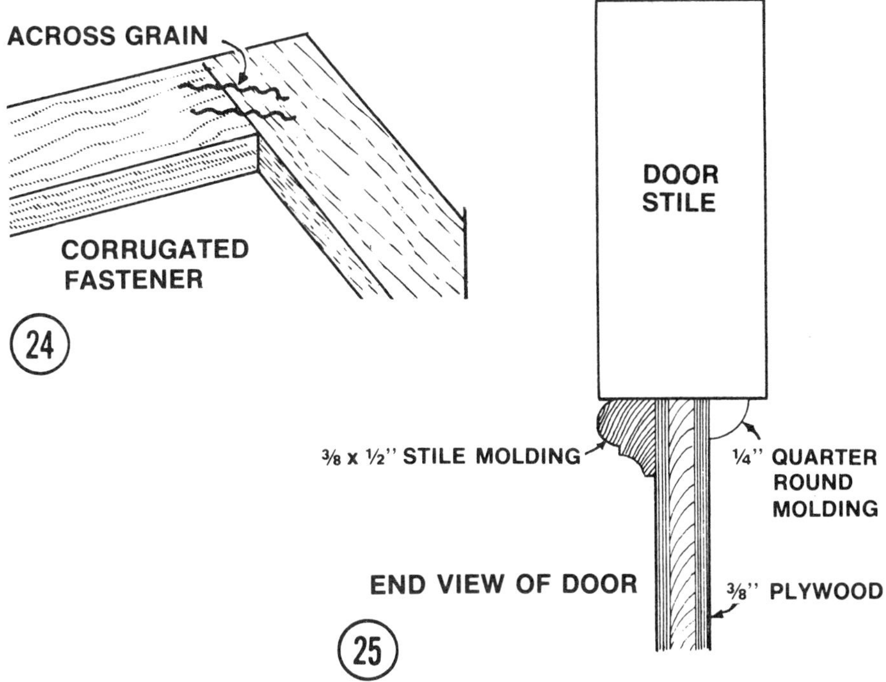

Notch L and K to receive 2½ x 1 1/16'' loose pin butt hinges, Illus. 23. Locate hinges 2½'' from top, 3'' from bottom. Plane frame to fit opening.

Cut stiles L from 5/4 x 3''. Cut rail MM from 5/4 x 4''. Apply glue and fasten with two ⅜'' corrugated fasteners at each corner. Drive in across grain in back, Illus. 24. Countersink fasteners, cover with wood filler. Sandpaper smooth.

Miter cut ¼'' quarter round molding to fit around inside edge, Illus. 25. Apply glue and nail in place with ¾ or 1'' brads in position indicated.

Cut ⅜'' plywood panel N to fit opening, Illus. 23. Apply glue and place N in position. Miter cut ⅜ x ½'' stile or glass bead molding to fit around outside face, Illus. 25. Apply glue and nail in place. Countersink brads. Cover with wood filler.

Bore holes to receive door pull or knob, 10'' down from top, 15/16'' from outside edge, Illus. 26.

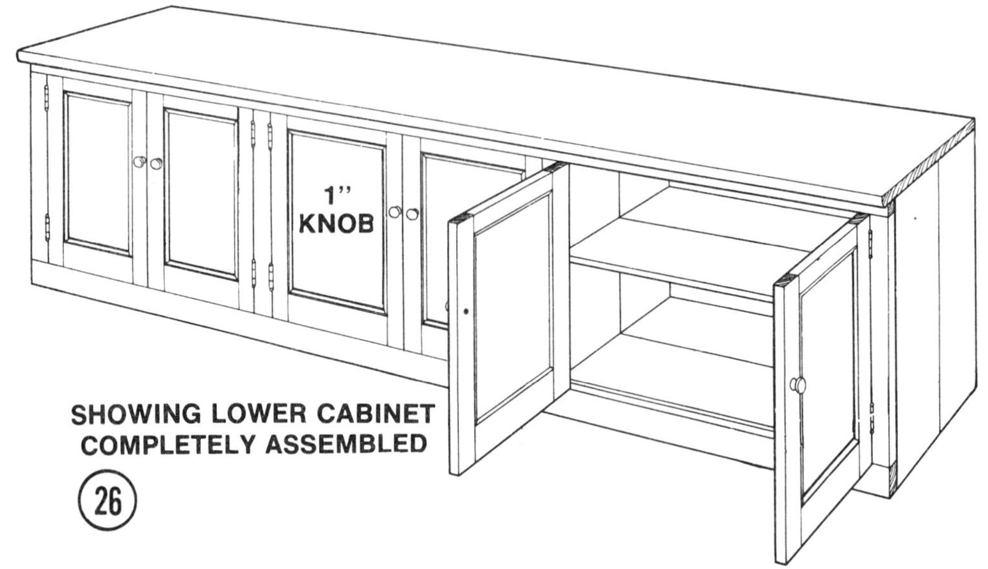

**SHOWING LOWER CABINET
COMPLETELY ASSEMBLED**

26

Fasten magnetic or Tutch Latch, Illus. 27, or equal, to door and to shelf. Follow manufacturer's directions.

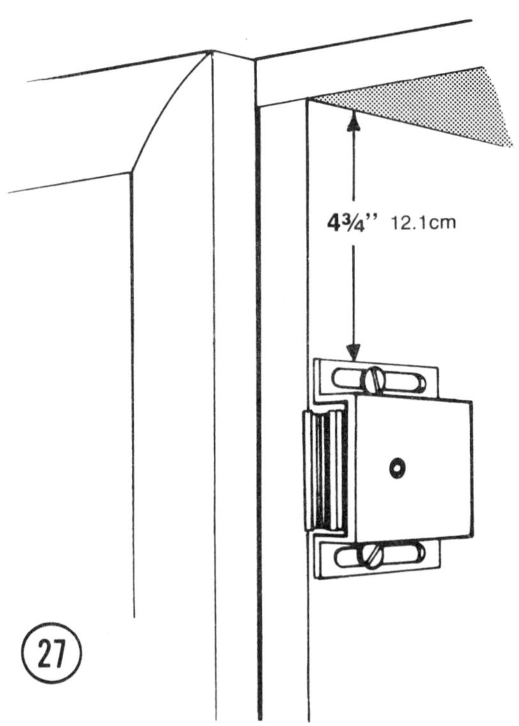

27

28

29

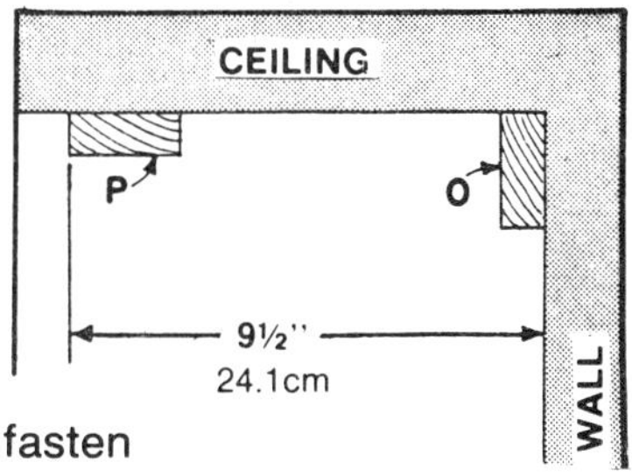

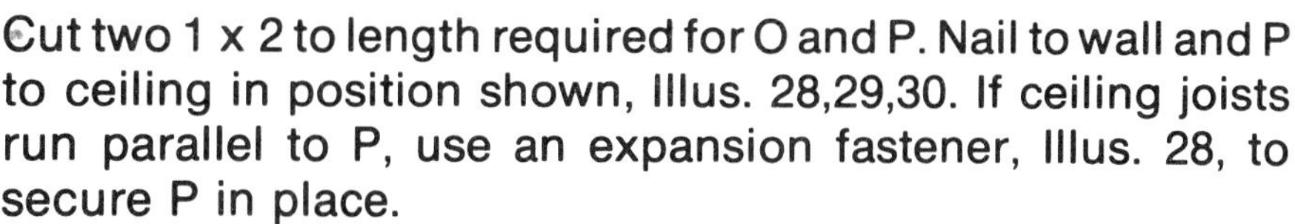

Nail P and O to Q. Do not fasten to wall or ceiling in rented space.

30

6'' — 15.2 cm
8'' — 20.3

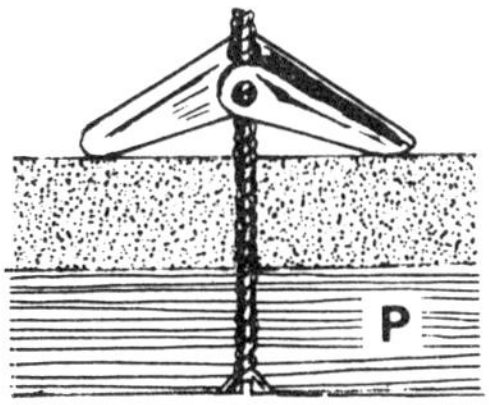

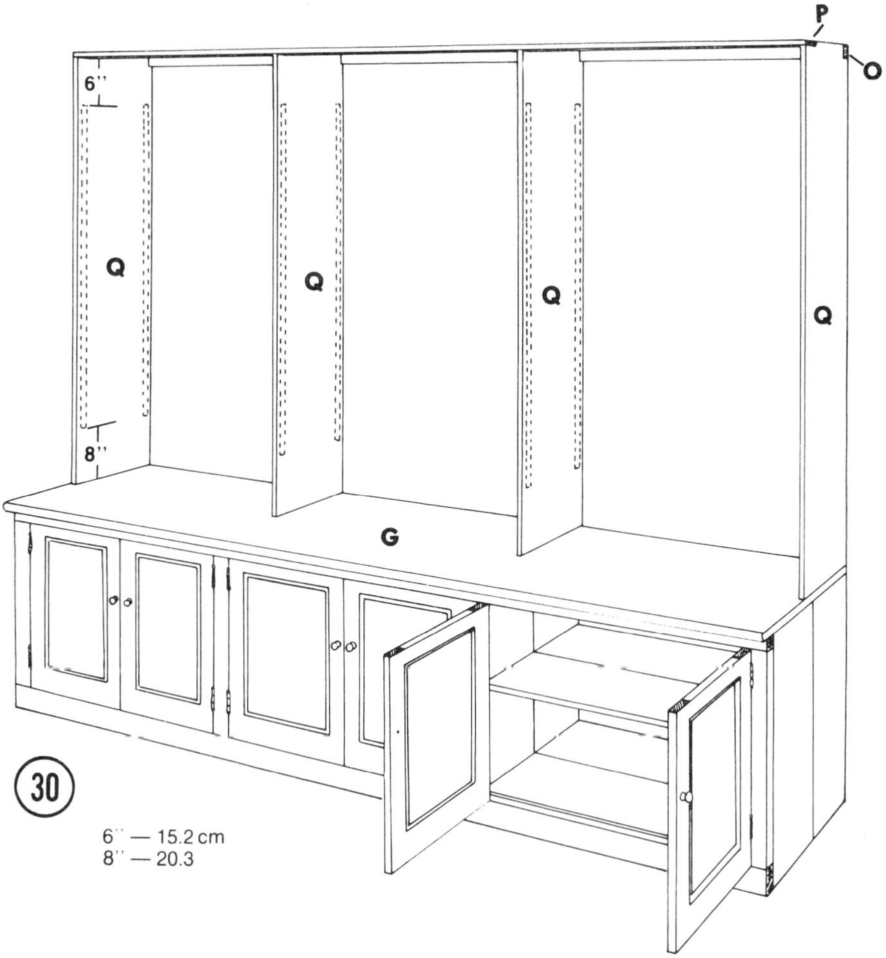

Cut two 1 x 2 to length required for O and P. Nail to wall and P to ceiling in position shown, Illus. 28,29,30. If ceiling joists run parallel to P, use an expansion fastener, Illus. 28, to secure P in place.

SHELF STANDARD

Place shelf brackets
at desired height.

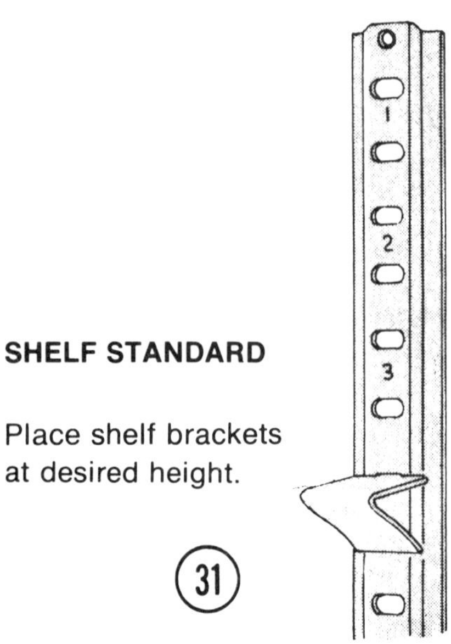

(31)

Cut 1 x 10 Q, Illus. 30, to length required. You can also use ¾"
plywood. Notch top to receive O and P.

Cut metal shelf standards, Illus. 31, to length required. Screw
in position indicated, Illus. 30. Shelf standards have
numbered holes to receive brackets. Be sure the same
numbered hole in each standard is equal distance from G, is
level and plumb with each other. Follow manufacturer's
directions to install accurately.

Apply glue to notch in Q. Position Q over partitions in base
cabinet. Check both edge and side of Q with a level. When
plumb, toenail Q to P, O and G with 6 penny nails.

Cut 1 x 6 R, Illus. 32, to length required. Nail in position
shown with 6 penny finishing nails.

Cut four stiles S from 1 x 3. Center and nail S to Q in position,
Illus. 32.

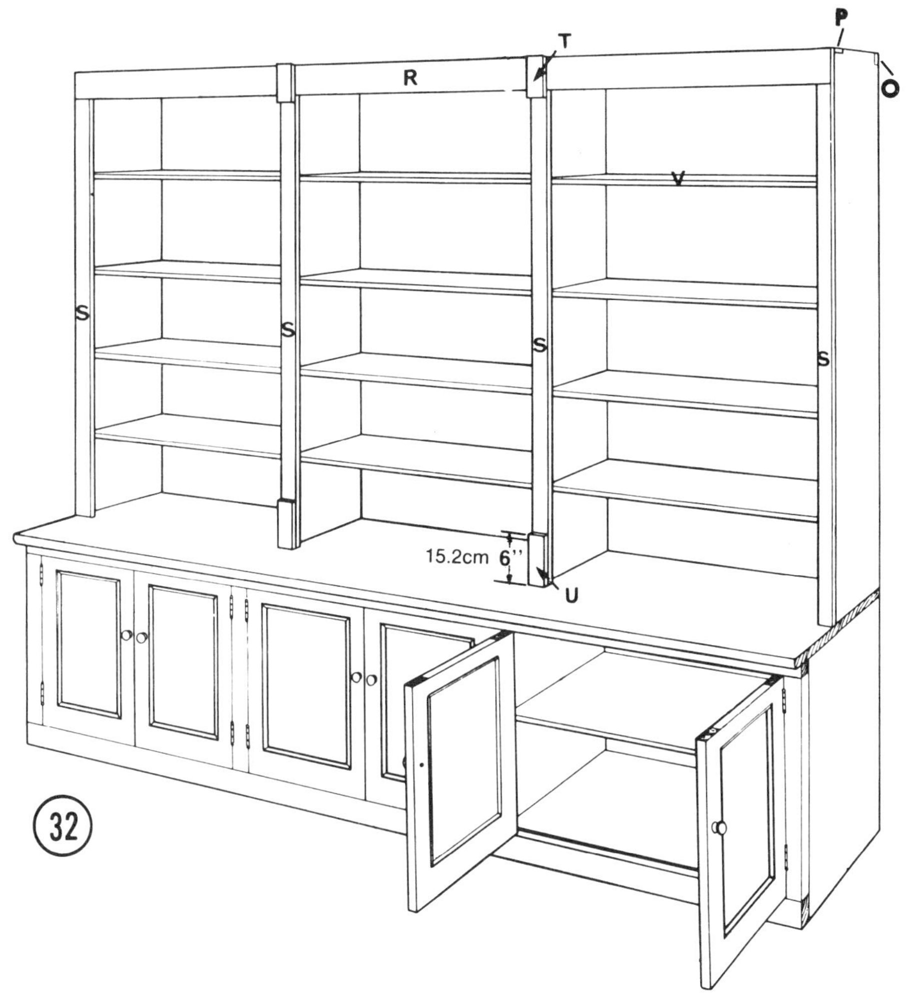

Place shelf brackets in position desired. Cut shelves V to length required from 1 x 10 or ¾" plywood, Illus. 32.

Cut two top pilasters T - 5/4 x 3 x 6¼"; two bottom U - 5/4 x 3 x 6", Illus. 32. Apply glue and nail in position with 4 penny finishing nails.

Cut ¾ x 2¼" pilaster molding, Illus. 33, to length required and nail in place between U and T, Illus. 33.

You can finish bookcase at ceiling with molding that matches that on other walls, or use crown molding, Illus. 34. Cut ceiling molding or crown following this procedure.

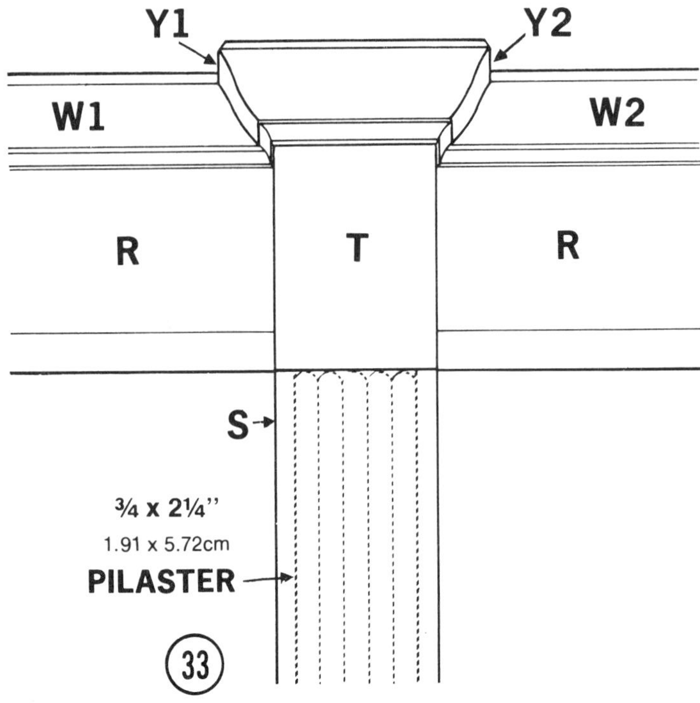

Block molding in miter box in position shown, Illus. 35. Cut ends of W - 45°, to length required to cover R and butt against T, Illus. 33.

Miter cut ends of X and Y to angle shown, Illus. 36. When all pieces are cut to angle and length required, they fit in position shown, Illus. 37,38, with bottom edge down.

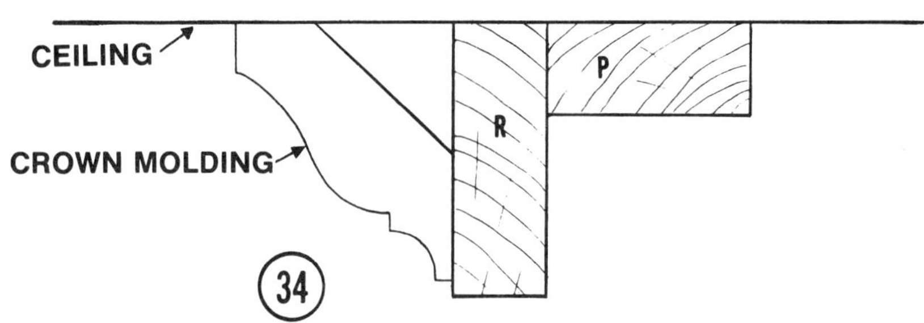

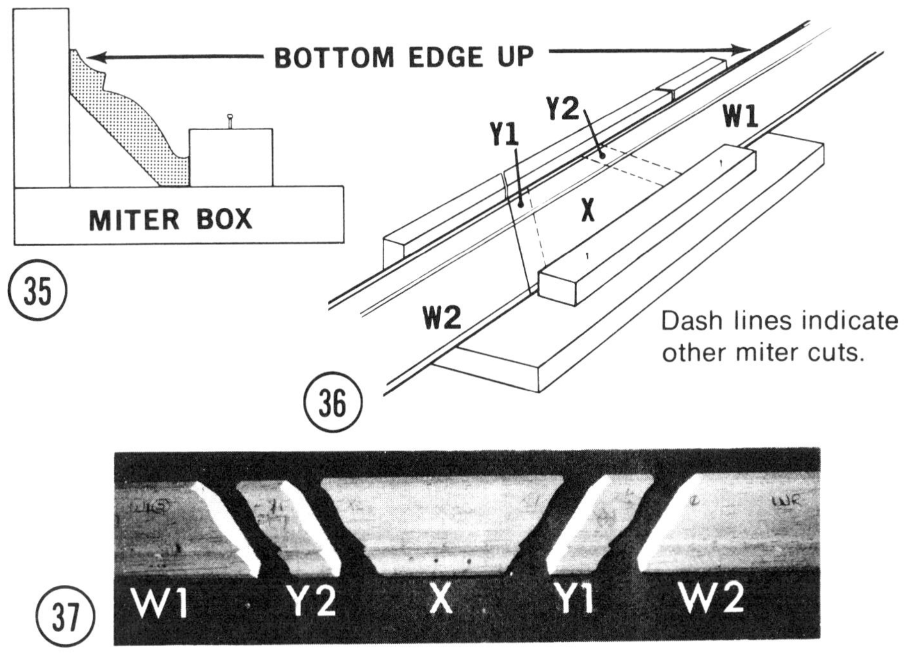

Bottom edge of X equals width of T, Illus. 38.

Glue and brad X to Y1, Illus. 37. When glue sets, apply glue and brad assembled XY1 to T and W1. Glue and brad X to Y2 and W2. Use a nailset to countersink nailheads, Illus. 38.

Fill all nail holes with wood filler, sandpaper smooth.

If you are building a bookcase using ¼" prefinished plywood over ½" flakeboard, both faces of the standing partitions Q, Illus. 31, would need to be covered with ¼" prefinished plywood. Use ½" flakeboard for Q.

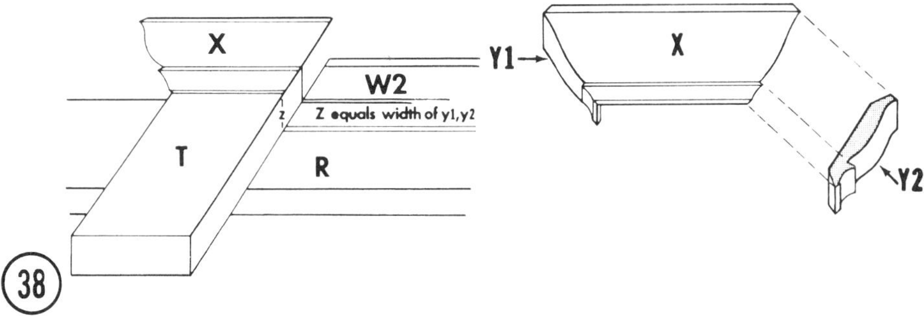

FREE STANDING BOOKCASE

A freestanding bookcase, measures 35½'' wide, 6'6¾'' high, can be built from 1 x 12 clear pine, surfaced four sides (S4S). Cut B,E,H and top shelf to length required.

LIST OF MATERIAL

Use clear pine or ¾" plywood surfaced two sides.
1 x 2 — 2/8
1 x 3 — 1/8,1/12
1 x 12 — 2/2,1/14
¼ x 36 x 96" fir plywood good two sides
8 lineal ft. shelf standard shelf standard brackets
4 prs. cabinet door hinges
4 magnetic catches
4 — 1" door knobs or door hardware to suit

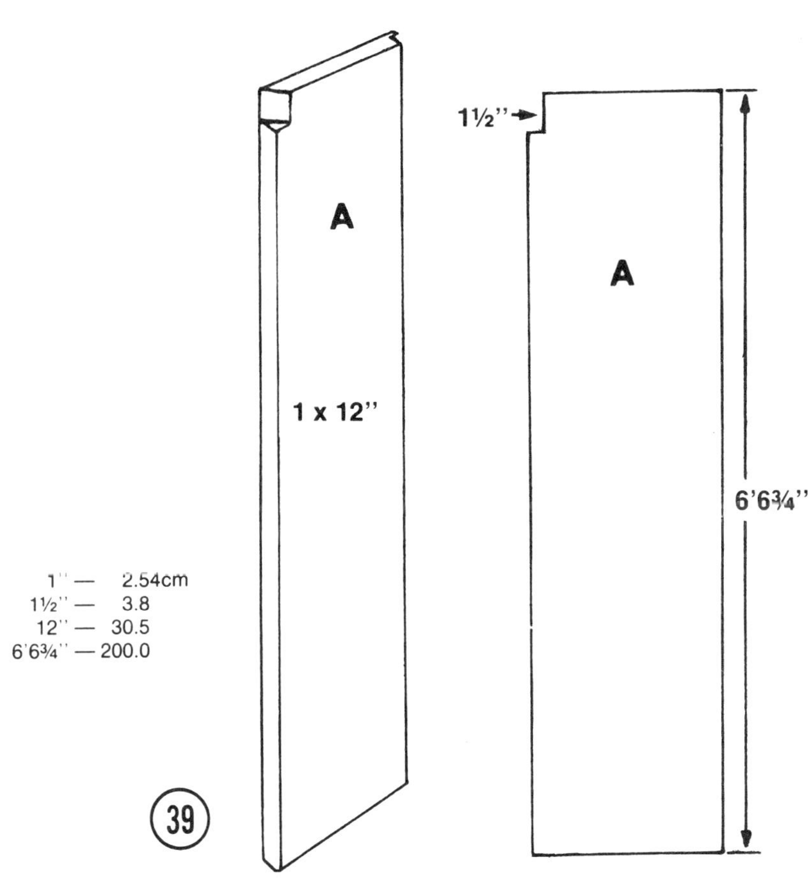

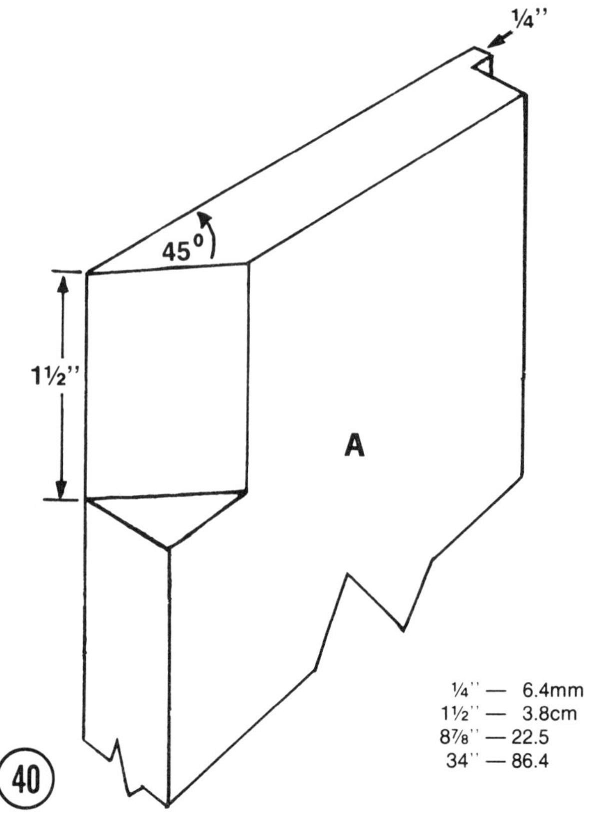

Cut two sides A - 1 x 12 x 6'6¾", Illus. 39. Using a table saw, electric or hand saw, notch back edge ¼" deep, ½" wide, to receive ¼" plywood back D, Illus. 40,41.

Saw top inside front edge to 45°, 1½" down, Illus. 40.

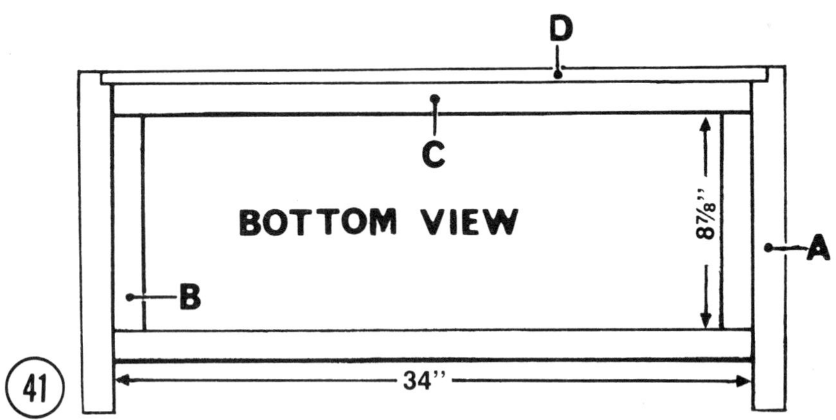

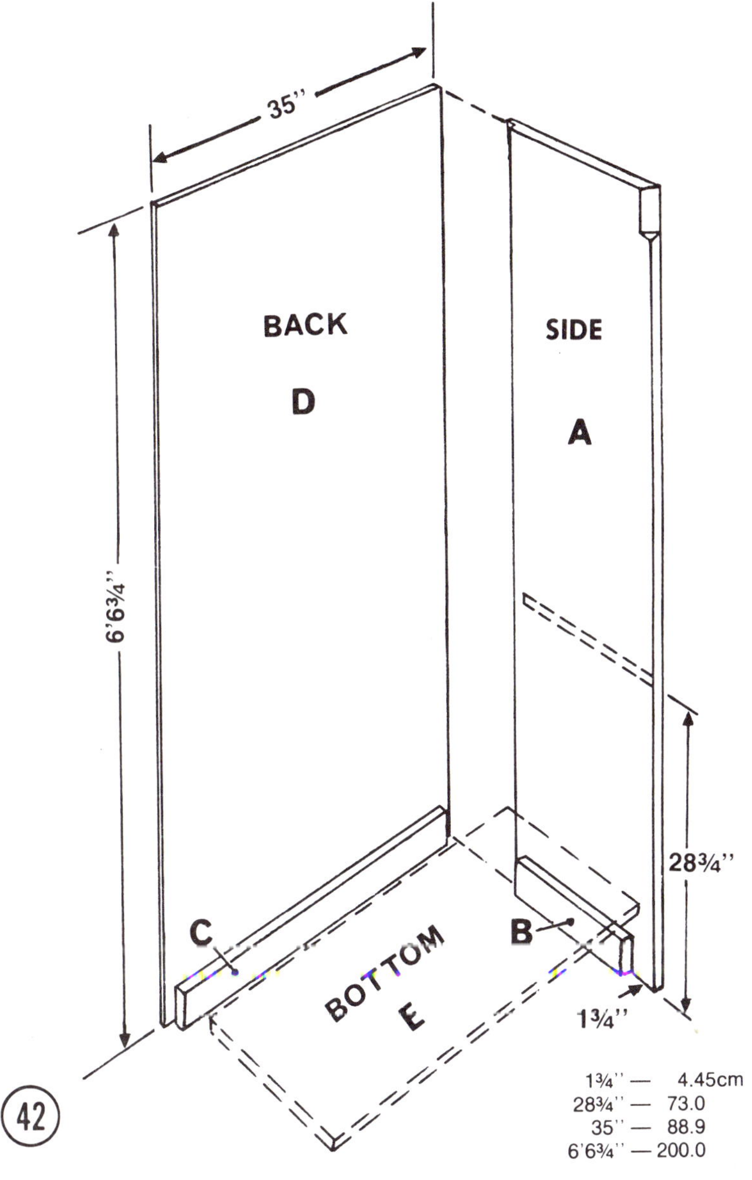

Cut two cleats B, Illus. 41, 1 x 2 x 8⅞". Cut two cleats C, 1 x 2 x 34". Apply glue and nail C to B with two 4 penny finishing nails, Illus. 41.

Apply glue and screw B to A. Keep B and C flush with bottom of A, Illus. 42.

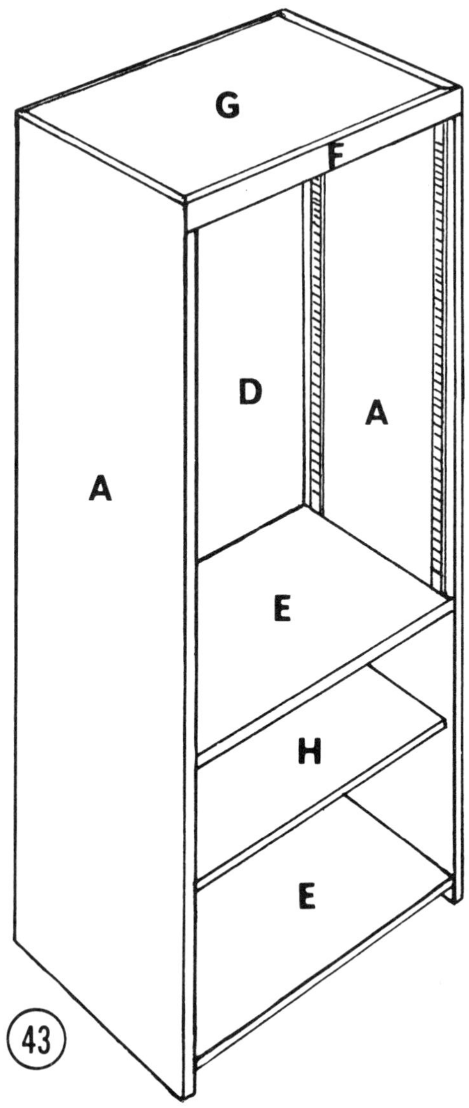

Cut ¼'' plywood back D - 35 x 6'6¾'', Illus. 42. Apply glue to notch in A. Nail D to A with 1'' brads spaced about 12'' apart.

Cut two shelves E from 1 x 12 x 34''. Apply glue to back edge and ends, and to top of B and C. Nail E to B and C with 4 penny nails, Illus. 42.

Check assembly with a square. Nail D to E. Nail top shelf E, 28¾'' from bottom of A, Illus. 42.

After assembling ABCD and E, check size of additional parts
before cutting.

Miter cut ends of 1 x 2 x 35½'' for F, Illus. 43,44. Glue and nail
F to A in position shown, Illus. 43,45.

Cut top G from 1 x 12 to size required, Illus. 45. Apply glue
and nail A,F and D to G.

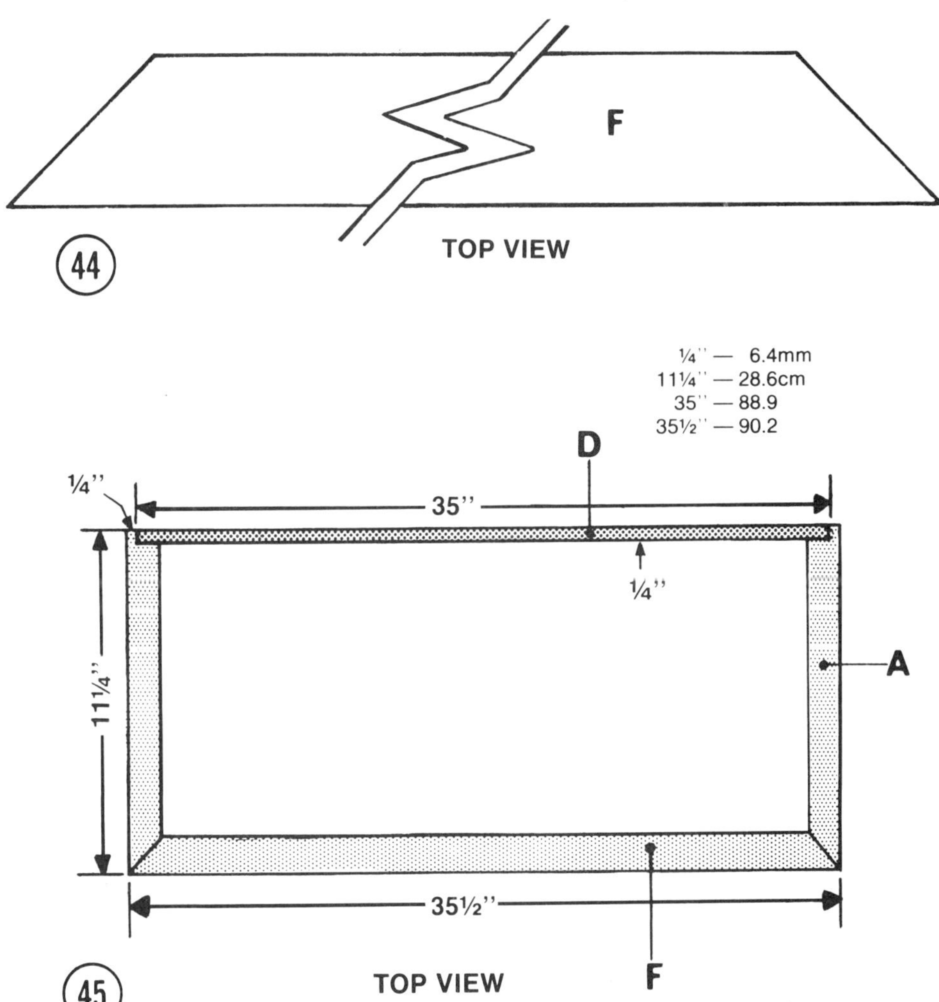

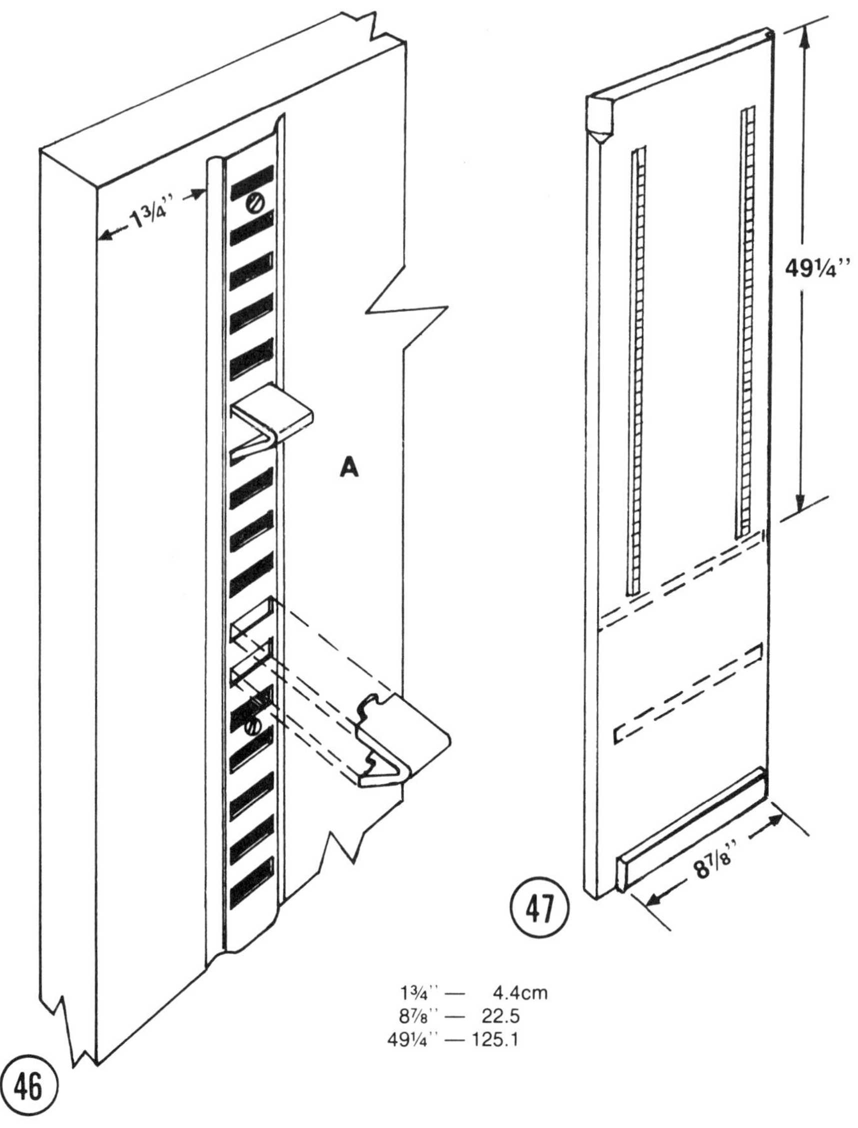

Cut shelf H, Illus. 43, 1 x 10⅝ x 34" or size required. Apply glue and nail A and D to H in position shown.

Countersink all nailheads, fill holes with wood filler.

Cut metal shelf standards to length required to fit in position shown, Illus. 43,47. Notches in standards are numbered. Cut each to line up with others.

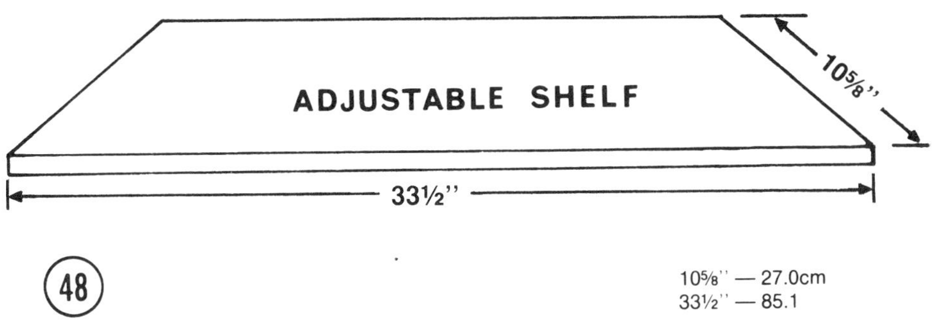

Fasten standard to A, 1¾" from front, Illus. 46, and 1" from D. Fasten front standard in place with one screw at top. Check with level, when plumb fasten other screws. Place rear standard in position, use level to make certain the same numbered notch is on line. After putting in top screw, use level to make certain it's plumb. Use level to draw lines across D and A. Standards must be level and plumb.

Insert adjustable brackets in standards. Cut shelves from 1 x 12, Illus. 48, to size required to fit between standards.

Make glass doors for top cabinet, Illus. 49,50,51,52. Build doors to fit opening.

Cut four stiles L - 1 x 1¾ x 47½", Illus. 50, or length required. Stile L should equal distance between F and E, Illus. 43, less thickness of a 6 penny finishing nail. Using a ¼" drill and chisel or router, notch top and bottom of L - ¼ x ⅝ x 1", Illus. 51. Then rout center ⅛ x ⅝" deep to receive glass.

Cut rail M, 1 x 1¾ x 14¾", or length required to maintain 17", or one half of opening. Cut rail N, Illus. 52, 1 x 1¾ x 14¾".

Cut tenon in N to size and shape shown, Illus. 52. Position of tenon in M is shown in Illus. 50.

Apply glue and fasten L to M with ½'' brads. Cut glass to size opening requires and slide into position.

Do not apply glue when installing N. Slide N in position, Illus. 50. Fasten with two ½'' No. 6 flathead wood screws at each corner. Countersink heads slightly, then cover with a wood filler. If glass breaks, remove screws, lift N out of slot.

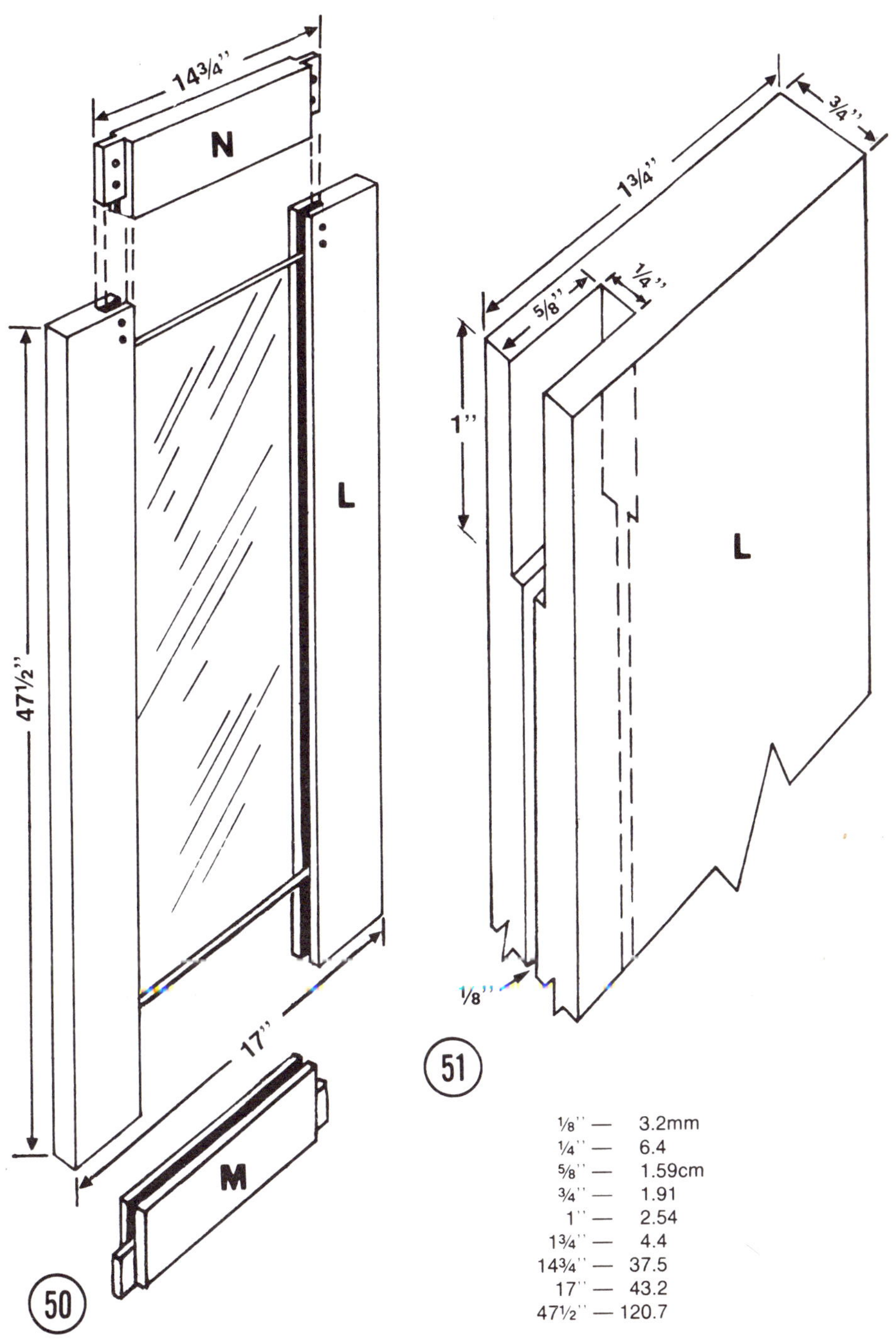

14³/₄"
N
L
47½"
17"
M
50
1³/₄"
3/4"
5/8"
1/4"
1"
L
1/8"
51
1/8" — 3.2mm
1/4" — 6.4
5/8" — 1.59cm
3/4" — 1.91
1" — 2.54
1³/₄" — 4.4
14³/₄" — 37.5
17" — 43.2
47½" — 120.7

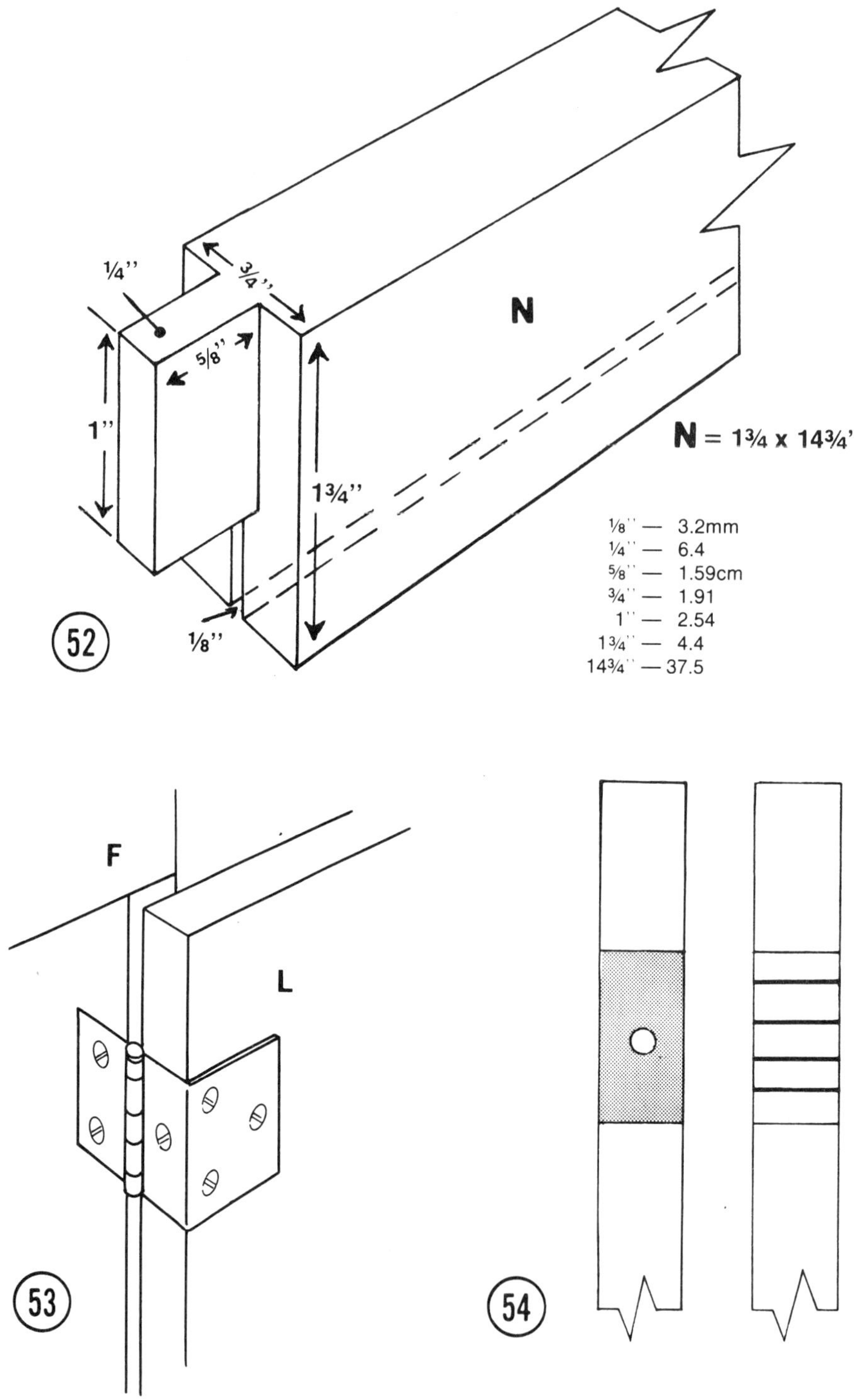

¼''
¾''
5/8''
N
1''
1¾''
1/8''
N = 1¾ x 14¾''
⅛'' — 3.2mm
¼'' — 6.4
5/8'' — 1.59cm
¾'' — 1.91
1'' — 2.54
1¾'' — 4.4
14¾'' — 37.5
52
F
L
53
54

Hinge doors in position with a pair of 1½" cabinet hinges for flush doors, Illus. 53. Place hinges 1¾" down from top, same distance from bottom. Mortise edge of door, Illus. 54, to receive full thickness of hinge. Draw outline on edge of door, Illus. 55. Using a coping saw, saw notches to depth of hinge. Using a ½ or ¾" wood chisel, chisel out mortise.

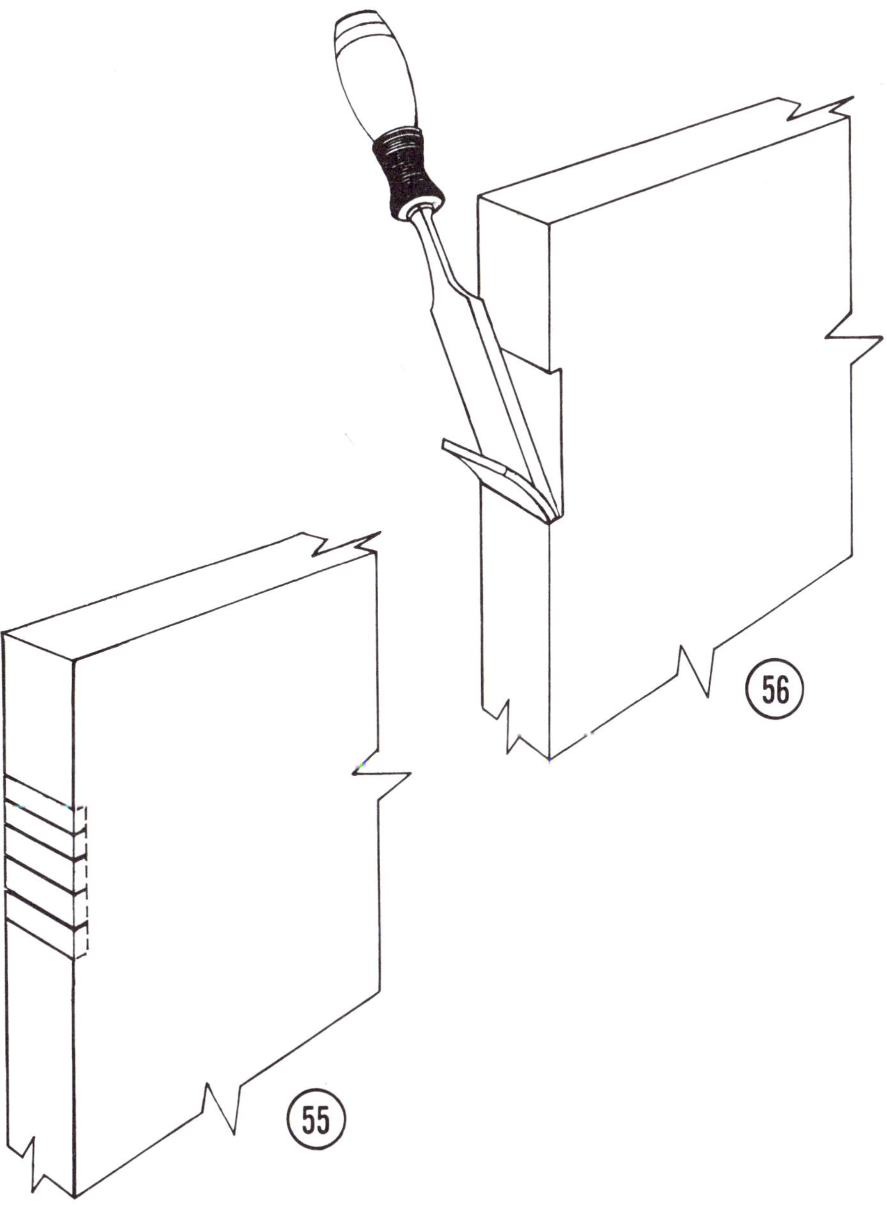

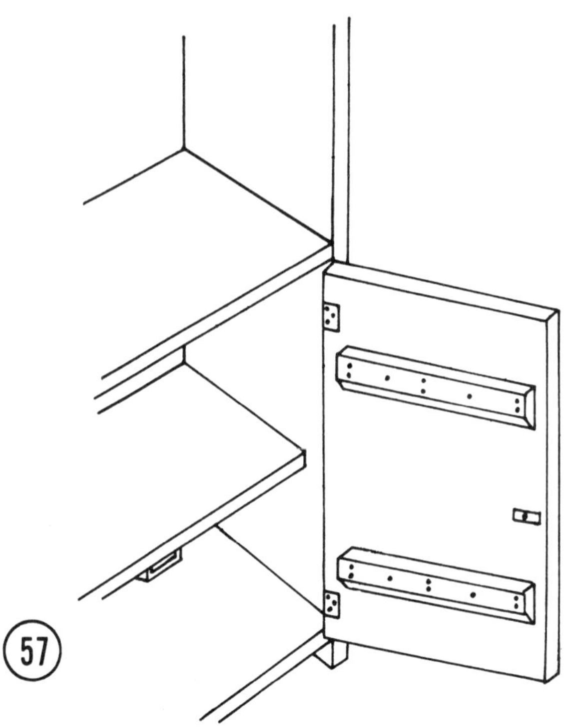

Install magnetic door catches, Illus. 57, to door and shelf. Follow manufacturer's directions.

Doors for lower cabinet can be made by gluing up 1 x 12 boards to width opening requires, then sawing in half.

To prevent warping, glue and screw two 1 x 3 x 15'' battens to inside face of each door, Illus. 57. Bevel edge as shown. Glue and screw to door 4'' from top and same distance up from bottom with 1¼'' No. 8 flathead screws.

Another way of making a door is shown in Illus. 58. You can use ¼'' prefinished plywood glued to ½'' flakeboard or use ¾'' flakeboard. Frame with picture frame molding. The molding is miter cut to length required, then glued and nailed to flakeboard. Use cabinet hinges for 1⅛'' thick flush doors.

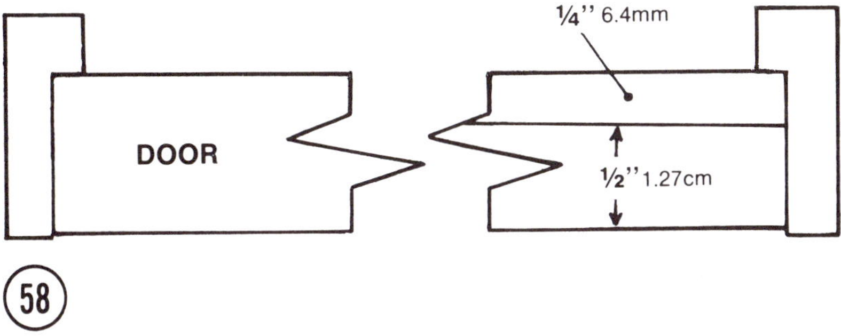

Apply 1" door knobs. These can be fastened at center, 1" in from edge.

A free standing, prefinished hardwood plywood bookcase can be made by gluing ¼" prefinished plywood to both sides of ⅜" flakeboard. When edge is banded with matching wood tape, or equal paper thin veneer, it makes a handsome, professional looking cabinet. Cut parts to size required.

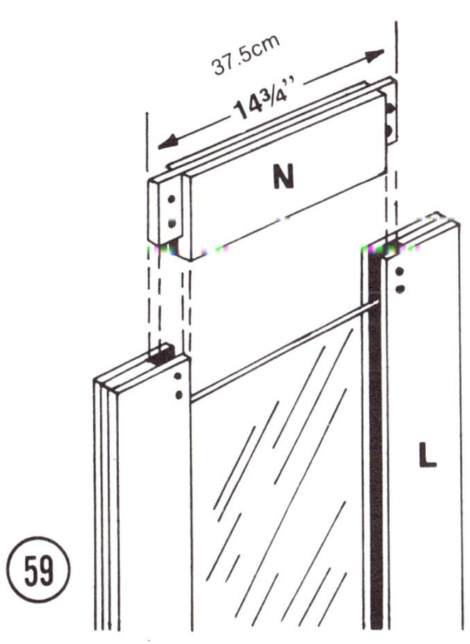

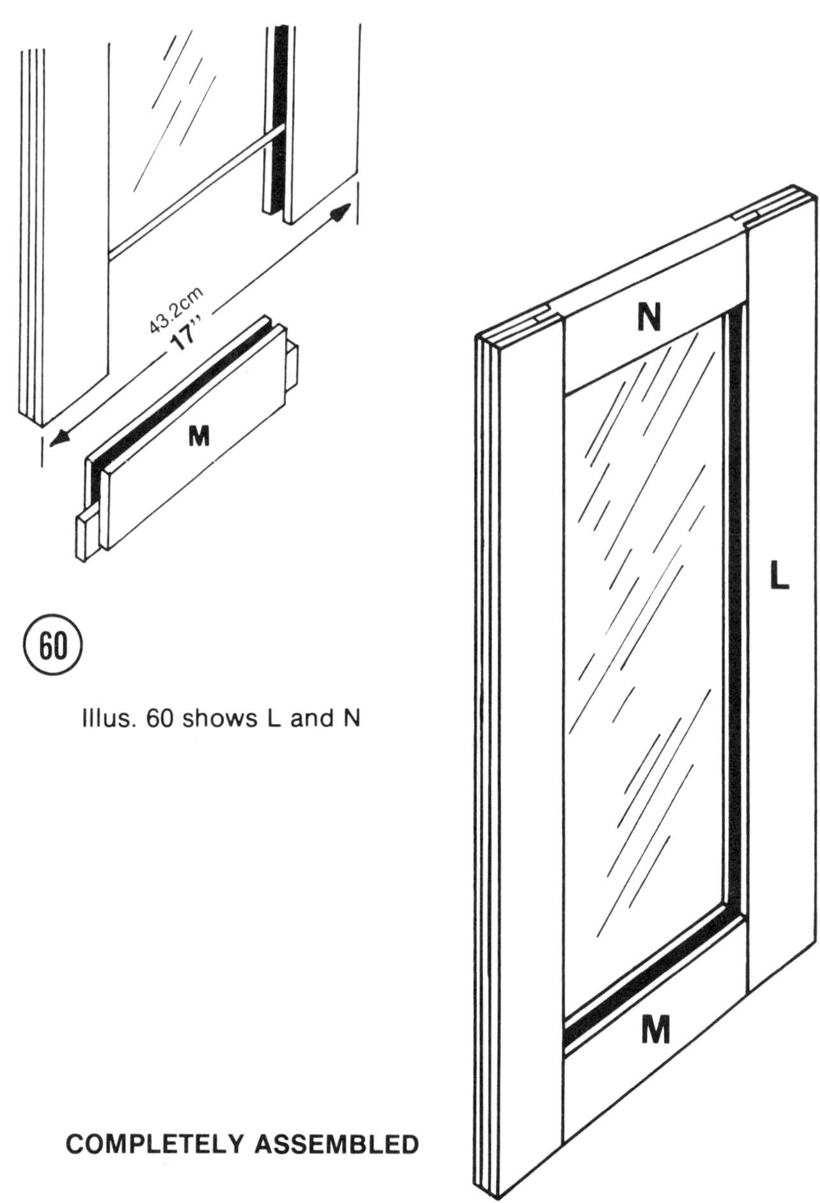

Illus. 60 shows L and N

COMPLETELY ASSEMBLED

Doors can be made with two thicknesses of prefinished plywood, plus a core of ⅛" hardboard, Illus. 59. By cutting the hardboard ⅝" less than width of stile L and rail M and N and placing it flush with outside edge of LNM, you create ⅛" channel for the glass, Illus. 60. Only apply glue to tenon on M.

Free standing cabinets, built to width needed to fill area on both sides of a door or window, provide excellent storage space. When installed in your home, finish area above by nailing O, P and R, Illus. 30,32. In an apartment, cut a 1 x 12 to length needed to provide a shelf over top of cabinets and door opening.

TO FRAME A PICTURE WINDOW OR MIRROR

Those who wish to build bookcases to frame a picture window, a large mirror or mural, will find the design shown has great appeal. It can be built as a sectional unit or built-in.

LIST OF MATERIAL

Material noted is sufficient to build a record and bookcase cabinet where width of window or mirror (X), Illus. 61, does not exceed 39''; overall height (Y) doesn't exceed 7'0''; and shelves in bookcases are approximately 18'' long.

3 — ¾'' x 4 x 8' flakeboard or plywood good two sides
1 — ⅜'' x 4 x 8' flakeboard for backs and valance
½ lb. 6 penny finishing nails
¼ lb. 4 penny finishing nails.
One fluorescent fixture (Optional)

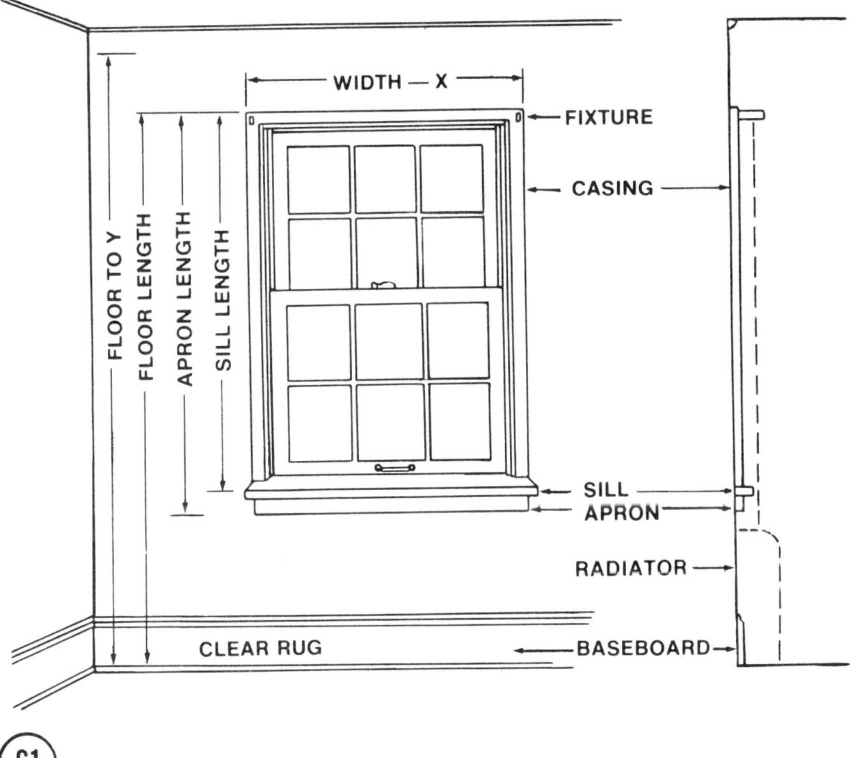

61

To ascertain exact size, measure space needed on each side for draperies. Measure width of window, casing to casing. Add amount required when drapery is folded. This could be 4 to 10'' on each side.

Next consider length of draperies. Do you want them to hang to window sill or apron length? Or do you prefer them to hang 4 to 6'' below apron? It will be necessary to build the base to acceptable height.

If you want to frame a door with this unit, consider whether you can still move a large chair, table or sofa in or out of the room after a bookcase cuts down the area of maneuverability.

If you are building bookcases around a mirror, designers frequently frame the mirror with a wide frame, then build right up to the frame.

Always apply glue before joining parts.

When building units around a mirror, measure width of X, frame to frame.

If you plan on covering base cabinet with a cushion, or with plastic laminate, use ¾'' flakeboard, or fir plywood good two sides.

Build base, Illus. 62, to overall length required. This could be X, plus space for draperies, plus 36'', or any other length for bookcases.

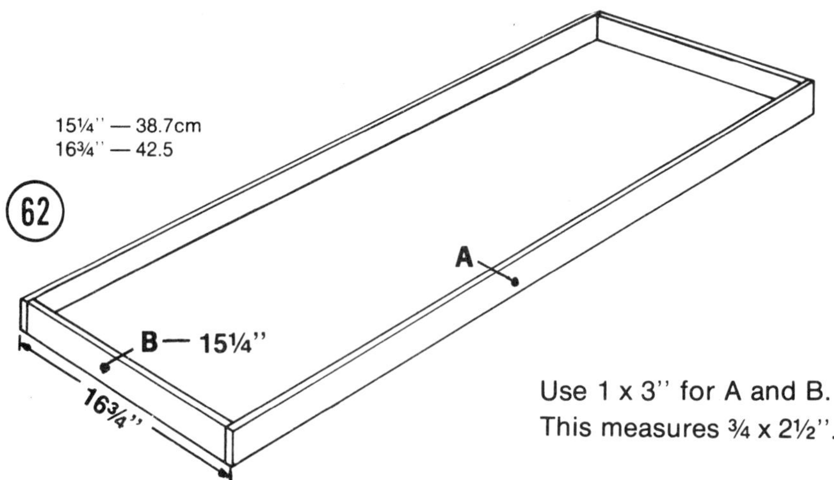

Use 1 x 3'' for A and B.
This measures ¾ x 2½''.

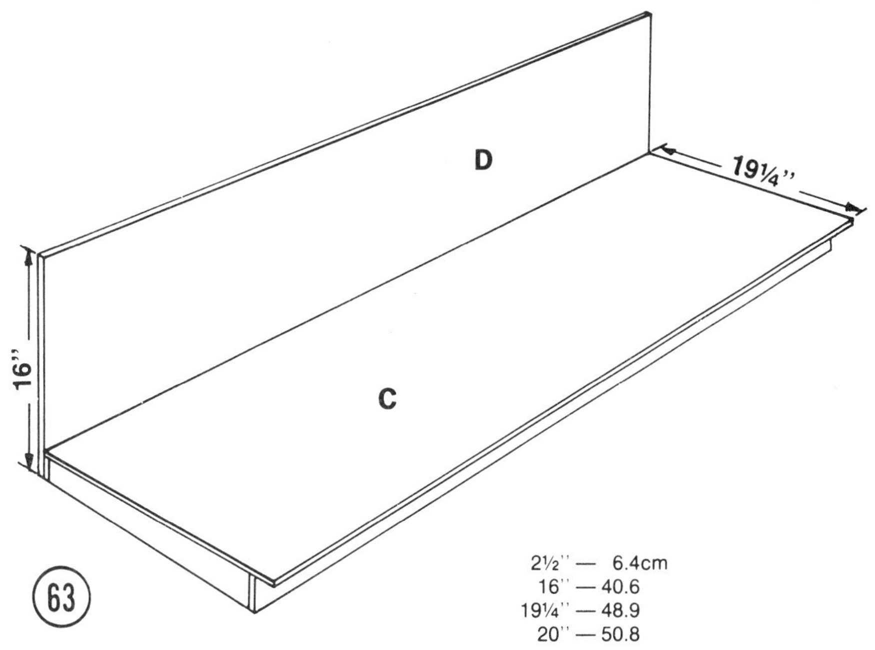

X plus space for draperies, plus 36", allows for two 18" wide bookcases. Since bookcases can be built 30, 36" or any other length on each side, cut A,C,D,E, Illus. 62,63, to length required.

Cut two A and two B, Illus. 62. Cut A - ¾ x 2½" to length required. Cut two B - ¾ x 2½ x 15¼". This provides a base cabinet with 20¾" overall dimension. Alter length of B if you want a wider or narrower base cabinet. Apply glue and nail A to B with 6 penny finishing nails. Check corners with square.

Cut C, Illus. 63, ¾ x 19¼" by length of A. Apply glue and nail C to A and B.

Cut back D, ¾ x 16" by length of A, Illus. 63. If you use a 2" thick cushion, this provides a bench 18¾" high. Glue and nail D in position to assembled A,B,C.

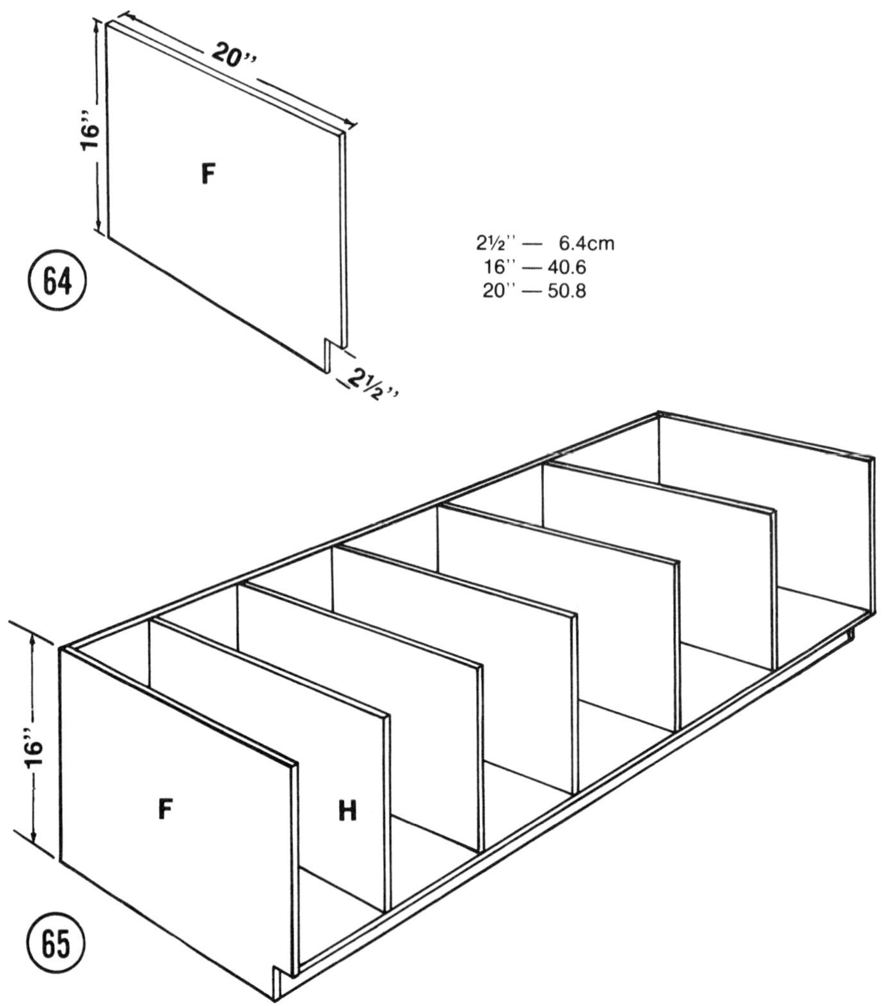

Cut ends F - 16 x 20", and to shape shown, Illus. 64.

Nail F to A, B and D with 6 penny finishing nails spaced 6 to 8" apart, Illus. 65.

Divide C into equal size compartments. Cut partitions H, 19¼" in depth and to height your cabinet requires, Illus. 65. Nail partitions H in position. Nail through C and D into H.

Cut two rails J - ¾ x 1½ by length needed, Illus. 66. Nail J in position.

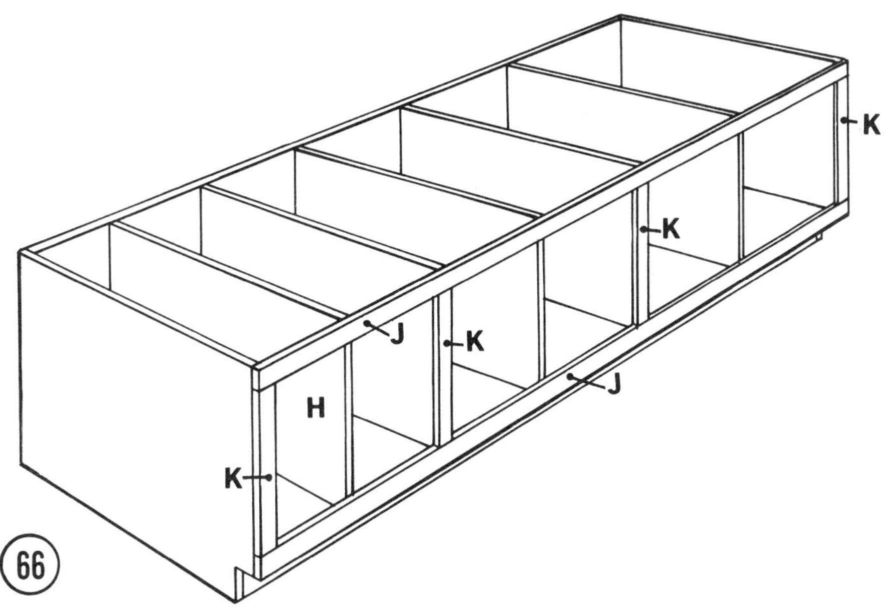

Cut four stiles K - ¾ x 1½ by length needed. Nail K in position.

Cut E - ¾ x 20¾'' to length of A, Illus. 67. Nail E to D and F.

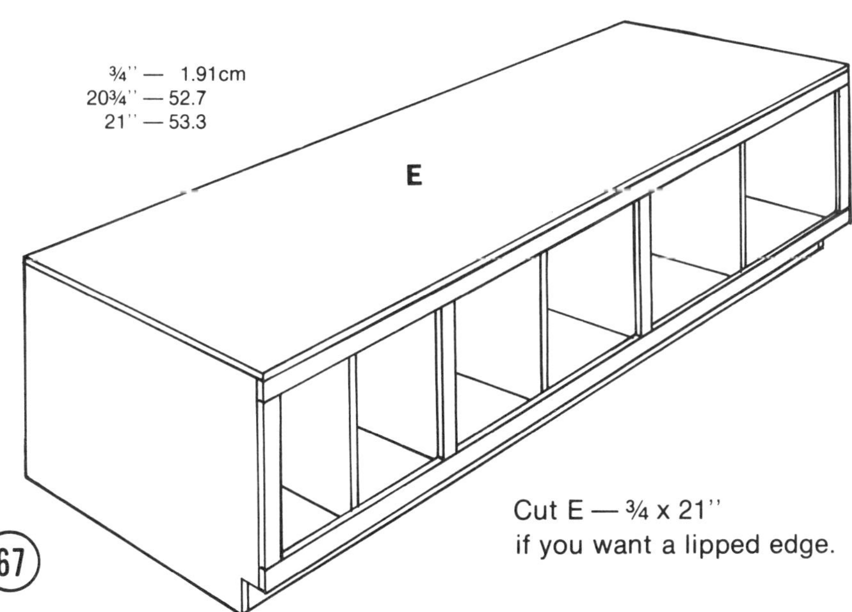

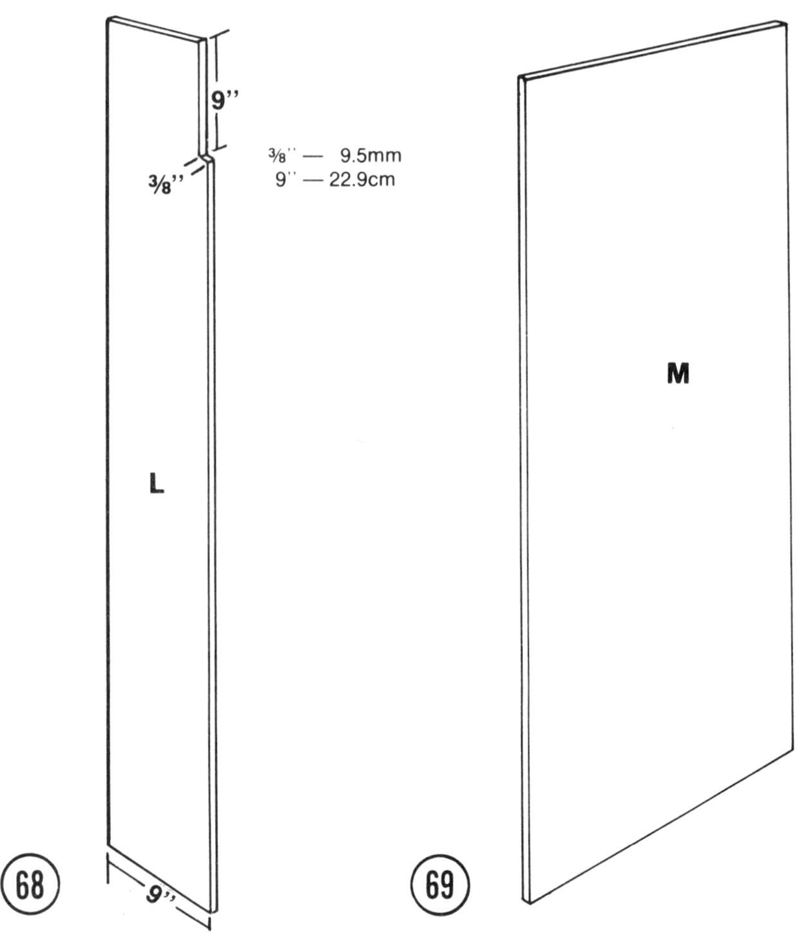

Prior to placing base and bookcases in position, remove shoe molding within area of base. Run BX wiring if you want to install fluorescent lighting. Book #694 Electrical Repairs Simplified explains how to conceal wiring, or fixture can be connected to an extension cord with a line switch, Illus. 73.

Place base in position. Check with level. If necessary, shim base plumb and level with pieces of wood shingle.

Cut sides L, 9" by length required, from ¾" flakeboard, Illus. 68. Notch top ⅜ x 9" for valance board.

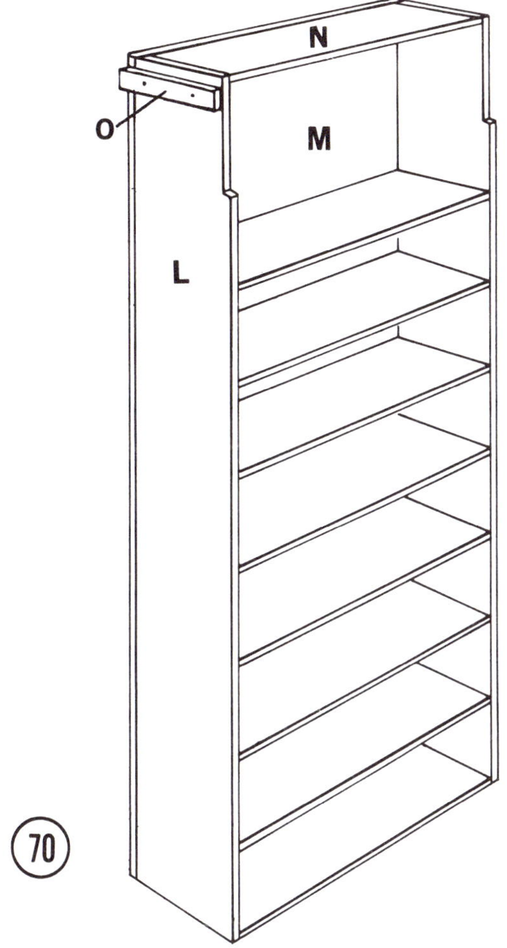

Cut shelves N to size required. Nail L to N at top and bottom. Square up frame. Cut ⅜" plywood back M, Illus. 69, to width and length of L. Nail M to L and N. Space shelves to accommodate your books. Place large books on lower shelves. You can install shelves using shelf standards, Illus. 47, or nail L to each shelf.

If bookcase is built clear to ceiling, remove ceiling trim within area. If you want to fasten BX cable on surface, cut ceiling panel, Illus. 71, ¾ x 8" by length needed. If you recess BX in ceiling or wall, cut ceiling panel ¾ x 8⅝" by length needed.

Cut 1 x 2 for O, Illus. 70. Screw O to L ¾" from top.

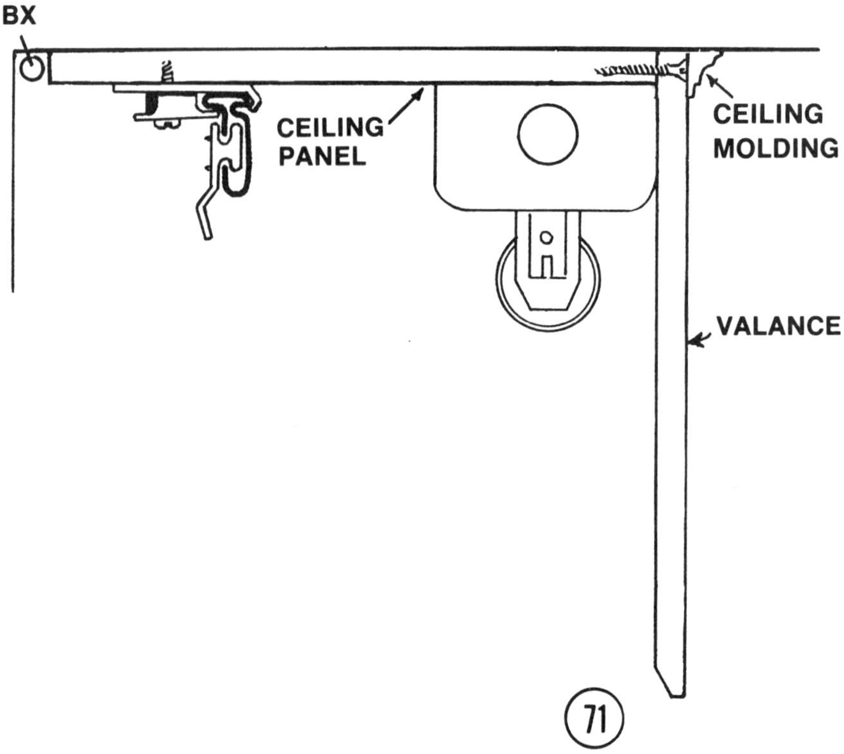

The ceiling panel provides a base for fluorescent fixture and drapery track, Illus. 71. Fasten fluorescent fixture to panel. Slide panel in position on top of O, Illus. 70. Fasten ceiling panel to ceiling joists, Illus. 29.

Fasten bookcase to wall and/or to base cabinet. Connect BX to fluorescent fixture.

Cut ⅜ x 9'' plywood by length required for valance, Illus. 71. Nail or screw valance to L and to ceiling panel. Nail ceiling molding to valance.

The front edge of E can be finished with molding, Illus. 22.

Doors can be made to size required, Illus. 23, or from ¾'' flakeboard.

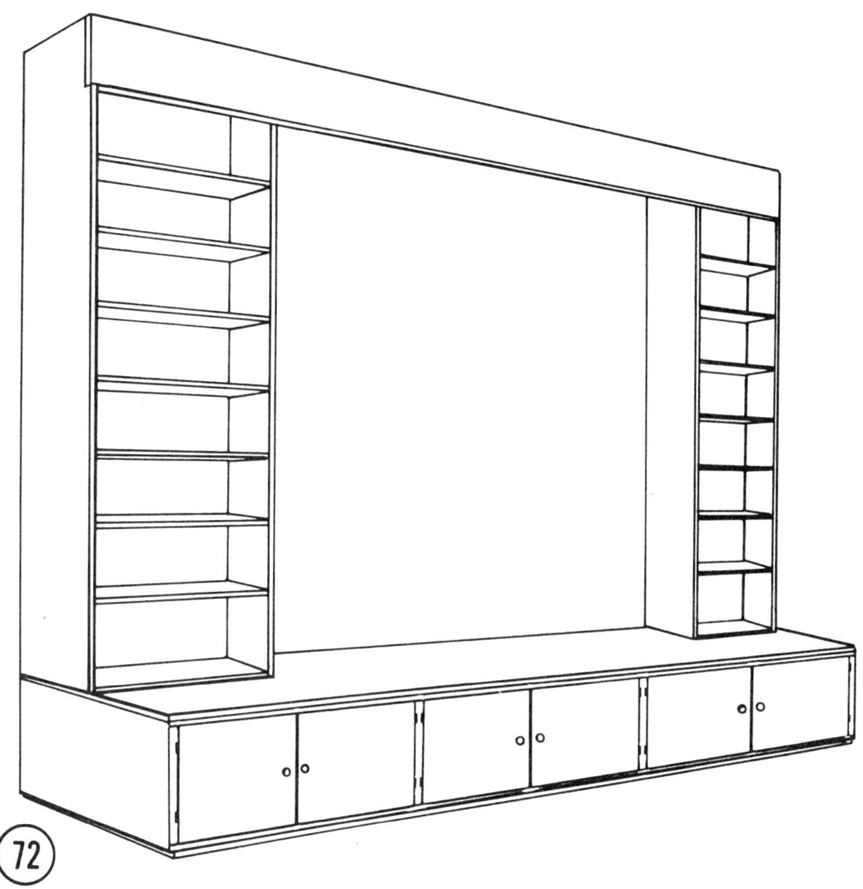

Hinge doors following directions on page 47. Doors should meet over center of H. Fasten roller door catches to both sides of H.

After painting cabinet, or veneering with woodgrain plastic laminate, drill holes and install 1'' brass door pulls, Illus. 72, following directions on page 88.

WIRING

Fluorescent lighting, as described in this book, performs best when used on a grounded wiring system. It is a simple matter to wire fluorescent channel with a grounding type extension cord to wall outlet.

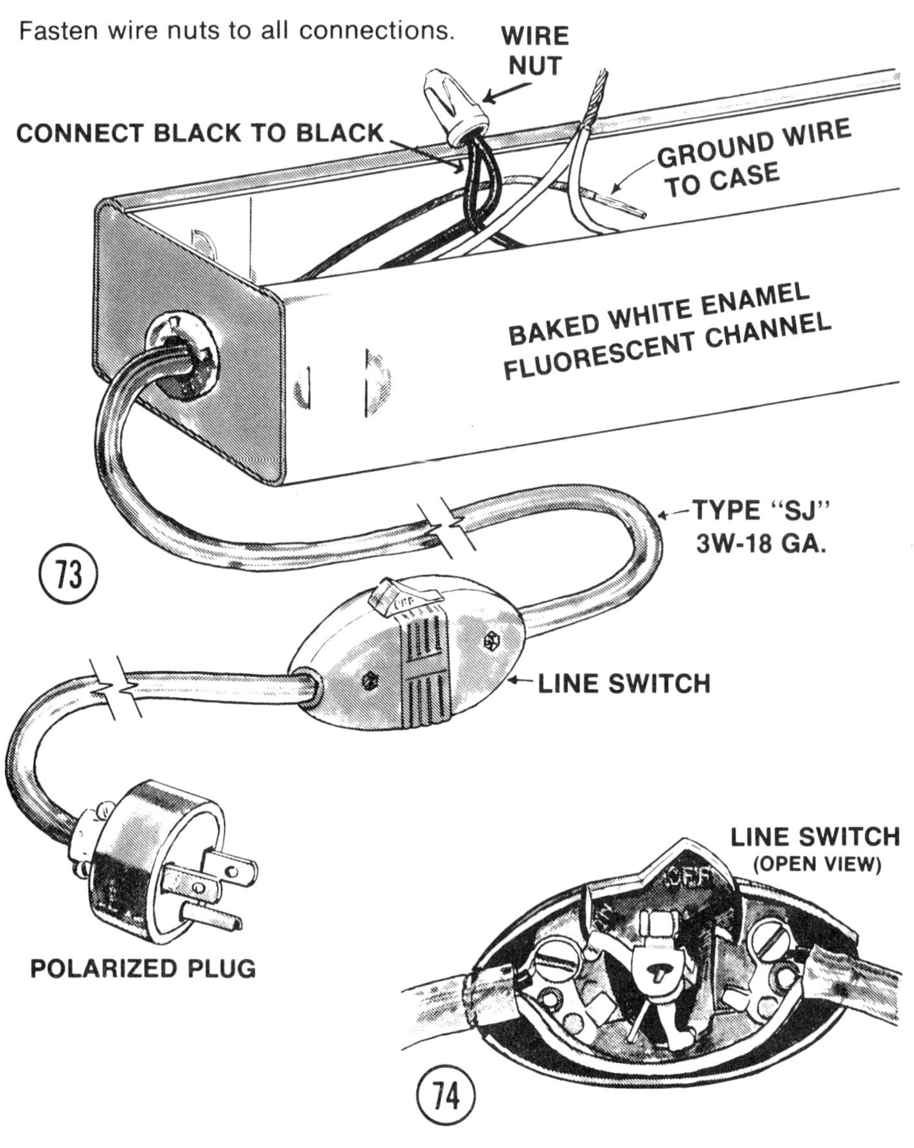

Illus. 73,74 show how this is done with a switch in cord. 3w type "SJ" 18 gauge, heavy duty cord should be used to connect channel to wall outlet. Cut and fasten black to screws. White is continuous. Use polarized rubber plug. Install switch in line at convenient height. Fasten plug on cord. Since the cord is usually placed behind draperies, it makes an inexpensive, easy and safe way of wiring.

WALL TO WALL BOOKCASE WITH DRAWERS

Free standing units measuring 48¼", Illus. 75, or 6'0", Illus. 76, can be constructed following these directions. A wall to wall built-in with drawers and cabinets can also be constructed to fill any space available. These units can also be used to frame a door, window or mirror. While directions simplify building drawers, many hardware, lumber and home improvement centers sell preformed plastic drawers complete with drawer glides. These can be faced with hardwood plywood as directions explain.

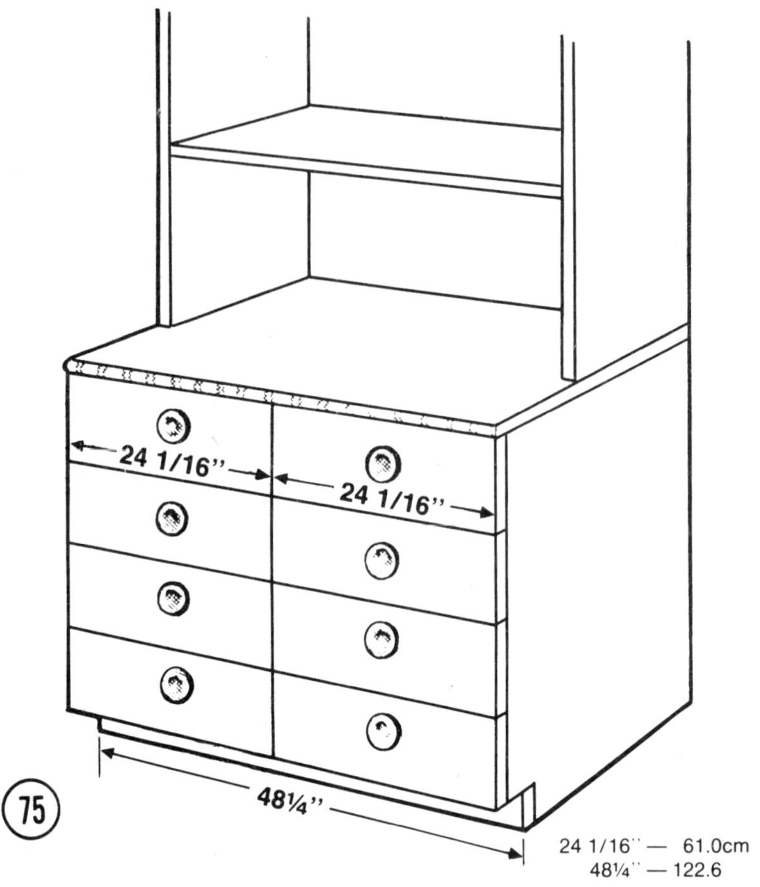

To build a 48¼" wide unit, Illus. 75, you will need the following:

LIST OF MATERIAL

1 x 2 — G,R,S and braces
1 x 3 = A,B,F
1 x 6 — U
1 x 10 — T,V
¾" x 4 x 8' — C,D,E,H,K,M,N,P
Use ¾" hardwood plywood or flakeboard for
C,D,E,H,K,M,N,P,T,U,V
Pair concealed hinges
Drawer knobs
Carved wood trim
1¼" No. 8 flathead wood screws.

64

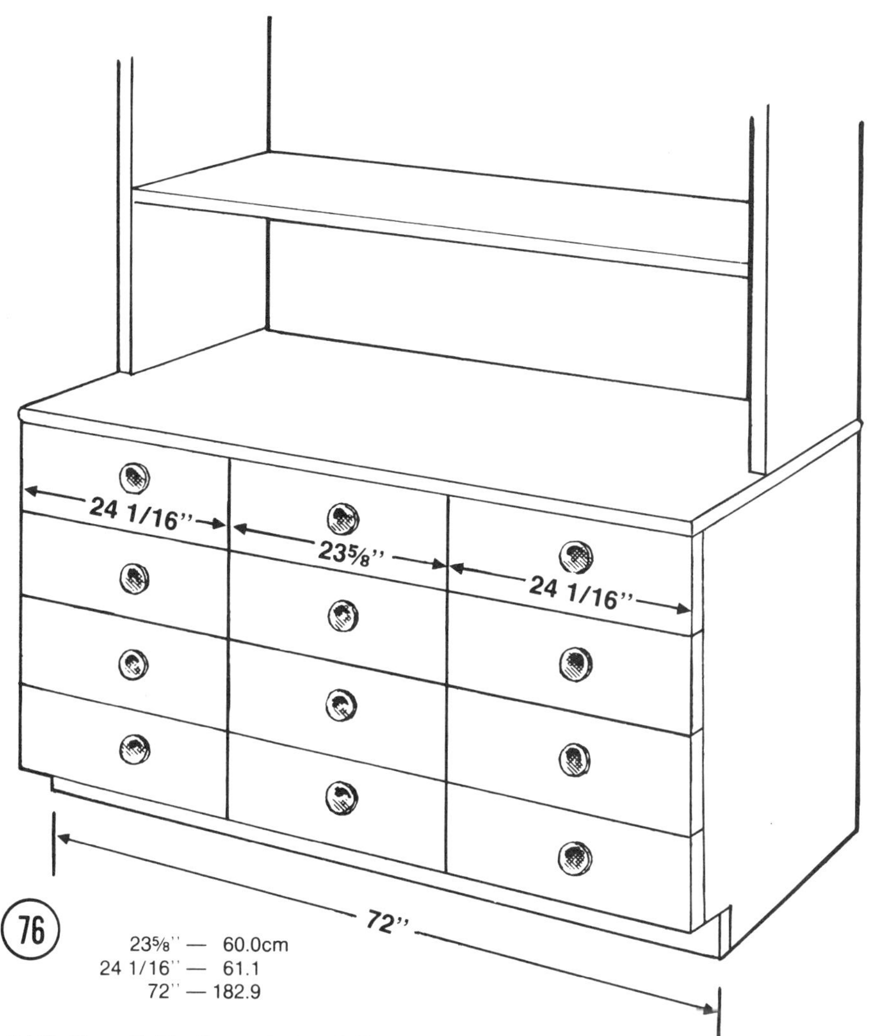

⅝" No. 5 flathead wood screws
1½" No. 7 flathead wood screws
6 penny finishing nails

1 x 2 measures ¾ x 1½"
1 x 3   "   ¾ x 2½"
1 x 6   "   ¾ x 5½"
1 x 10   "   ¾ x 9¼"

To build the 48¼" wide unit, cut two A from 1 x 3 x 46¾",
Illus. 77. Cut three B, 1 x 3 x 11⅞". Apply glue and nail A to B
with 6 penny nails.

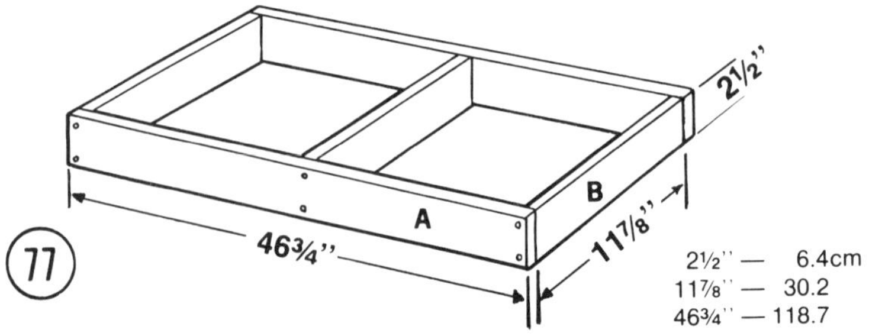

Cut two C - 16 x 30 9/16'', Illus. 78, from ¾'' plywood. Notch corner 2½ x 2½'' or to width of 1 x 3.

Cut one D, 16 x 27 3/16'', Illus. 79. Using a square, draw lines on C and D to indicate top edge of drawer guides provided by manufacturer of drawers.

If you prefer to build drawers, cut 1 x 1'' aluminum angle, Illus. 80,81, for drawer guides. A single drawer, Illus. 82, can be built 17'' wide; a double drawer 23''. Dimensions shown, Illus. 83, allow ⅛'' clearance between face panel on drawers.

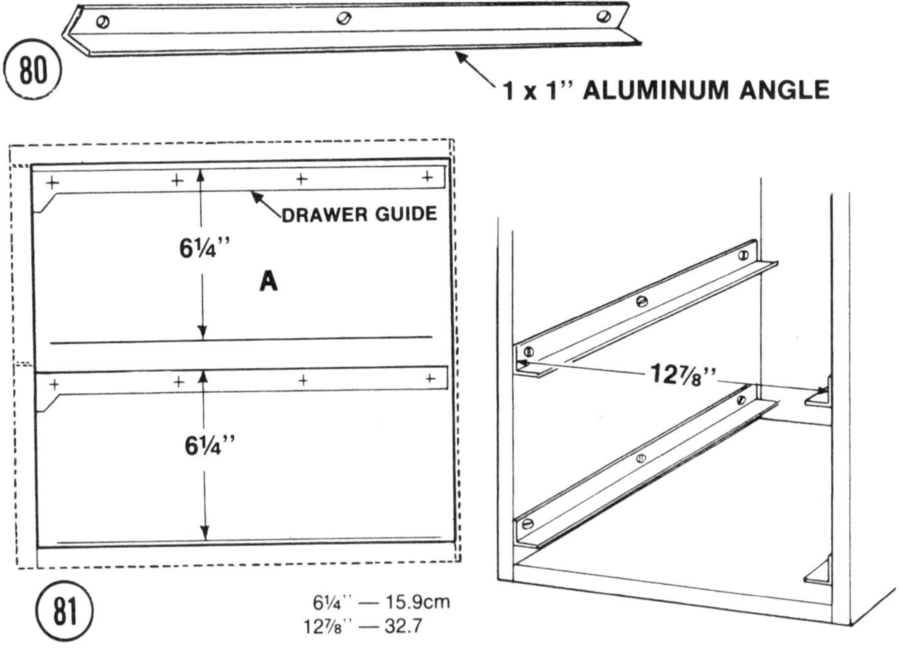

66

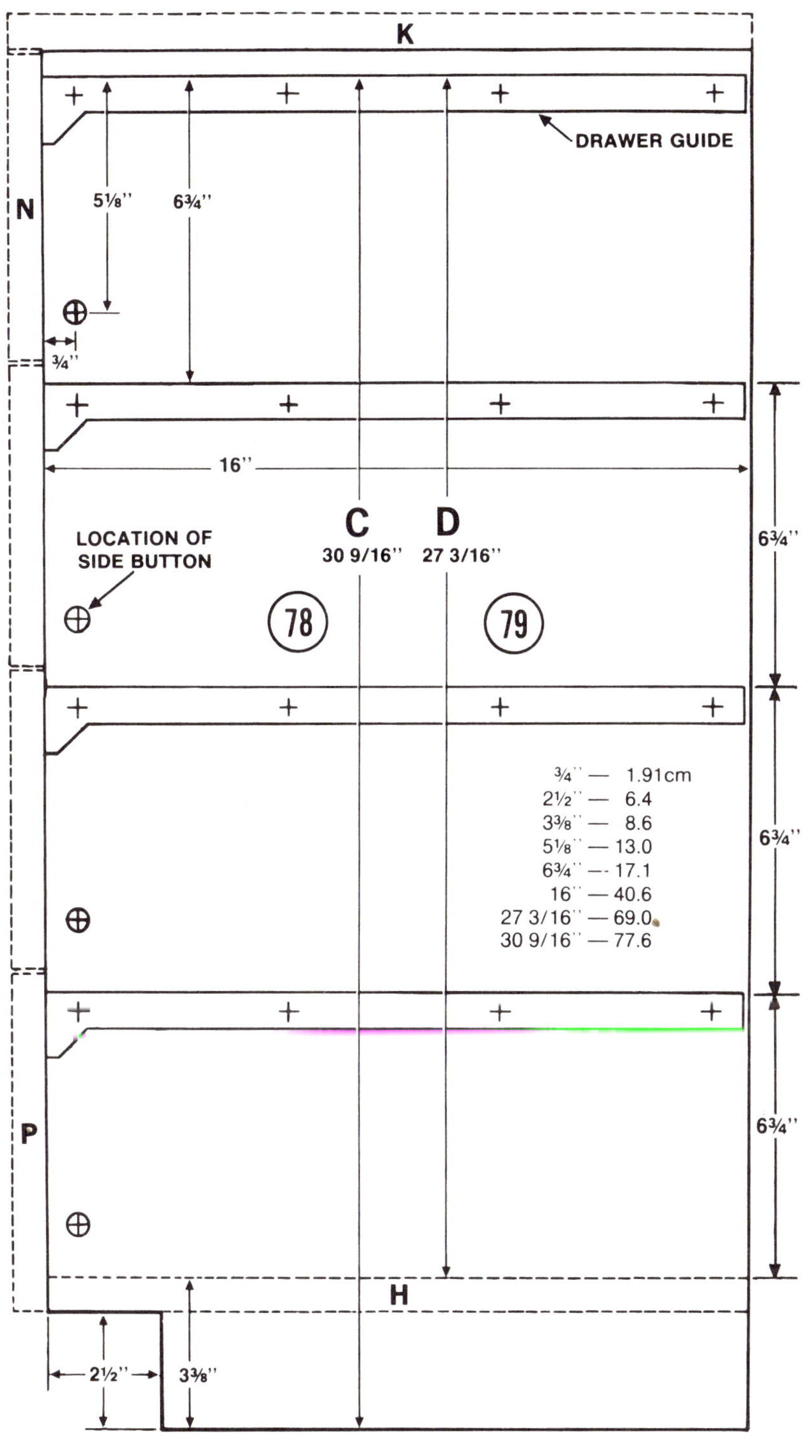

K
DRAWER GUIDE
N
5⅛''
6¾''
¾''
16''
LOCATION OF
SIDE BUTTON
C
30 9/16''
D
27 3/16''
78
79
6¾''
6¾''
¾'' — 1.91cm
2½'' — 6.4
3⅜'' — 8.6
5⅛'' — 13.0
6¾'' — 17.1
16'' — 40.6
27 3/16'' — 69.0
30 9/16'' — 77.6
P
6¾''
H
2½''
3⅜''

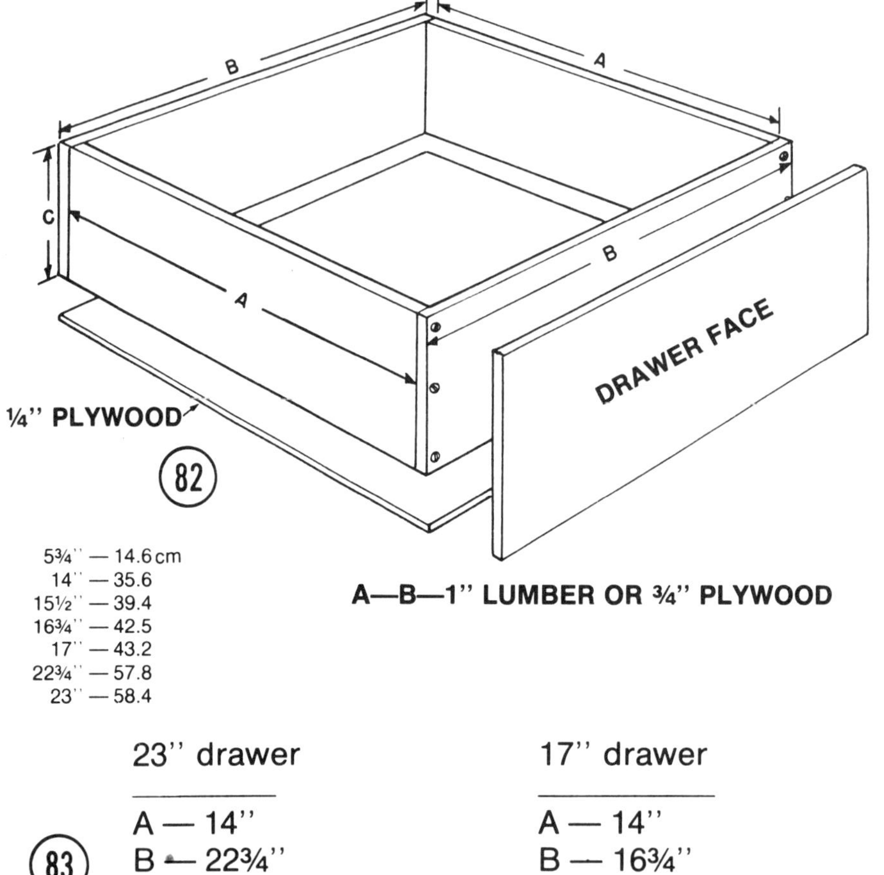

	23" drawer	17" drawer
83	A — 14"	A — 14"
	B — 22¾"	B — 16¾"
	C — 5¾"	C — 5¾"
	bottom — 15½ x 22¾"	bottom — 15½ x 16¾"

Dimensions offered are based on use of ¾" plywood or 1" lumber and ¼" plywood bottom. If ⅜" is used for A and B instead of ¾", make A 14¾". Use shorter screws.

The manufacturer of plastic drawers provides guides and stop buttons. Fasten guides and stop buttons, Illus. 84, to C and D in position noted, Illus. 78,79, or in position manufacturer specifies.

Fasten C to assembled base, Illus. 85.

68

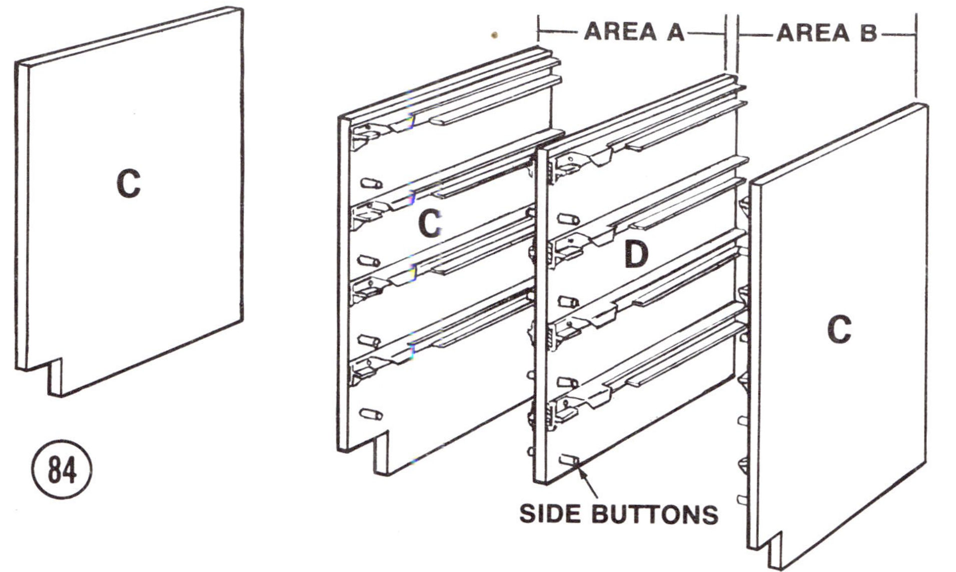

C
84
AREA A
AREA B
C
D
C
C
SIDE BUTTONS

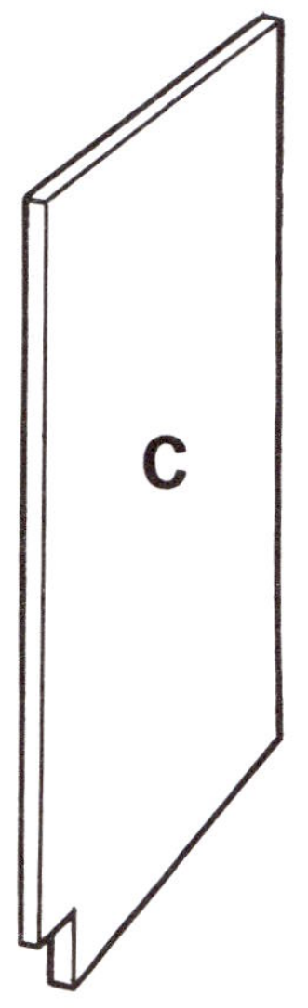

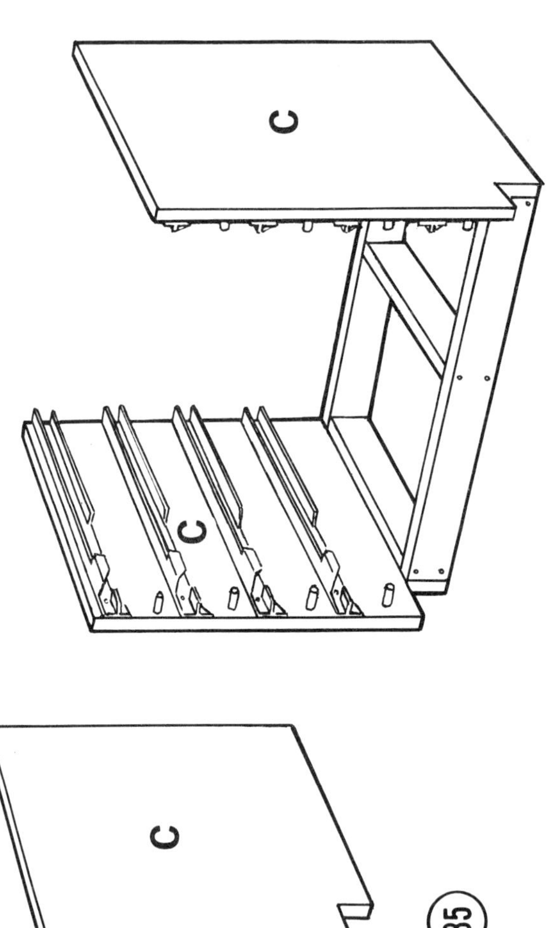
C
C
C
85

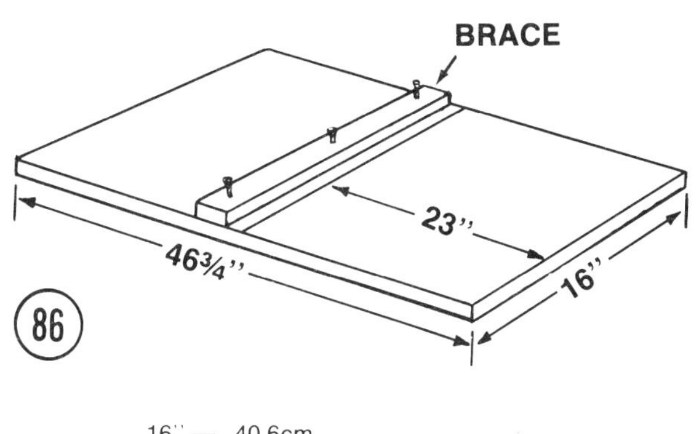

16" — 40.6cm
23" — 58.4
46¾" — 118.7

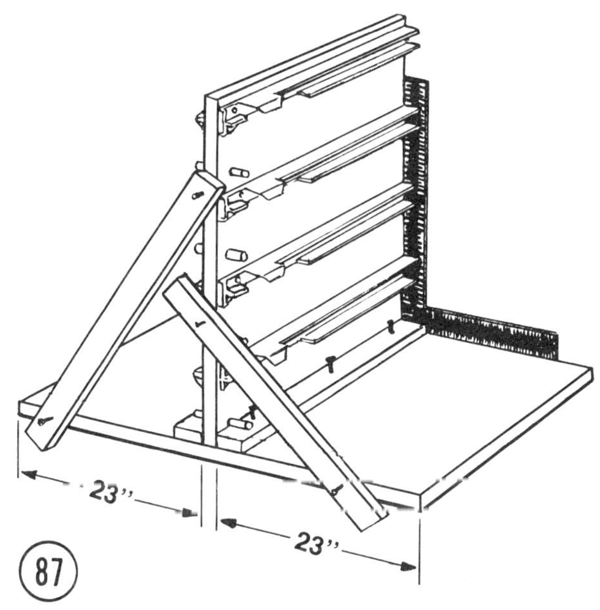

Cut bottom E, Illus. 86, ¾ x 16 x 46¾". Using a square, draw lines 23" from end. Nail 1 x 2 braces temporarily along line.

Apply glue and nail E to D, Illus. 87. Check with level. When plumb, brace in position. Allow glue to set before moving ED.

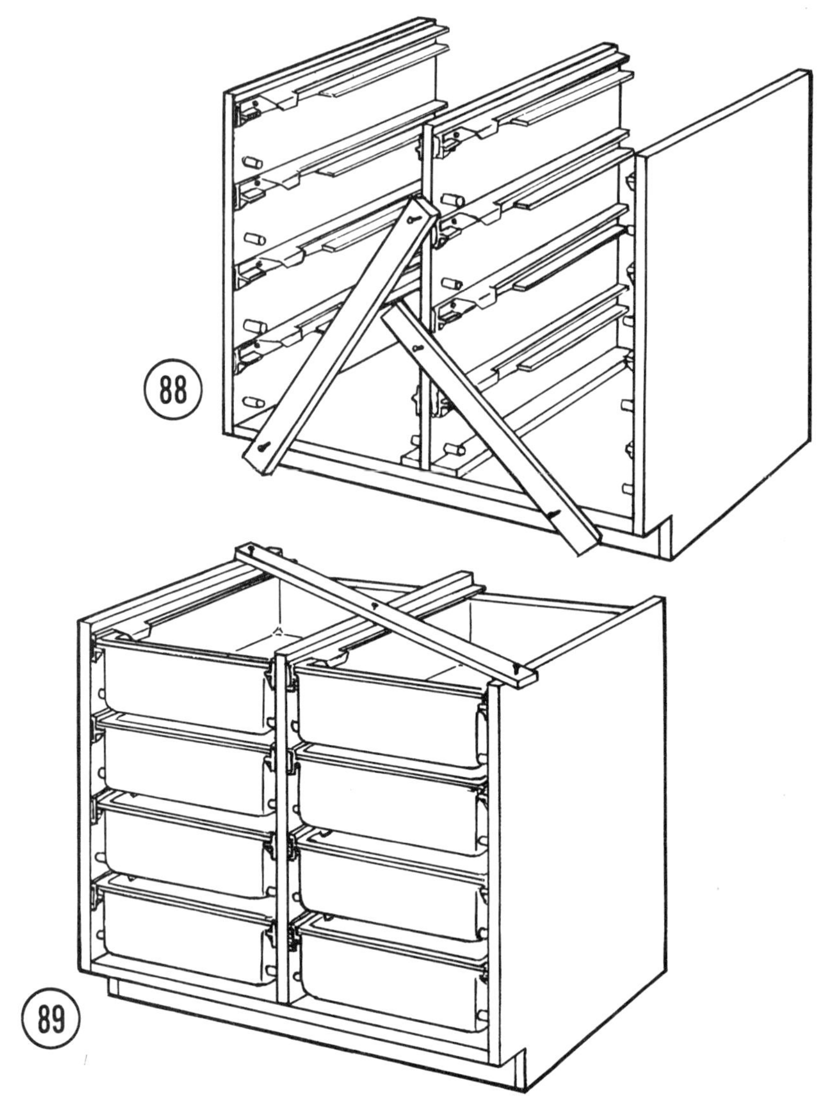

Fasten E to A, Illus. 88. Remove braces and test plastic drawers in guides. When drawers work smoothly, nail 1 x 2 braces diagonally across top, Illus. 89.

In a wall to wall installation, this unit should be centered as shown, Illus. 90. Cut F to length required. Glue and nail F to B,end C to B. Glue and screw 1 x 2 shelf support in position shown.

Cut K and L to overall length required, Illus. 91.

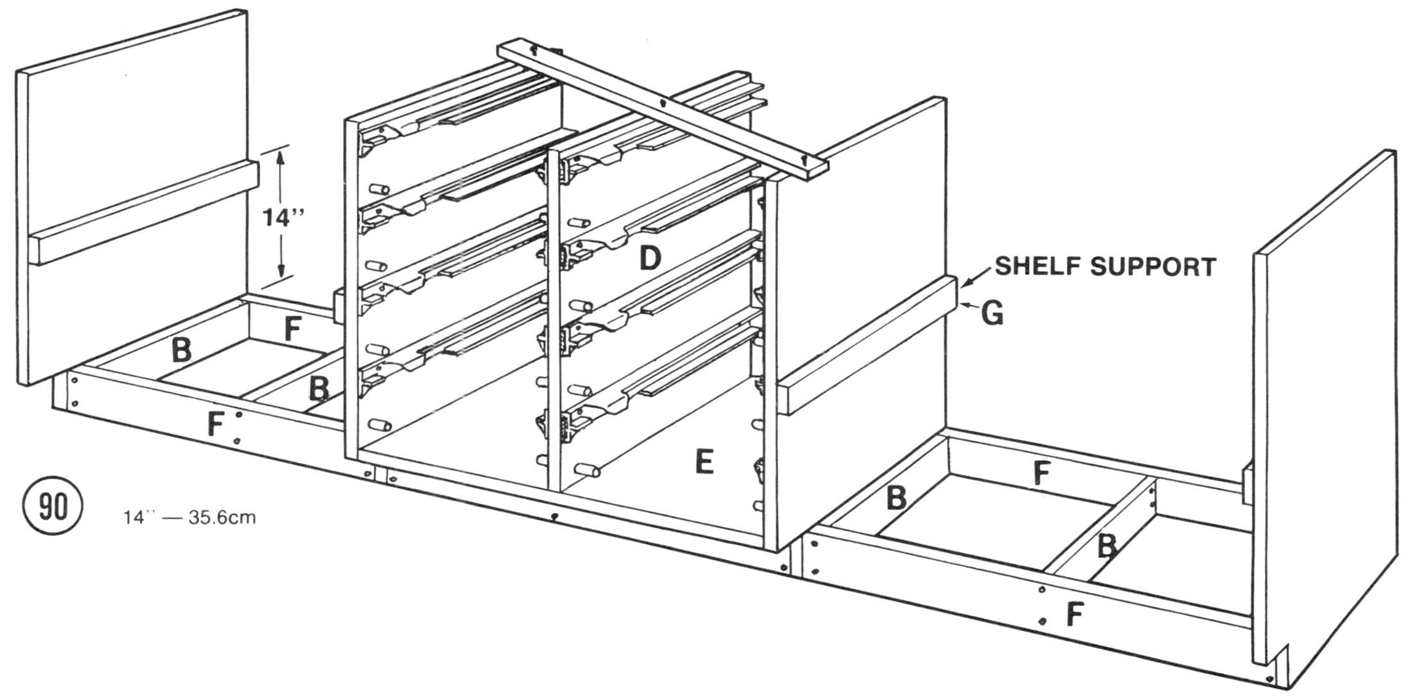

73

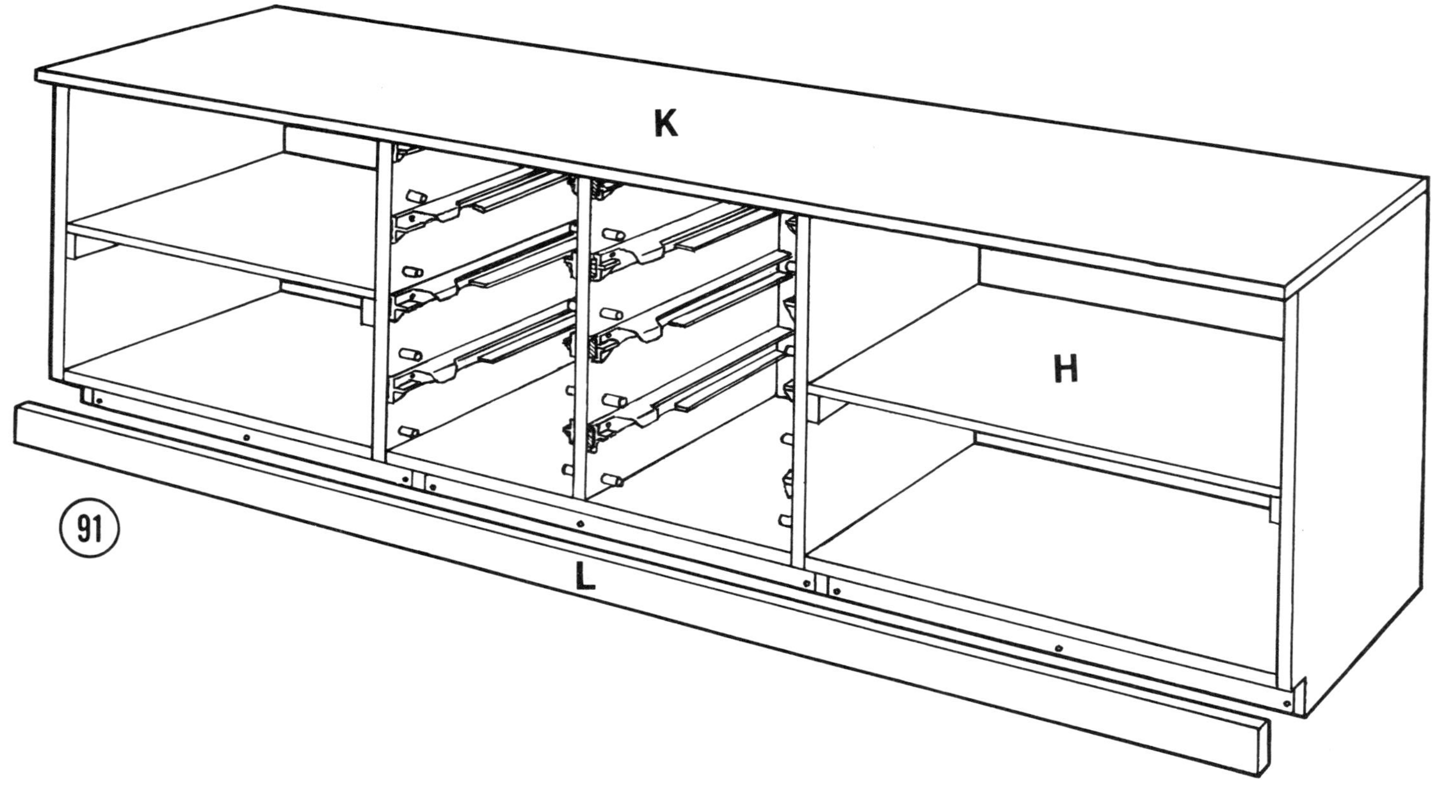

K
H
L
91

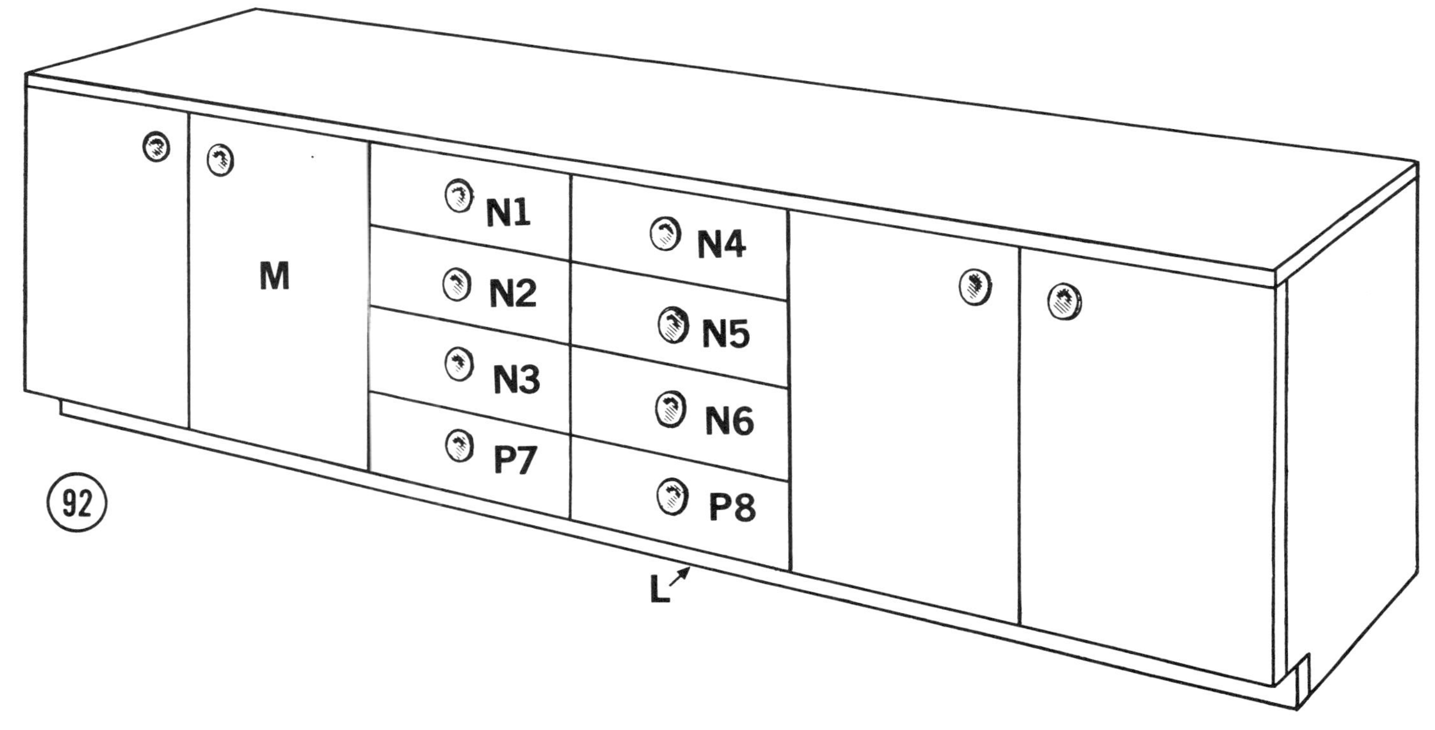

M
N1
N2
N3
P7
N4
N5
N6
P8
L
92

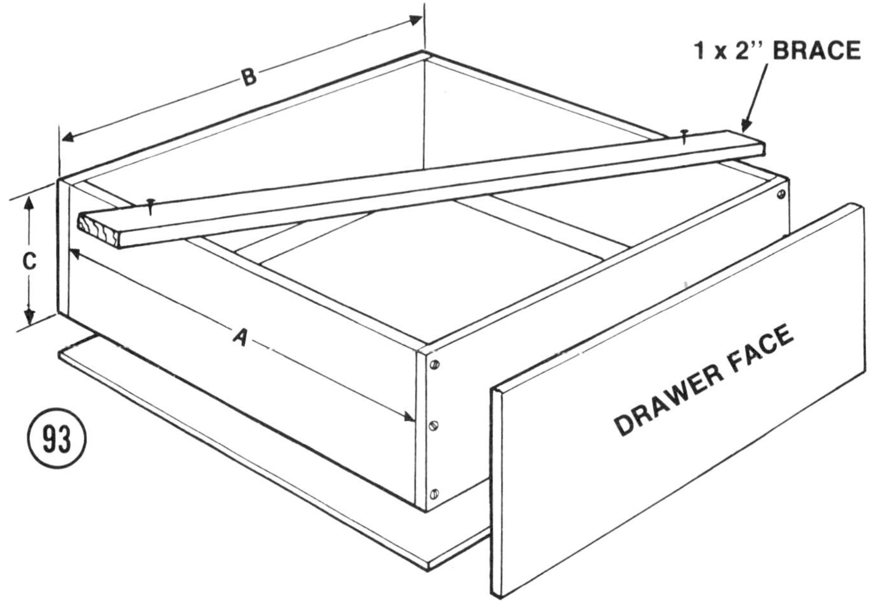

Cut top K to width required to finish flush with drawer face N, and doors M, Illus. 78,92. Remove top brace. Check to make certain drawers move freely. Apply glue and nail through K into C and D with 6 penny finishing nails. Countersink heads. Fill holes with wood filler.

Cut L 2½" wide by length required, Illus. 91. Glue and nail in position.

If you decide to build drawers, cut parts, Illus. 82,83, to size noted or to size your construction requires. Sides A and B can be cut from 1" lumber, ⅝ or ¾" plywood.

Apply glue, screw or nail B to A. Check with square. Hold square with 1 x 2 cross brace, Illus. 93. Glue and brad 3/16" hardboard or ¼" plywood bottom to sides. Allow drawer to set time glue manufacturer specifies.

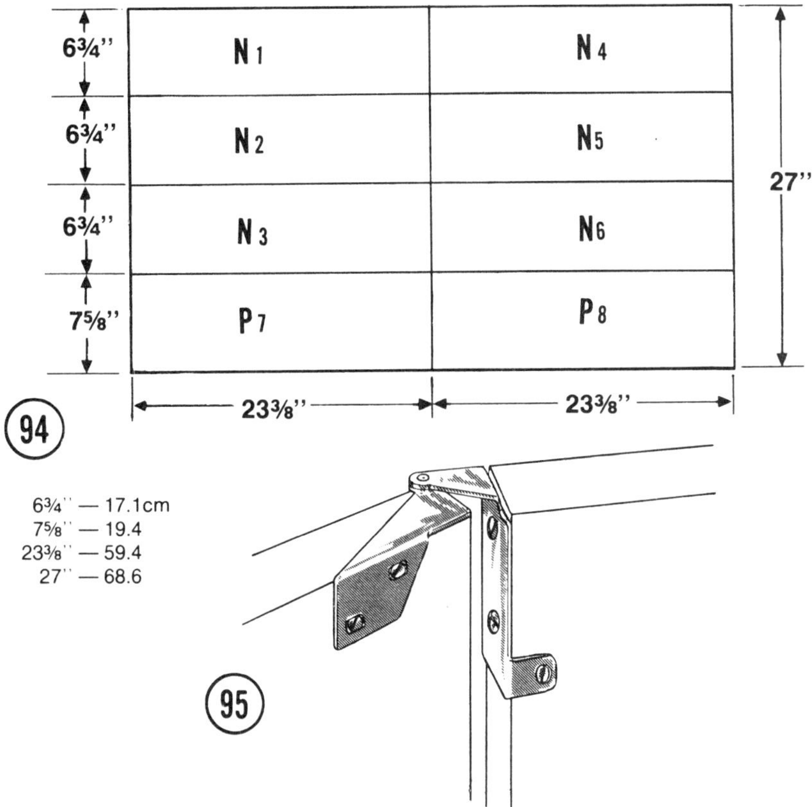

(94)

6¾" — 17.1cm
7⅝" — 19.4
23⅜" — 59.4
27" — 68.6

(95)

½" fir plywood faced with ¼" prefinished can be used for drawers. Build drawers to size required after unit has been assembled. If you want to face drawers and doors with ¼" prefinished plywood, cut all drawer faces from one panel so grain runs vertically, Illus. 94. Drawer fronts P7 and P8 cover edge of E, Illus. 75.

Apply glue and fasten B to ¼" face panel, Illus. 93. Apply clamp or weight until glue sets. Drill hole at center and fasten one knob in a 17" drawer, two knobs in a 23" drawer.

Door M, Illus. 92, should be cut 27⅞" high by width required. Cut panel to overall size of opening, then cut in half. Plane door to fit opening.

Hinge door to C with a pair of concealed hinges, Illus. 95. Follow hinge manufacturer's directions.

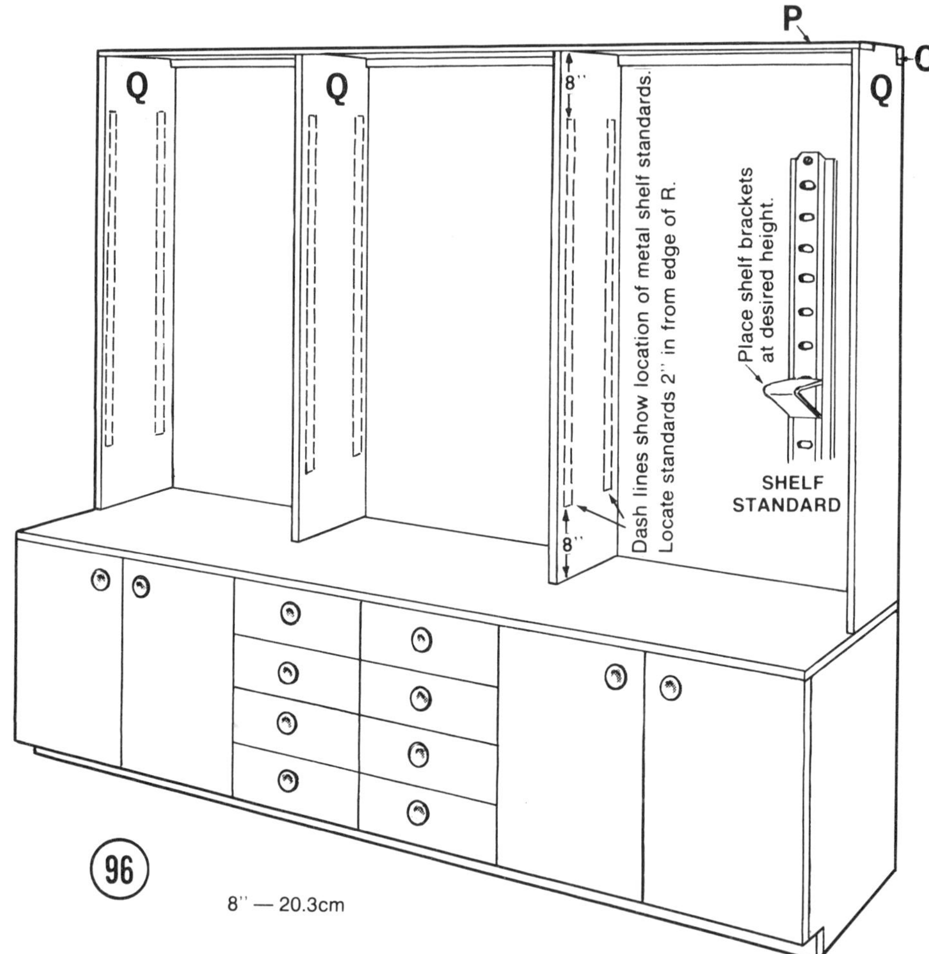

Cut 1 x 2 P and O, Illus. 96, to length required. Nail to ceiling following directions on page 31. Note direction of finished flooring on room directly above. Finished flooring is usually nailed across floor joists. Joists are usually spaced 16" on centers. If joists run parallel to P, drill holes and fasten P to ceiling with expansion fastener, Illus. 28. If joists run at right angles to P, measure 16" from a wall and try nailing P to a joist. When you drive a nail into one joist, measure 16" and locate others.

Cut 9½" wide partitions Q, Illus. 96, by length required. Notch top ends to receive P and O, and install following directions offered previously.

78

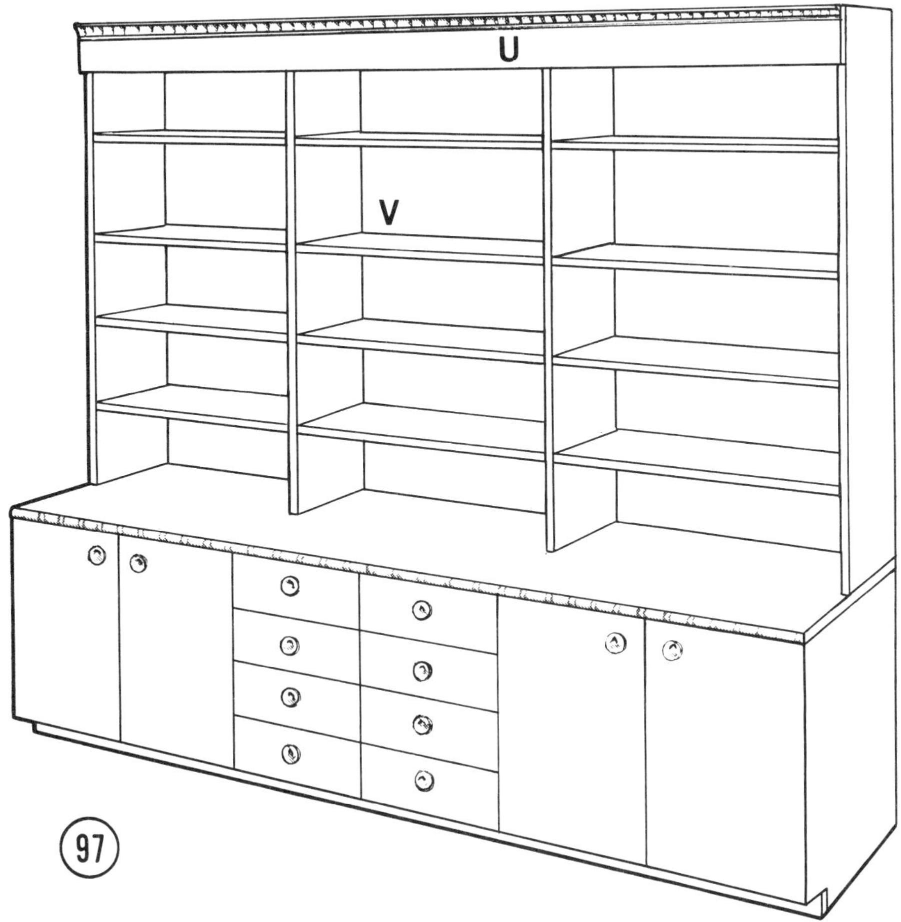

Fasten shelf standards, Illus. 96, to Q in position shown.

Cut twelve shelves V, Illus. 97, 9½'' by length required. Shelves can be cut full length and notched to fit around standards. This locks shelf in position. Insert brackets in standards and cut each shelf to exact size required.

Cut fascia U, 5½'' by length required. Glue and nail in position, Illus. 97.

To add a decorator touch, glue and brad carved wood trim in position shown to top of U and edge of K. On a free standing unit, miter cut and apply molding to front and end of K.

BOOKCASE, BAR, RECORD CABINET

This easy to build cabinet fills many needs. It can serve as a bookcase, bar, record cabinet or store linens and blankets. While directions suggest building a 14½ x 36 x 44'' unit, any other size can also be built. Since these cabinets provide handy storage space, they prove a popular project for students taking vocational education. Offer to paint or cover cabinet with fabric or washable wallpaper supplied by customer.

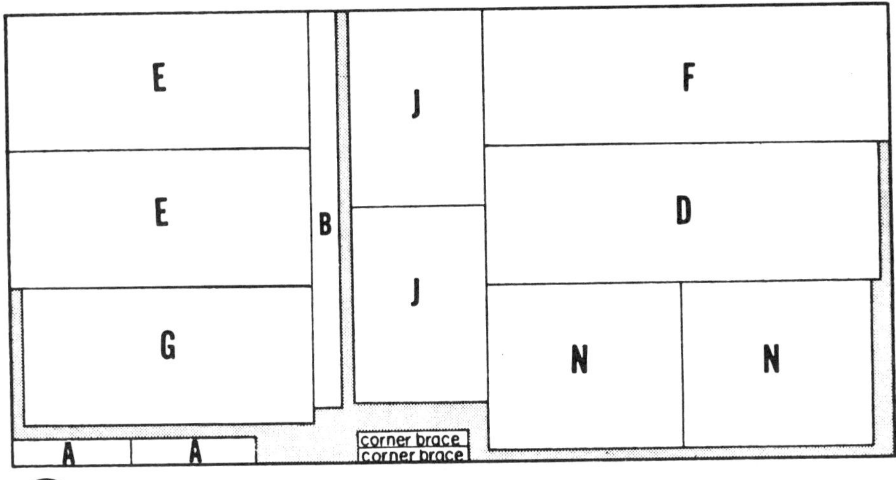

(98) **CUTTING DIAGRAM**

LIST OF MATERIAL

1 — ¾'' x 4 x 8' plywood or flakeboard, good two sides
1 — ⅛'' x 3 x 4' hardboard
1 — 7/16 x 1⅜'' x 5' stop molding
½ lb. 6 penny finishing nails
12 — 1'' No. 8 flathead screws
1 box 1'' brads
2 pr. 1½ x 1½'' loose pin butt hinges
4 — 10'' lid supports
2 — bullet type catches
2 — 2½'' cabinet knobs

Illus. 98 provides a cutting guide for the 4x8 panel. Cut two A, Illus. 99, ¾ x 3 x 13¼''.

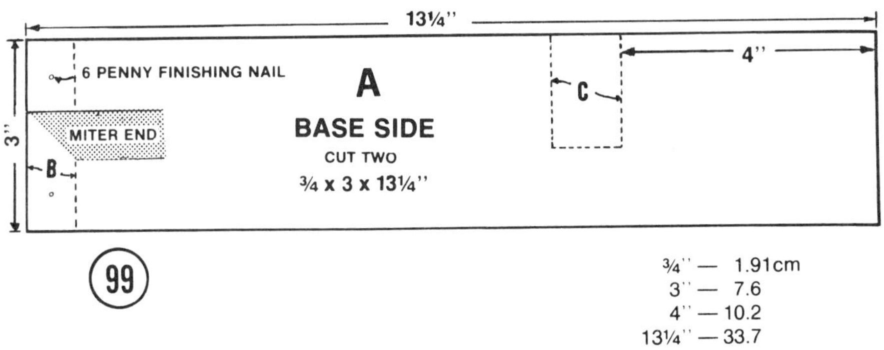

(99)

¾'' — 1.91cm
3'' — 7.6
4'' — 10.2
13¼'' — 33.7

81

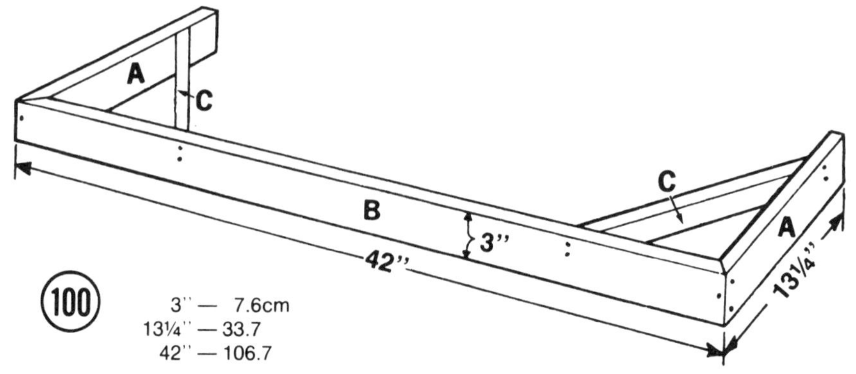

Miter cut ends 45°, Illus. 100,101.

Cut one B, Illus. 100, ¾ x 3 x 42". Miter cut ends. Apply glue and nail AB together with 6 penny nails. Check with square. Hold square with a temporary brace across top.

Cut two corner braces C, Illus. 100, 1¾ x 12". Miter cut both ends. Keeping AB square, apply glue and nail C to AB.

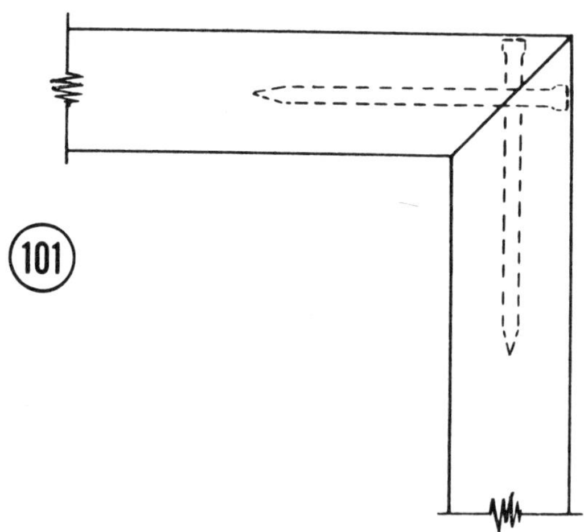

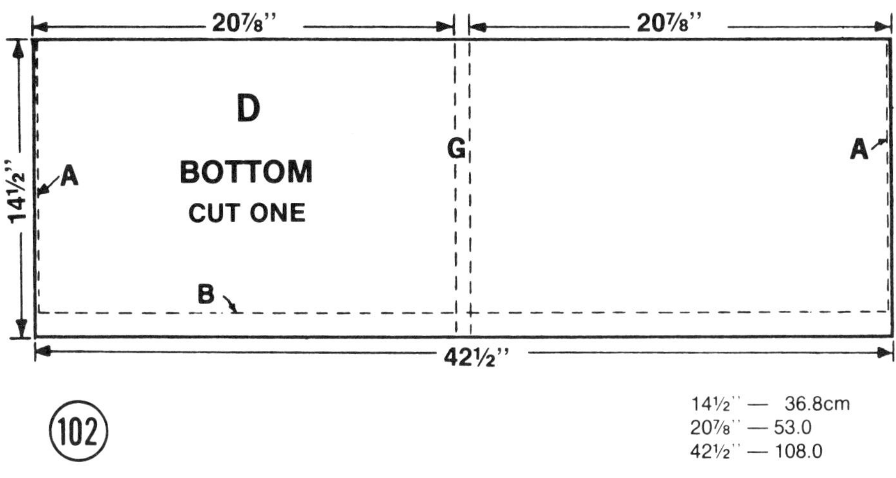

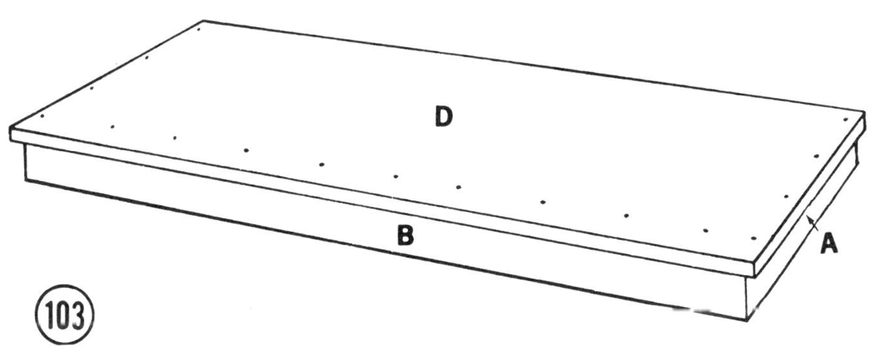

Cut bottom D, 14½ x 42½'', Illus. 102. Apply glue and nail D to assembled base with 6 penny nails spaced about 4'' apart, Illus. 103.

Cut two sides E, 14½ x 33'', Illus. 104. Miter cut top edge 45° as indicated. Miter cut so E forms a pair, one right, one left.

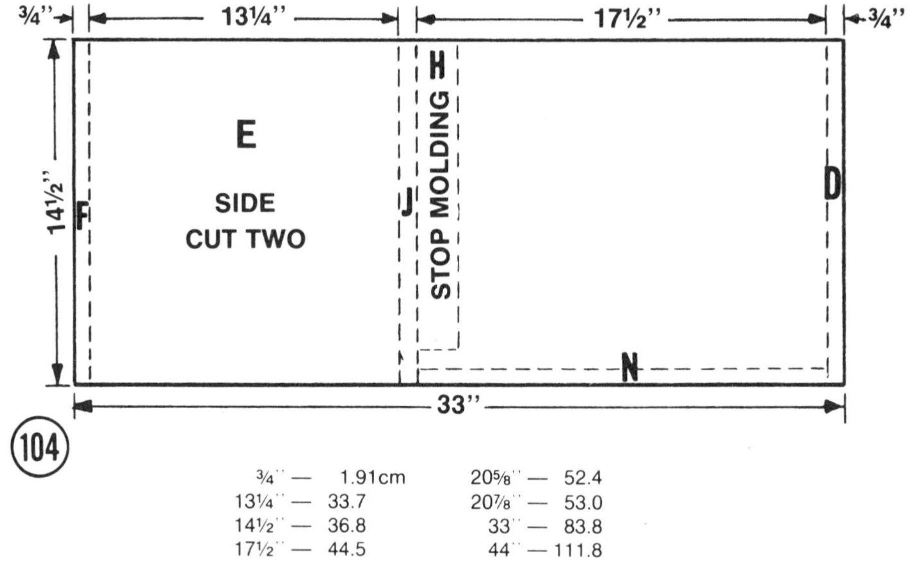

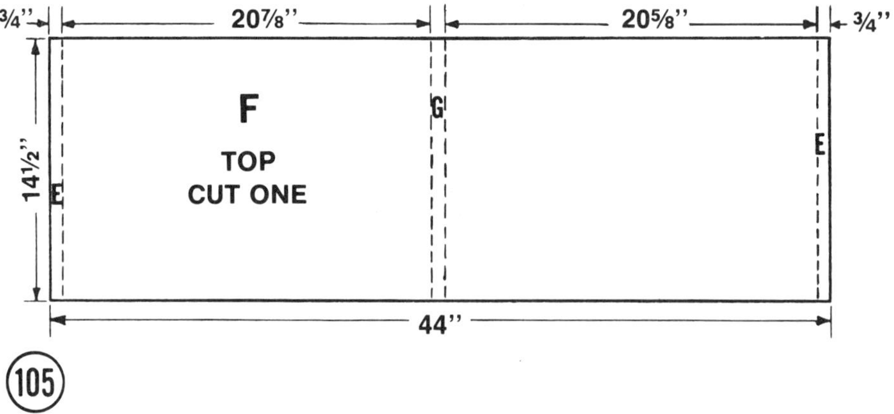

Cut top F, 14½ x 44", Illus. 105. Miter cut ends 45° to match sides E, Illus. 106.

Glue and nail E to D with 6 penny finishing nails. Glue and nail F to E. Check with square. Hold assembly square with 1 x 2 brace nailed diagonally across back.

Cut partition G, 14½ x 31½", Illus. 107. Be sure to check length against assembled unit. Cut to length unit requires. Glue and nail D and F to G in position shown, Illus. 102,106.

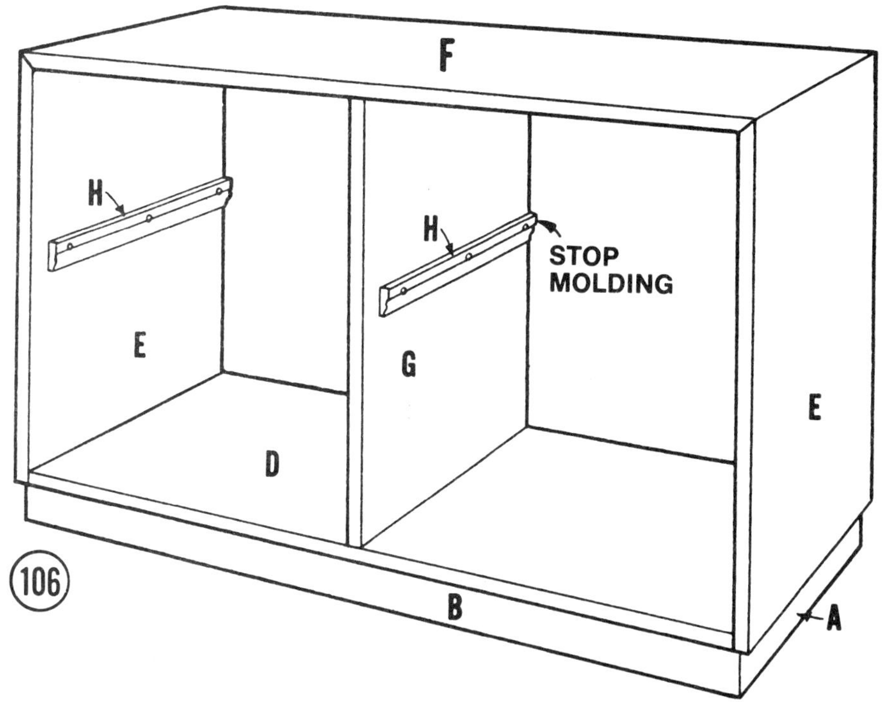

Cut four pieces of 7/16 x 1⅜ x 13" stop molding for shelf support H. Bore through H for No. 8 screws in position indicated, Illus. 106,107. Glue and screw H in position indicated. Screw H to both sides of G with 1" No. 8 screws. Stagger position of screws so they don't interfere.

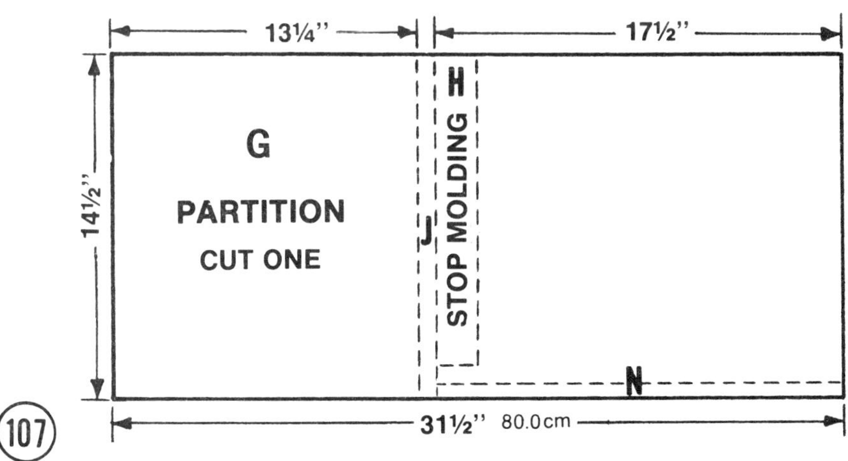

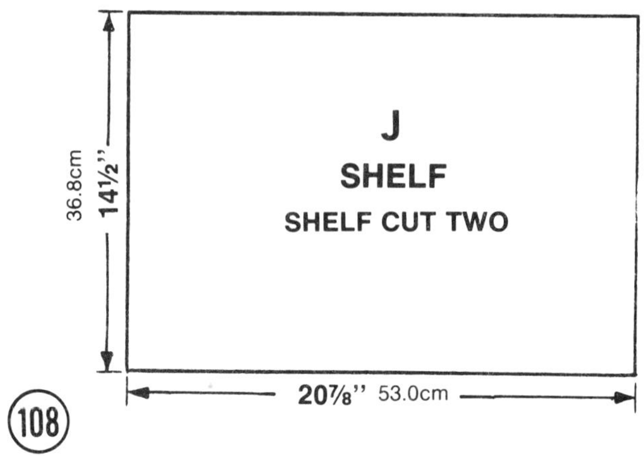

Cut two shelves J, 14½ x 20⅞", Illus. 108, or to size your unit requires. Place or nail shelves in position.

Cut back panel K from ⅛" hardboard. Before nailing back, check assembled cabinet with square. Apply glue to D,E,F. Position K about ¼" in from outside edge and nail in position with 1" brads spaced 4 to 6" apart.

Miter cut ends of ¾" wide molding L. Glue and brad in position, Illus. 109,110.

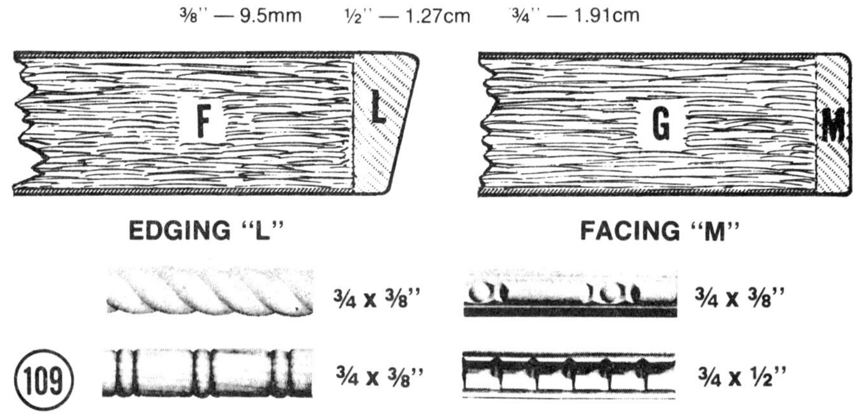

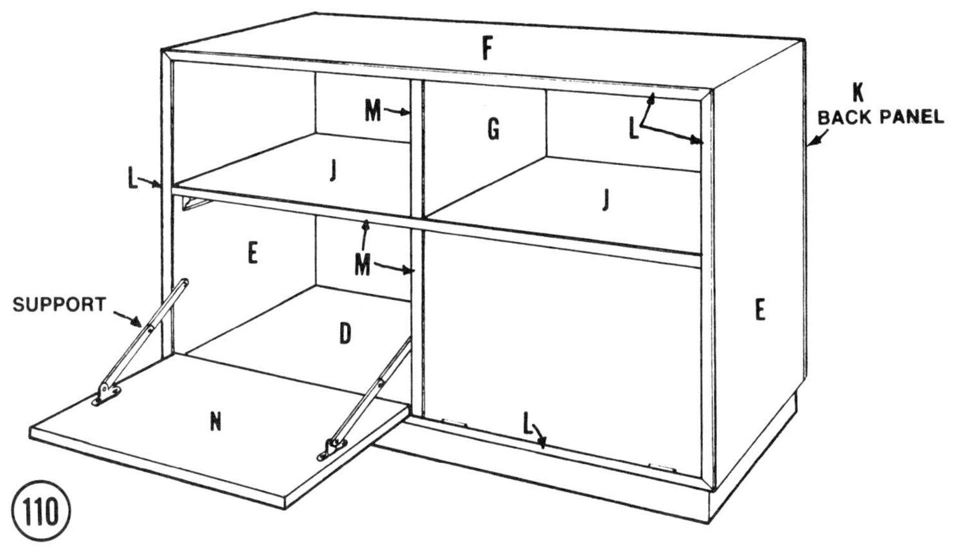

For that custom look, use carved wood trim in place of edging L.

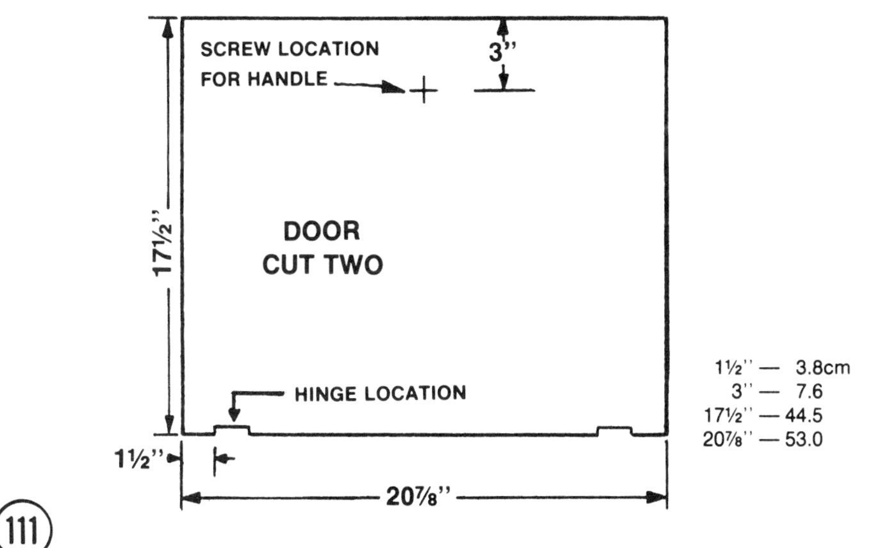

Cut two doors N, 17½ x 20⅞'', Illus. 111, or to size required. Notch bottom edge to receive full thickness of a closed 1½ x 1½'' loose pin butt hinge. Note position of hinge, Illus. 110,111. Cut notch to width and thickness hinge requires. Place door in opening. Plane or sandpaper to fit. Screw hinge in position using screws retailer recommends.

Prime coat project. When dry, sand smooth, then apply first coat of paint. Sand lightly then apply a second coat.

OPTIONAL TRIM APPLICATION

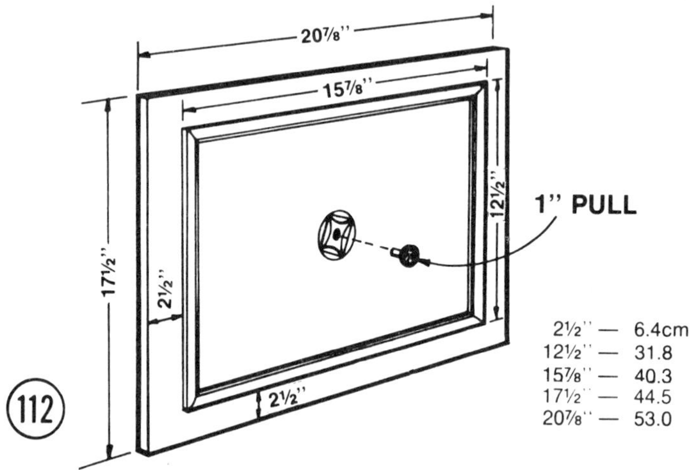

You can frame a door with molding as shown in Illus. 112. Miter cut four pieces 12½'', and four pieces 15⅞''. Glue and brad to doors in position indicated.

Locate center of door by drawing diagonal lines. Drill a hole through center to receive the door knob. Drill a hole through center of a rosette to receive bolt in knob. Apply glue to rosette. Fasten rosette and knob to door.

Apply lid supports as shown in Illus. 110. Fasten plunger type cabinet door catch to center of N and bottom of J.

NOTE: Position of shelf permits storing 12'' albums.

ROOM DIVIDER

An easy to build room divider can be built to any length required. While four foot dividers can be built from clear 1 x 10 pine, longer units should be built from 5/4 x 10. 10'' lumber measures 9¼''. This is an ideal width for shelving.

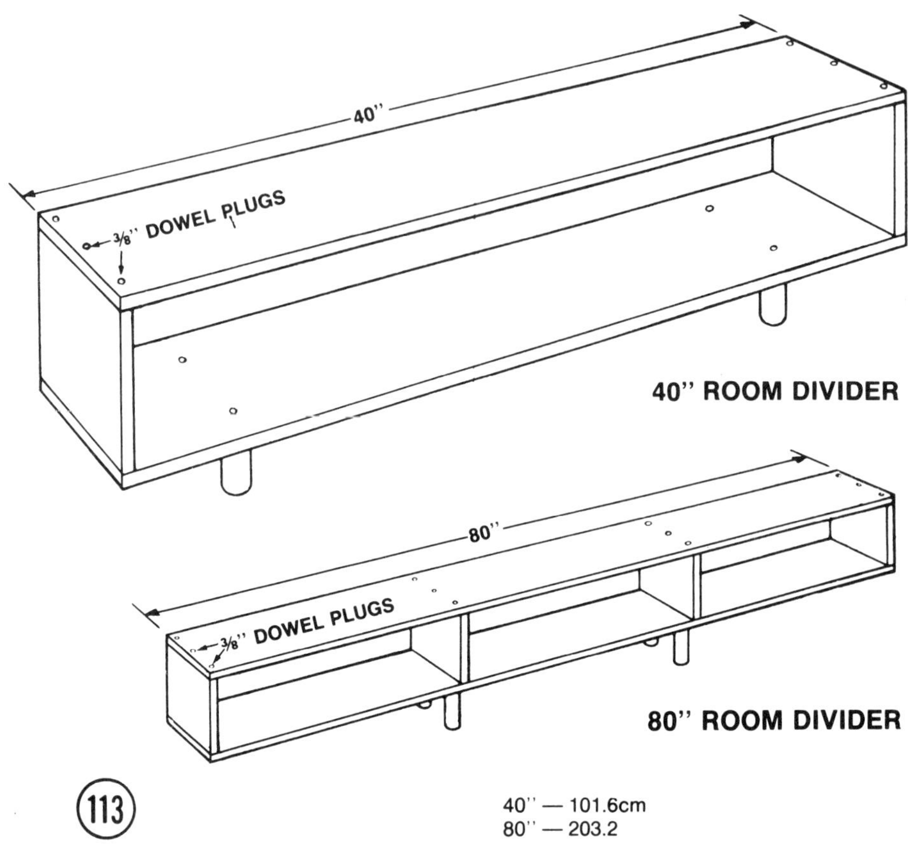

Illus. 113 shows 40 and 80" dividers. Construction of both follow the same general procedure. The only difference is the need for shelf supports C in the 80" unit.

For a 40" unit, cut A, 40". Bore 3/8" holes 3/8" deep at ends where indicated, Illus. 114, then bore 3/16" through to receive shank of No. 10 screw. If you use 1" lumber, a 1¼" No. 10 screw is sufficient. If you use 5/4" lumber, use 1½" No. 10 screw. Note Illus. 116.

Bore four 3/8" holes, ⅛" deep in top face of bottom A, Illus. 113,116. These permit countersinking screws needed to fasten legs to A.

90

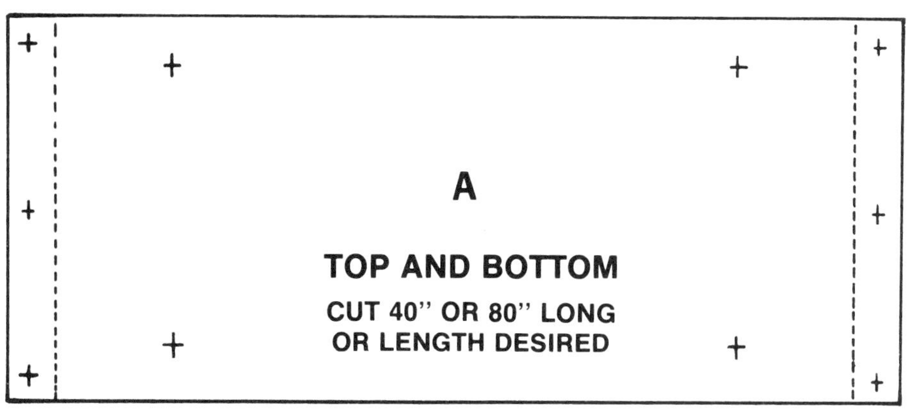

¾" — 1.91cm
1" — 2.54
2" — 5.1
4¼" — 10.8
6" — 15.2
8½" — 21.6

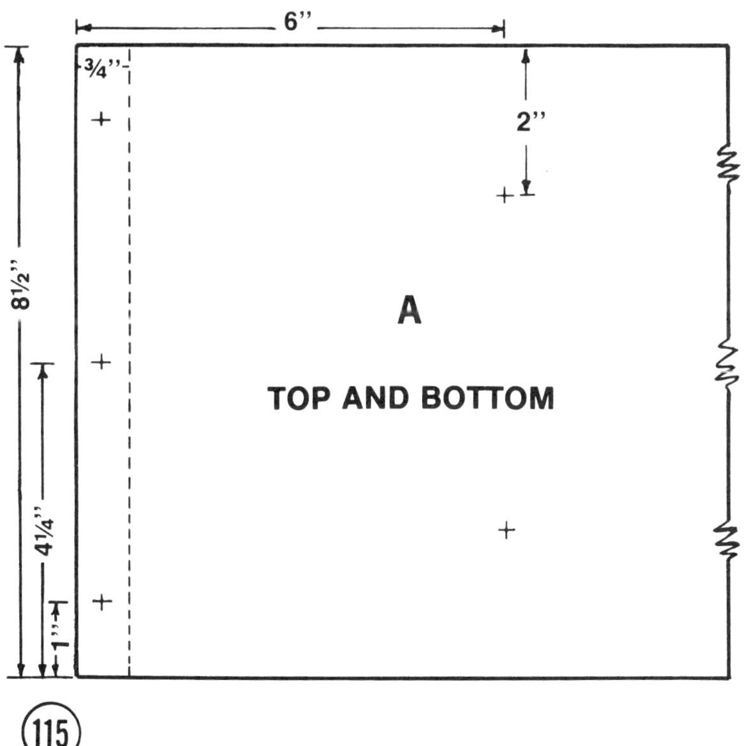

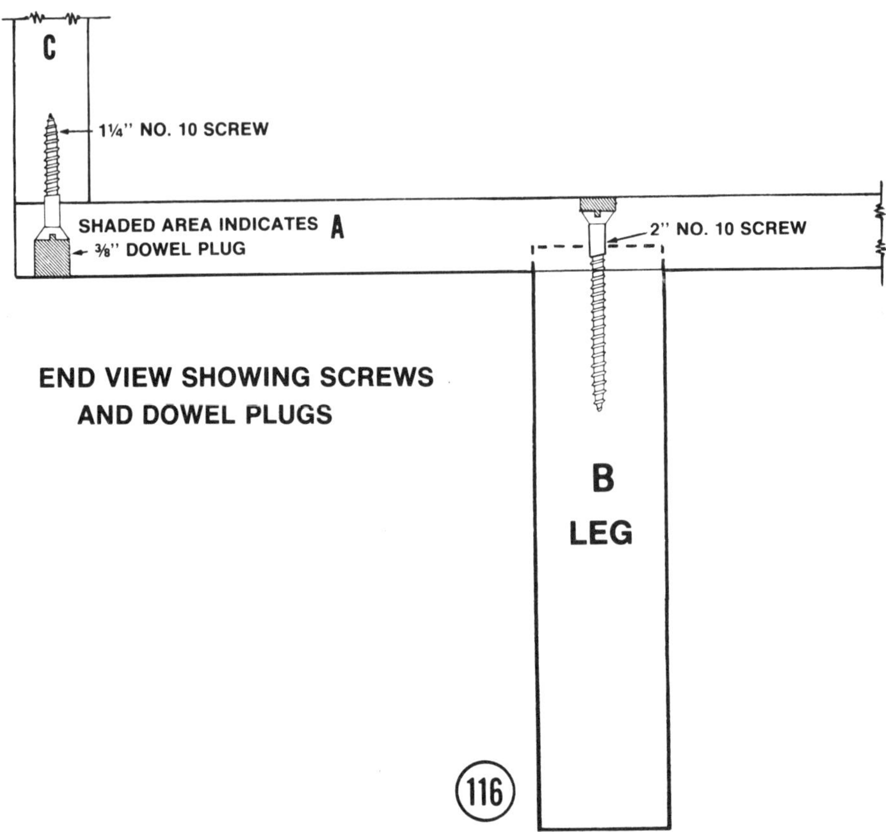

Bore four 1⅜" holes, ¼" deep in bottom face of lower A to receive 1⅜" clothespole used for legs. Using center of 1⅜" hole as a guide, continue boring 3/16" hole through to receive shank of No. 10 screw, Illus. 115, 116.

Cut two 10" ends C, Illus. 117. Apply glue and fasten top and bottom to C with 1¼" screws. Countersink heads, Illus. 116. Cut ⅜" dowel approximately 1". Apply glue and drive dowel into hole. Allow glue to set, then saw end of dowel flush with top. Use care not to mar surface. Sandpaper smooth.

Cut leg B from 1⅜" clothespole. While length of leg is optional, cut them oversize. If you want 6" finished leg, cut 7". Apply glue and insert leg into hole. Secure A to leg with a 2" No. 10 screw, Illus. 116. Fill hole over screw with wood filler or dowel.

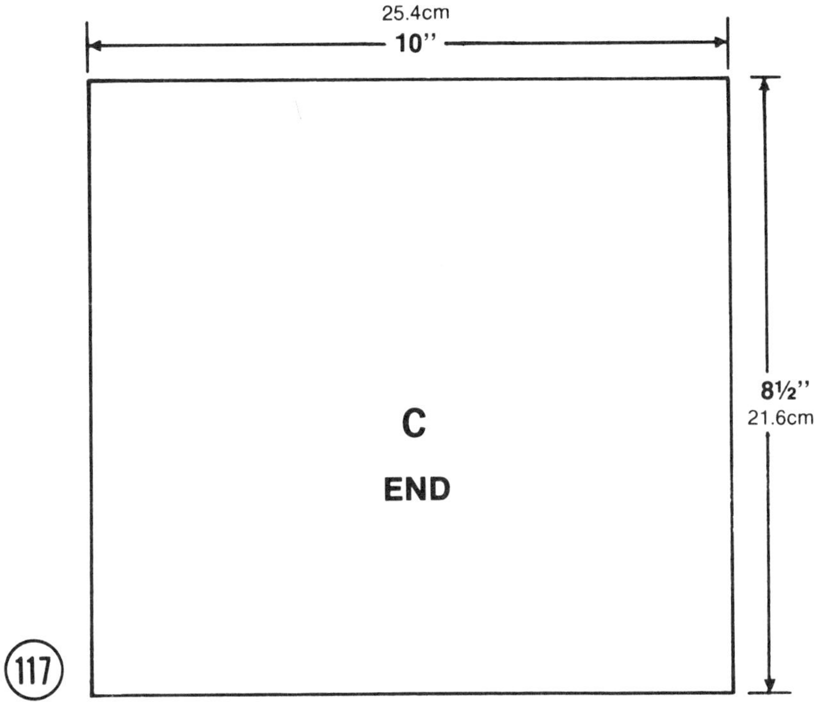

Allow glue to set thoroughly. To cut legs to exact length, use the "sawing guide," Illus. 118. Clamp two pieces of equal width lumber or plywood in position shown and saw legs flush with edge of guide.

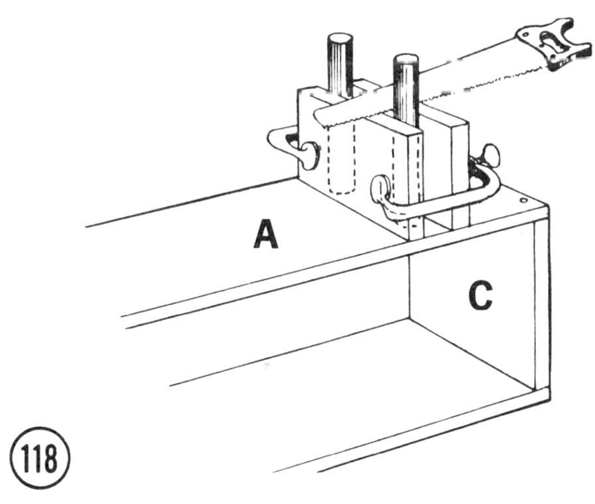

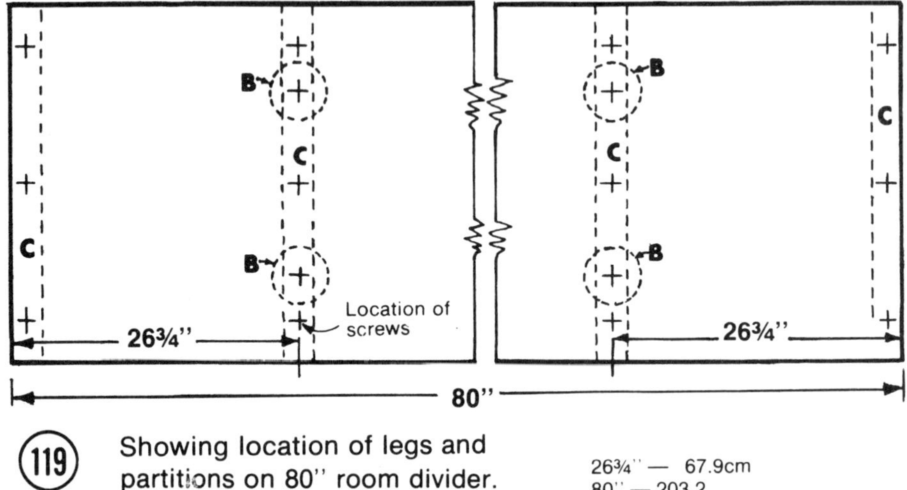

(119) Showing location of legs and partitions on 80" room divider.

26¾" — 67.9cm
80" — 203.2

Sandpaper end. Fasten domes of silence to bottom of leg to facilitate sliding over floor.

For an 80" room divider, cut top and bottom 80". Use clear, 5/4 x 10. Cut four C. Drill holes in position indicated, Illus. 119. Use 2½" No. 10 screws to fasten legs. It isn't necessary to countersink screws as partitions cover same.

When stacked one on top of another, these units make an ideal room divider and show place for prized bric-a-brac.

SECTIONAL BOOKCASES

Sectional bookcases provide an economical solution to a book storage and shelving problem. Since every home, apartment and office can use these, and most customers want cases to fill a specific area, the potential for a part or full time business is good. Step-by-step directions suggest using 1 x 12. Since all clear costs a bundle, use a grade with tight knots or cut ¾'' plywood, surfaced two sides (S2S), to width required.

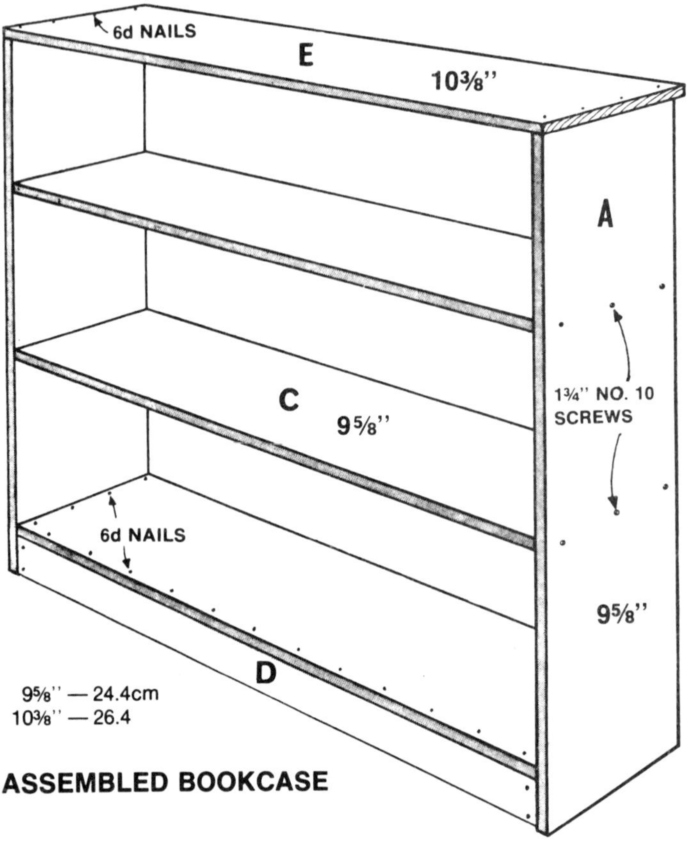

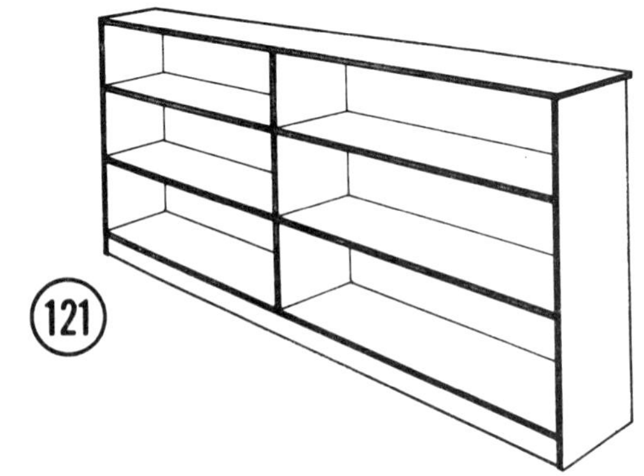

120

ASSEMBLED BOOKCASE

The case shown, Illus. 120, measures 36" long and stands 36½". The ends were cut to 9⅝" width, the top 10⅜". A 36" shelf can hold a fairly heavy load. If you build a longer length, install dividers every 30 to 36", Illus. 121, to provide additional support.

121

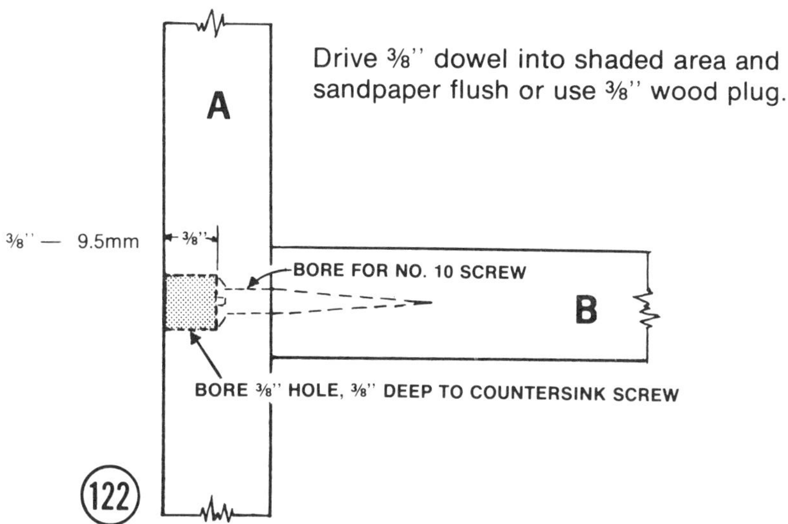

Sides should be screwed to shelves. To make like a "pro," countersink screw heads. Use a pilot hole bit or drill ⅜" hole, ⅜" deep, Illus. 122. Drill a 3/16" hole through A. Cut ⅜" dowel length required. Dip screw in glue before driving. After driving screw, glue dowel in position, sandpaper smooth.

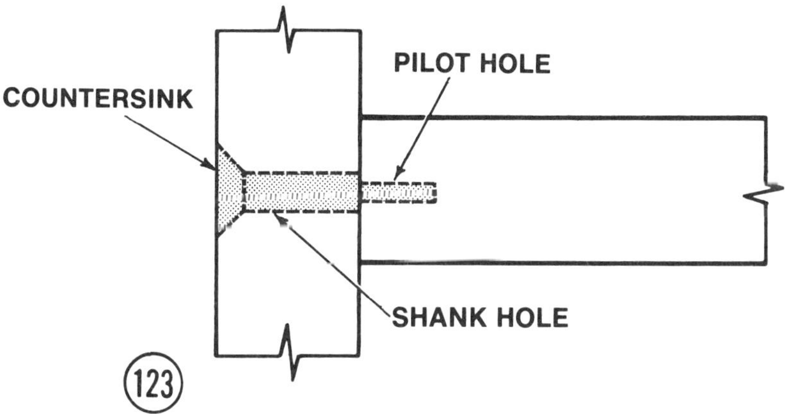

You can also use a screw pilot bit, Illus. 123, to countersink screw head. In this case, cover head of screw with wood filler. Always bore shank hole large enough to freely accommodate screw shank. Bore pilot hole slightly less than diameter of threaded portion of screw and only half the depth of threaded portion.

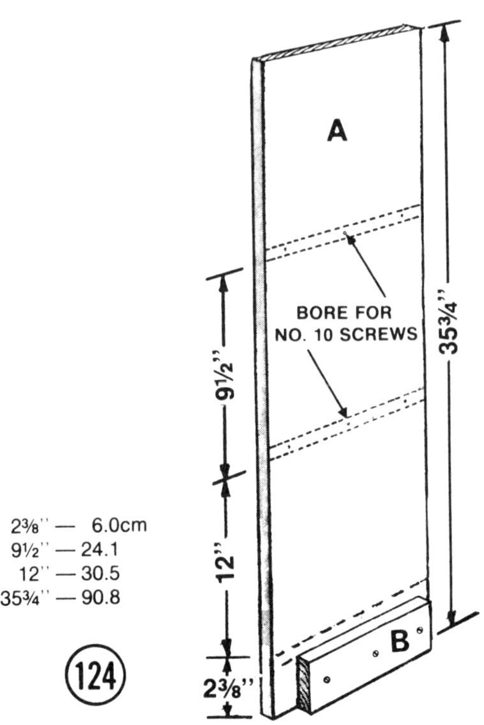

Cut two A, 9⅝ x 35¾", Illus. 120. Bore three holes in position required for each shelf, Illus. 122,124, then drill 3/16" holes through A to receive No. 10 screw.

Cut two cleats B, 1 x 1½ x 8⅞". Apply glue before nailing or screwing B to A.

Screw B to A, Illus. 124, ⅛" up from bottom of A. By keeping B and D ⅛" from bottom, it simplifies planing edge if slope in floor requires same. Use thickness of D, Illus. 120, to space B from leading edge of A.

Cut three shelves C, 9⅝ x 34½". Nail bottom shelf to B, Illus. 125, with 6 penny finishing nails.

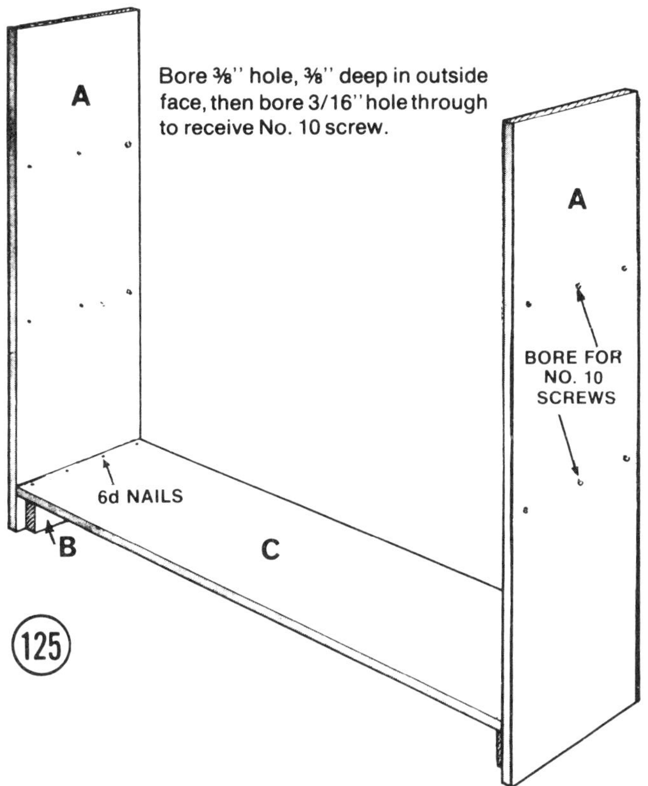

Cut D, 1 x 1½ x 34½'', Illus. 120. Nail D to B with 6 penny nails. Countersink heads. Fill holes with wood filler.

Check AC with a square. Hold square with a 1 x 2 brace nailed temporarily across front.

Fasten shelves C in position, Illus. 120, with 1½'' No. 10 screws or 6 penny finishing nails. Countersink screw heads.

Since a baseboard or baseboard radiation may position a bookcase ¾'' or more away from wall, cut top E, Illus. 120, to width required. Nail in position shown with E projecting over back edge. Follow same procedure when applying tops on matching cases.

If you want to build a longer one piece bookcase, cut partitions to size required, glue and nail in position.

OPEN END CASE

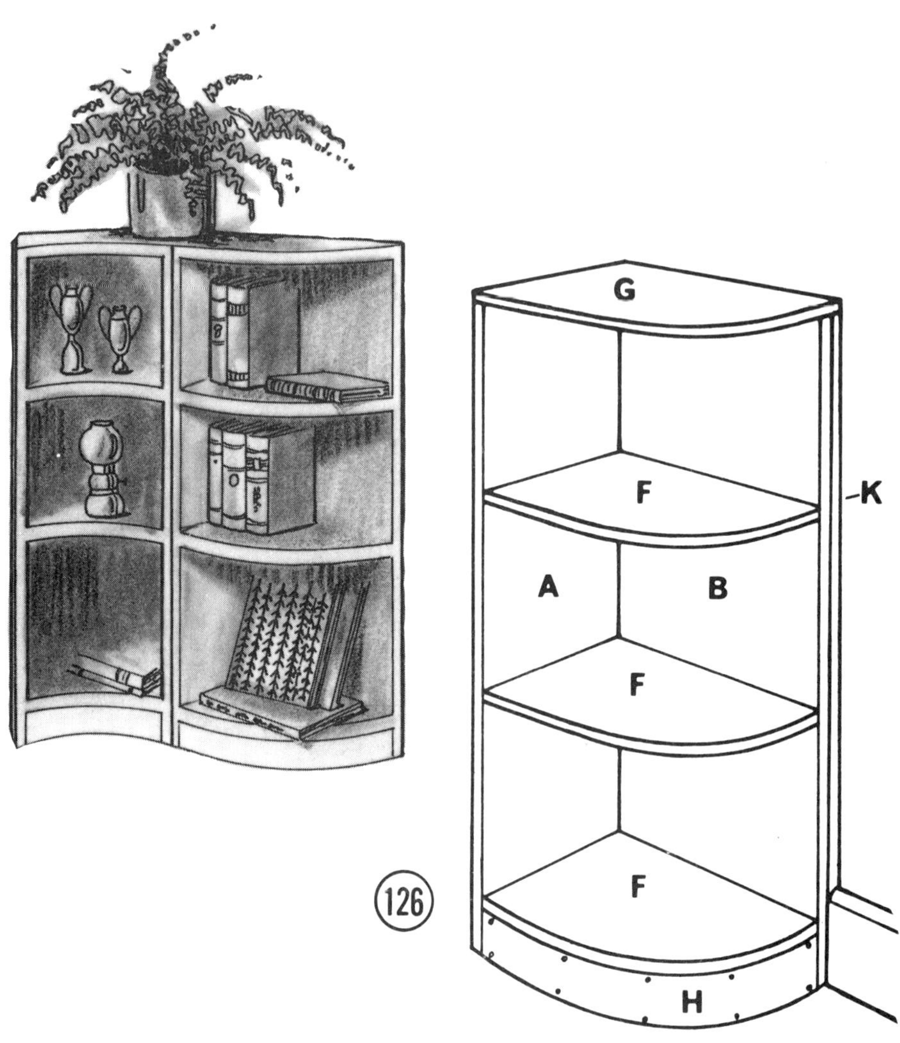

Build this end case from ¾'' plywood or 1 x 12 with tight knots. This can be built for a left or right end. To build a right hand end case, Illus. 126, follow these directions.

Cut one A, 9⅝ x 35¾'', Illus. 127. Bore 3/16'' holes through A where indicated to receive 1½'' No. 10 screws.

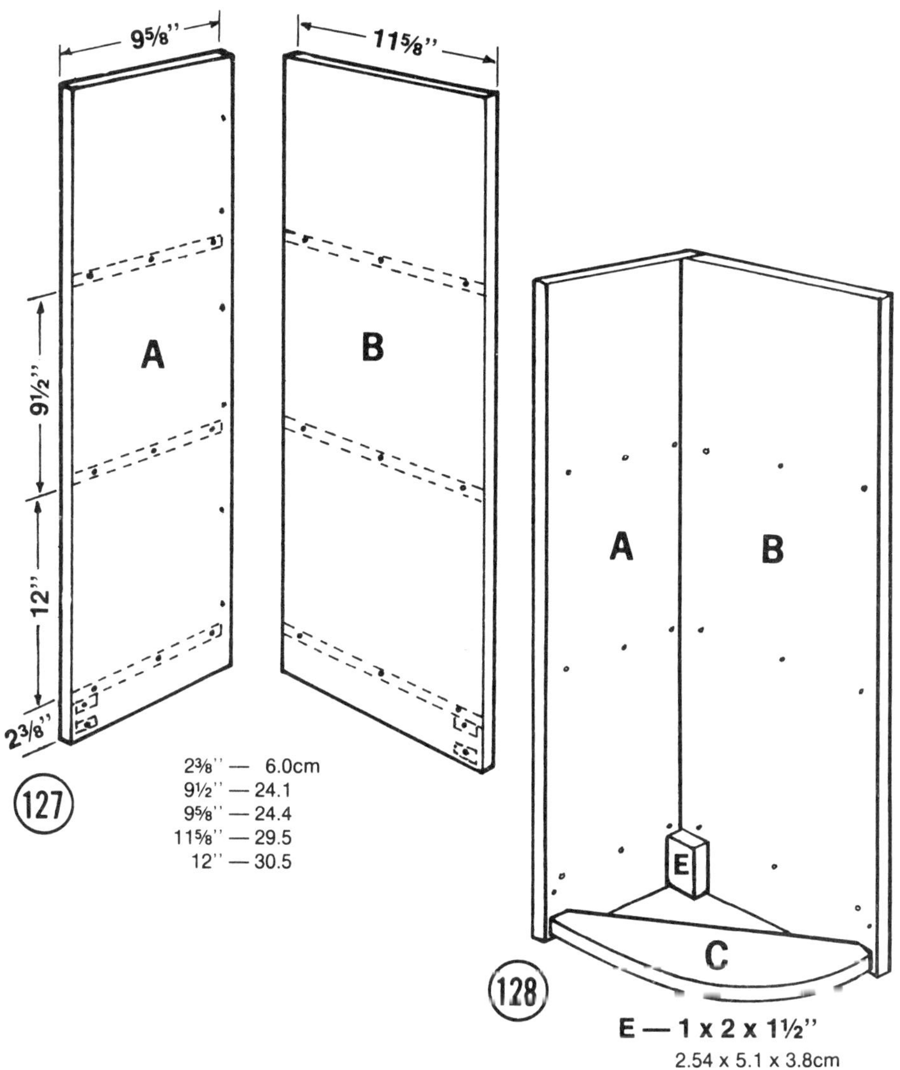

Cut B, 11⅝ x 35¾". Bore holes in B in same position as in A.

Cut cleat C to size and shape shown, Illus. 128,129,130. Join pattern with tape and trace full size outline to overall size required.

Glue and nail A to B with 6 penny nails. Countersink heads. Nail A and B to C. C is recessed ¼" from edge of A and B, and is raised ⅛" from bottom.

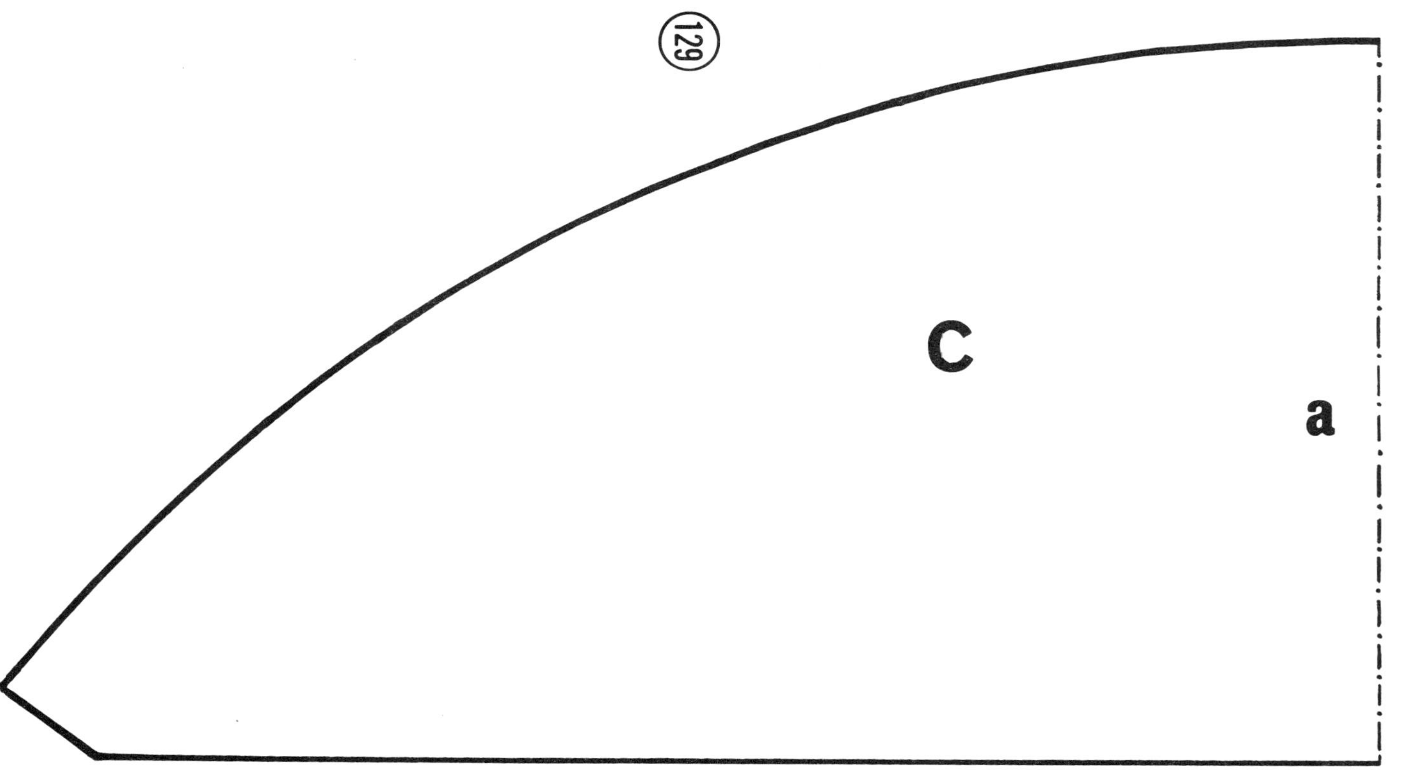

129
c
a

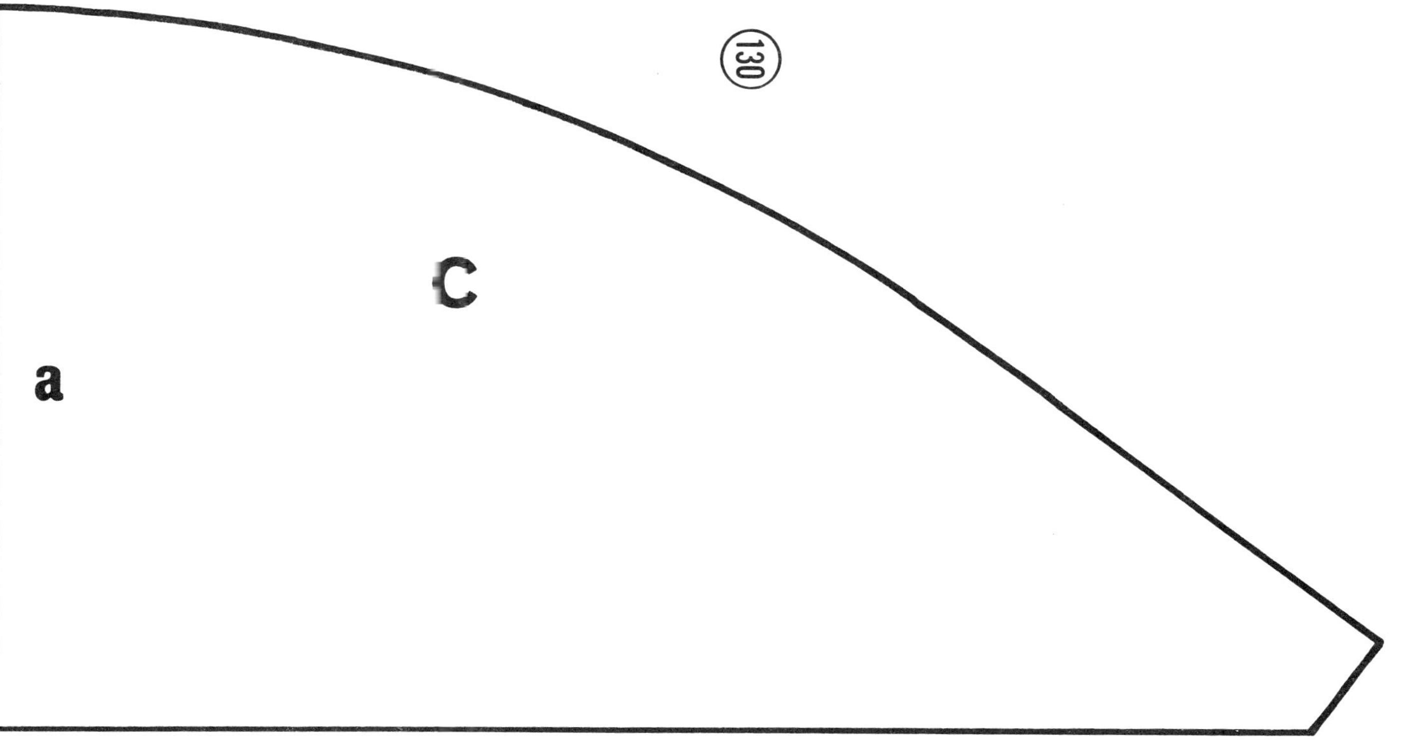
130
c
a

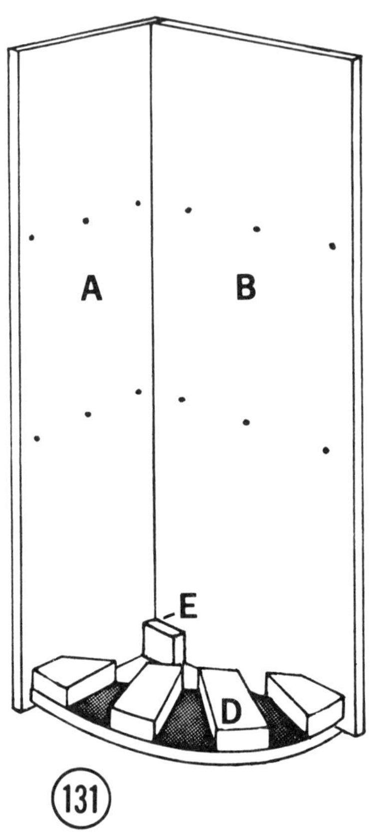

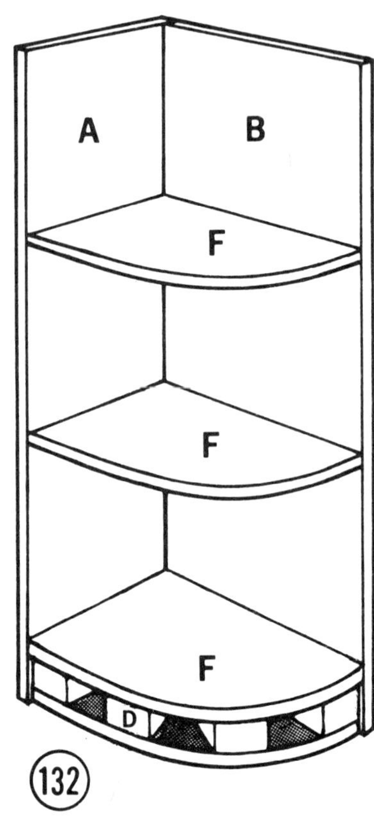

Cut 1 x 2 filler blocks D, Illus. 131. Nail in position flush with edge of C. Cut fillers D to width of C.

Cut 1 x 2 x 1½'' for E, Illus. 128. Place E ⅛'' from bottom of AB. Screw B to E. Top of E is on same plane as D, Illus. 131.

Cut shelf F, Illus. 132, to size and shape shown, Illus. 132, or to size required to finish flush with AB.

Using a nail, string and a pencil, draw curve of radius, Illus. 133,134. Cut two other shelves to same size and shape. Screw or nail AB to F in position shown, Illus. 127, or position preferred.

r = radius

Using a nail, length of string and
a pencil, draw curve to radius
indicated.

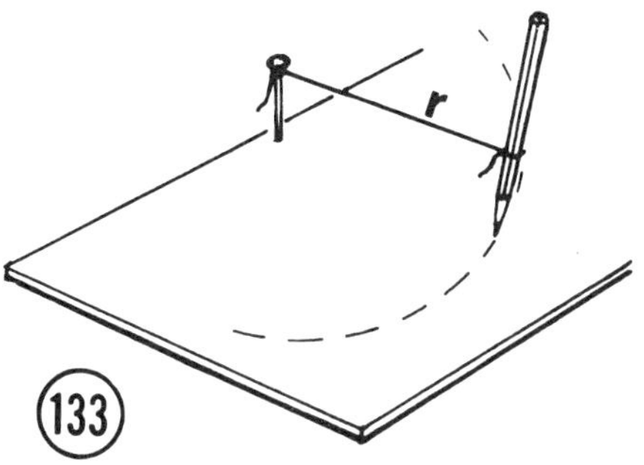

(133)

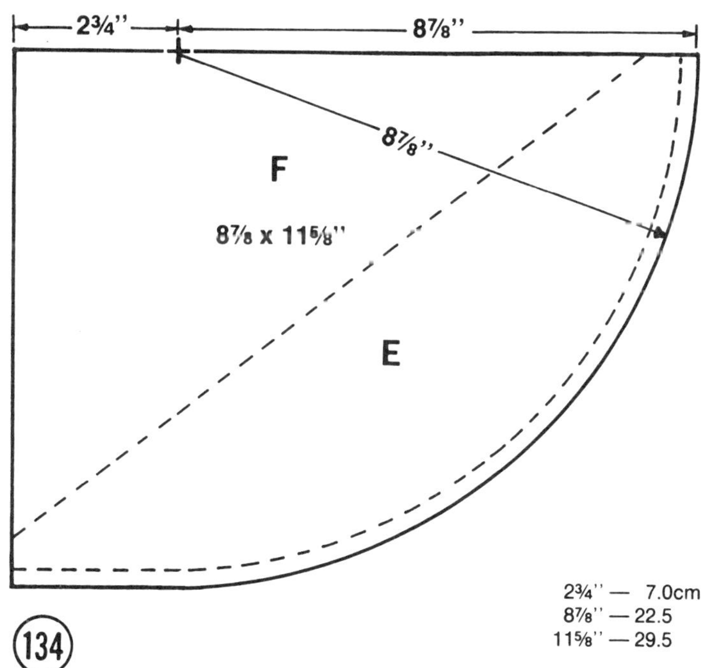

(134)

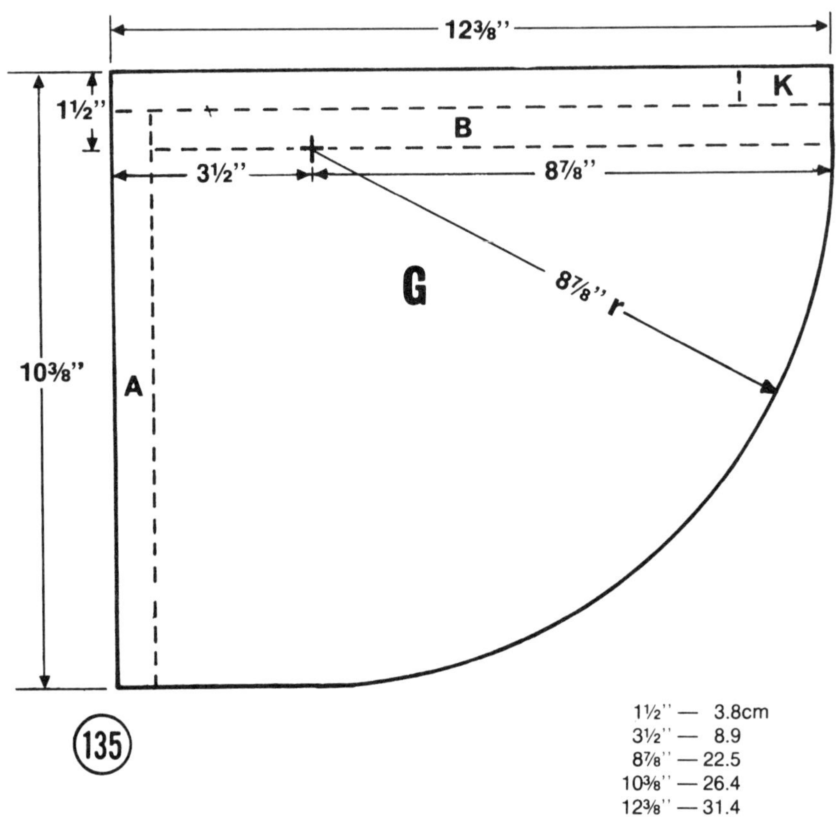

Cut top shelf G so it's flush with front edge of AB and butts against wall. Since a baseboard or baseboard radiation may keep a bookcase ¾" or more away from wall, cut G to overall size required, Illus. 135.

Cut ⅛" nontempered hardboard H, Illus. 126, 1½" by length required. Glue and nail to CD.

A 1 x 2 filler K, Illus. 126,135, can be cut to length required to fill space above baseboard. Nail to back of B.

106

CORNER BOOKCASE

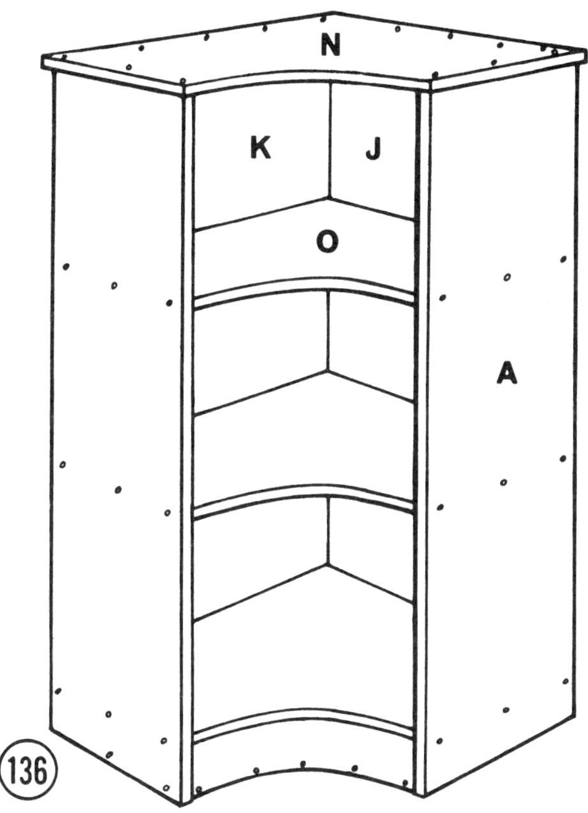

Building a corner bookcase follows the same general procedure as the end case. Cut K - 15¾ x 35¾''; J - 16½ x 35¾'', Illus. 136.

Cut M to size and curve indicated, Illus. 137, 138, 139.

Butt K against J. Nail J to K; KJ to M. Nail 1 x 2 x 1½'' E in position shown, Illus. 137. Be sure to raise M and E ⅛'' from bottom edge. Nail 1 x 2 D to M, as shown in Illus. 131.

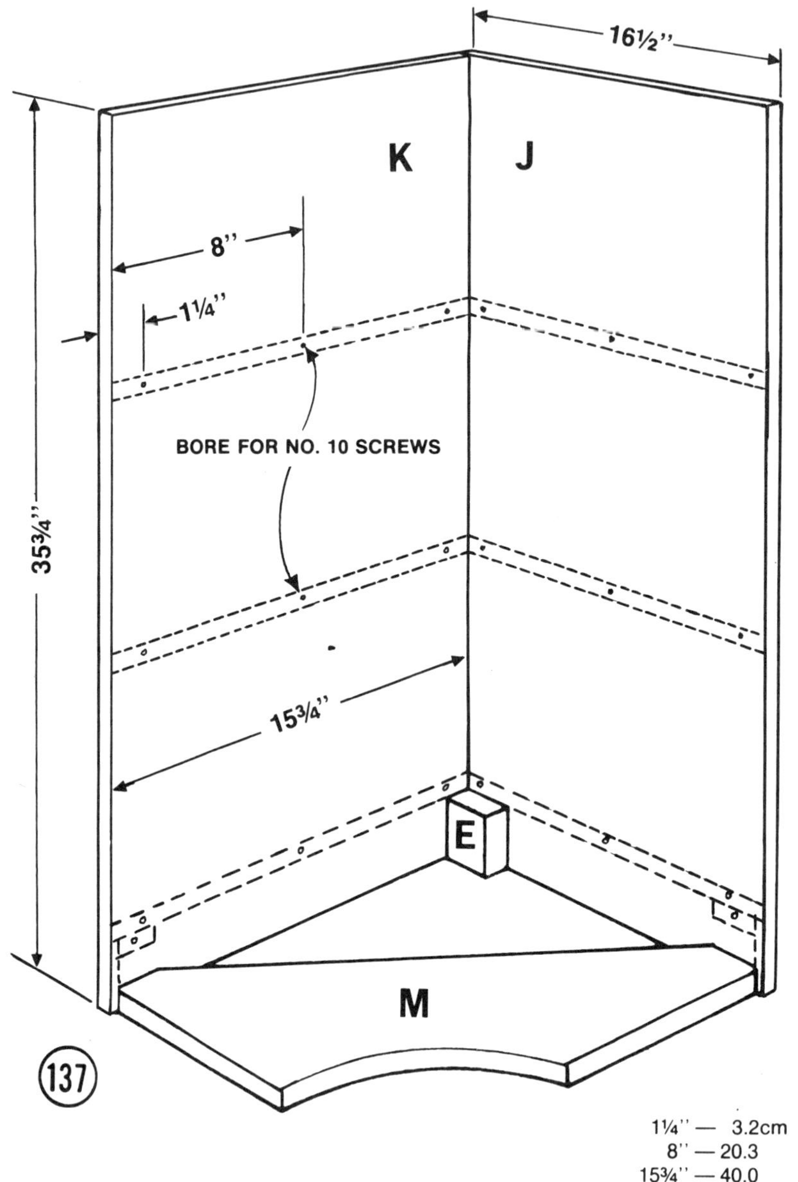

NOTE: Height of shelves is shown in Illus. 127.

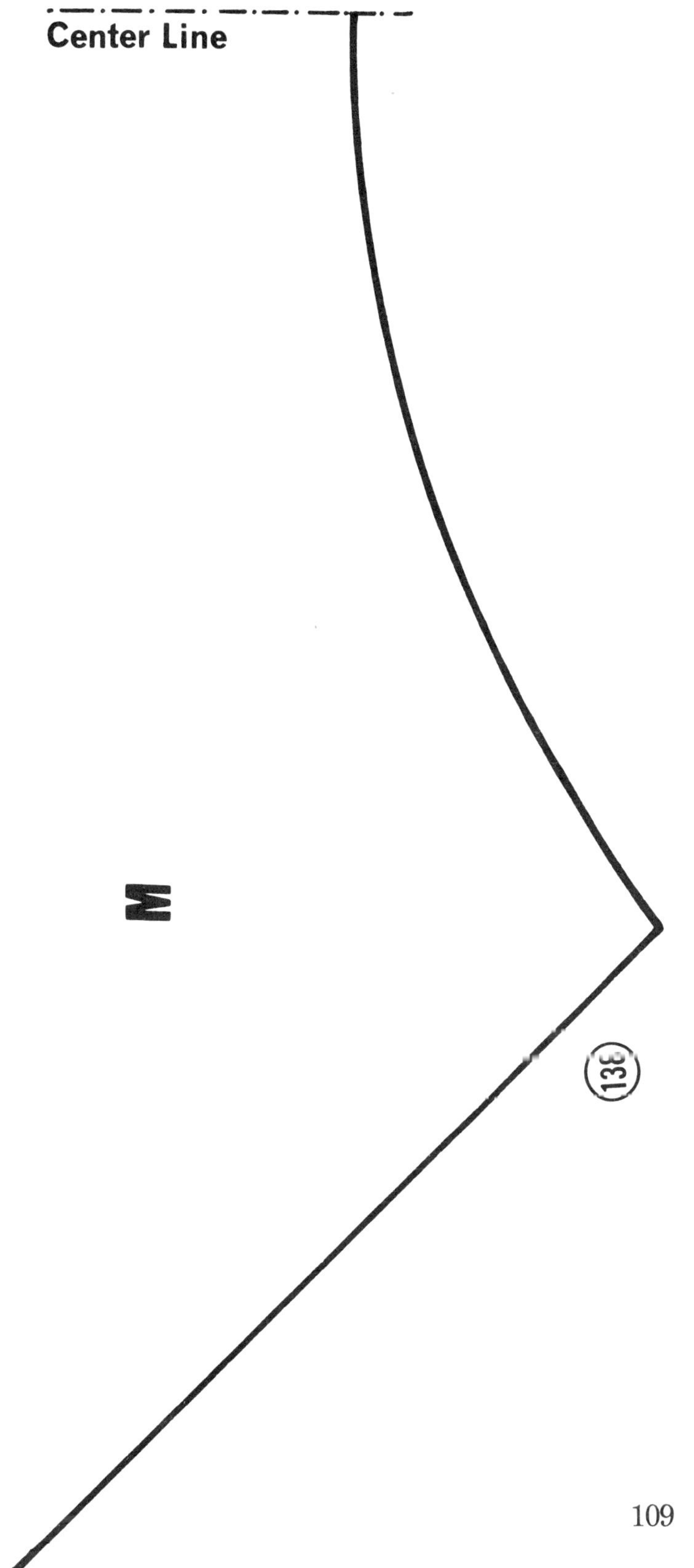

Center Line
M
138

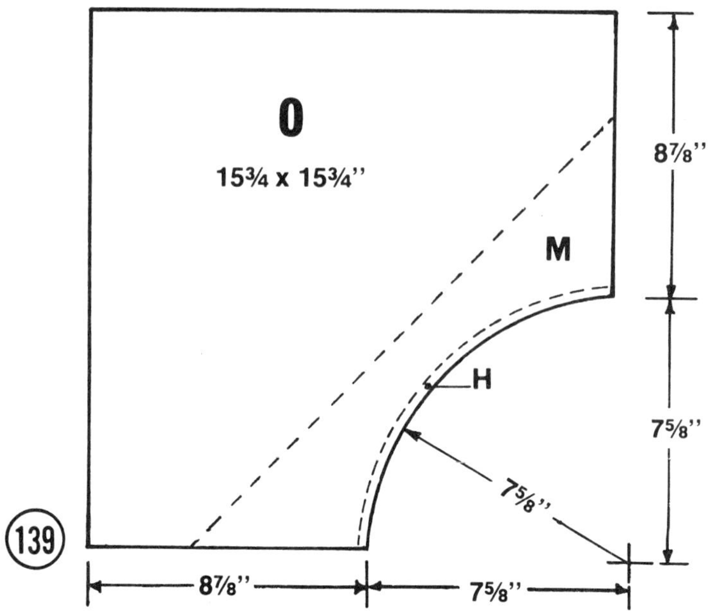

Cut shelf O to size shown, Illus. 139.

Cut top N, 18 x 18" or size required, Illus. 140. Assemble all parts following procedure outlined for each end case.

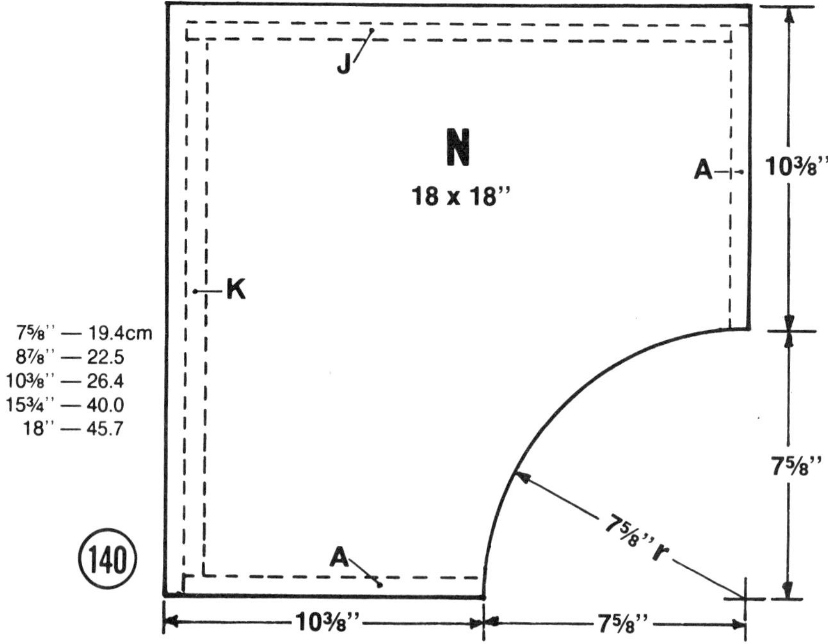

110

Stereo Cabinets

No matter where you live or how you earn a living, there comes a time in each day's rush through life when it's necessary to relax. While many do this without effort, those who need it most frequently find relaxing a difficult part of living. Almost before they realize what is happening, tensions mount, then explode. As we are all subjected to stress and strain, it's imperative to take time to escape, relax and contemplate living.

Since music stimulates, soothes and entertains, we can obtain the kind of relaxation we need if we tune in sound we find beneficial. Regardless of whether it's Bach, Strauss, "rock or pop," music we enjoy provides escape. It's probably the one form of therapy everyone can practice without special training. If you doubt the therapeutic value of sound, listen to music you like. Note how quickly your mind begins to discharge tension and recharges with a desire to do.

This book not only simplifies building a lowboy or highboy cabinet, but also cabinets wall to wall.

The simplified method of construction permits building cabinets and bookshelves to size desired. Directions also explain how to install an indirect lighting valance.

Before buying any material or equipment, read directions through completely. Measure space available. Since sound travels in waves that are reflected or absorbed by various material, placement of speakers is important. Plywood paneled walls provide excellent tonal reproduction while a brick wall or a large area of glass tend to reflect sound.

Everyone who walks into a stereo store for the first time invariably becomes slightly more than confused with the vast selection of components available. Even on return visits, few, except electronic wizards, develop sufficient talent to recognize all the plus and minus features credited to each component. Since most of today's quality speakers are front mounted on handsome, oiled walnut cabinets, they can be placed on shelves, on a floor base, or mounted on a wall. Selection of components should be made prior to building cabinets.

Give serious consideration to the location of a stereo system, and particularly location of speakers. What passes for music and relaxation for one member of a family can drive others up a wall. This is especially true during or immediately after an abrasive discussion. Since a stereo system can penetrate many areas, use extreme care in selecting a site where everyone can enjoy it or the peace and quiet they need.

Another facet that causes concern is the amount of space a system or its speakers require. Be sure all concerned are in agreement. Place speakers where a spouse feels they destroy the decor and every time she hears music it will remind her of how badly it looks. Building and installing a stereo music wall can prove a great conversation piece and ego builder. Don't permit any difference of opinion to lessen its psychological benefits.

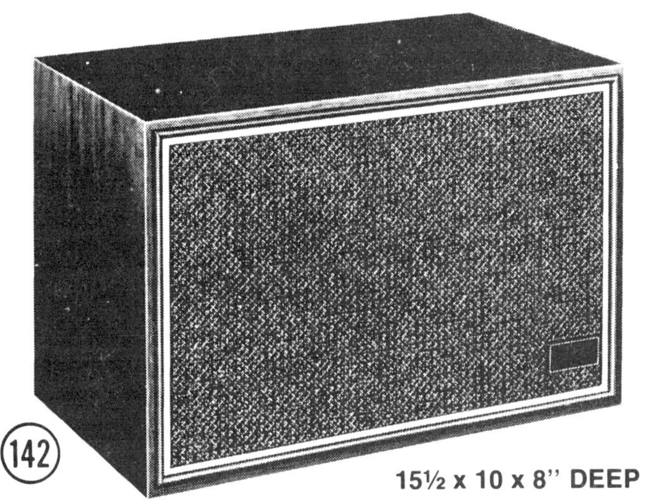

Much research has gone into the development of speaker systems. While we suggest placement, it is up to the reader to spend the necessary listening time to decide which provide the tonal results required.

Listening to speakers in a showroom, where the acoustics have been designed to complement each speaker, frequently provides a quality of sound the purchaser may not obtain when he installs the same components in his home. Consider the acoustics. Can you duplicate similar conditions in the rooms where speakers are to be placed?

Illus. 142 shows one popular priced speaker that provides excellent reproduction ranging from hard rock to the power requirements of a full symphonic orchestra. The big 8" woofer, Illus. 143, has an oversize voice coil. The cone assembly uses the latest neofrene suspension for practically distortion free reproduction of base frequencies. The quality is hard to believe. Crystal clear treble results from a new 2½" tweeter, offers a smooth, wide angle dispersion of sound.

In selecting speakers, a wide frequency range is your first consideration. Good speakers range from 35 to 18,500 Hz; 30 to 18,500 Hz; 30 to 20,000 Hz. The top quality range from 25 to 20,000 Hz; 20 Hz to inaudibility.

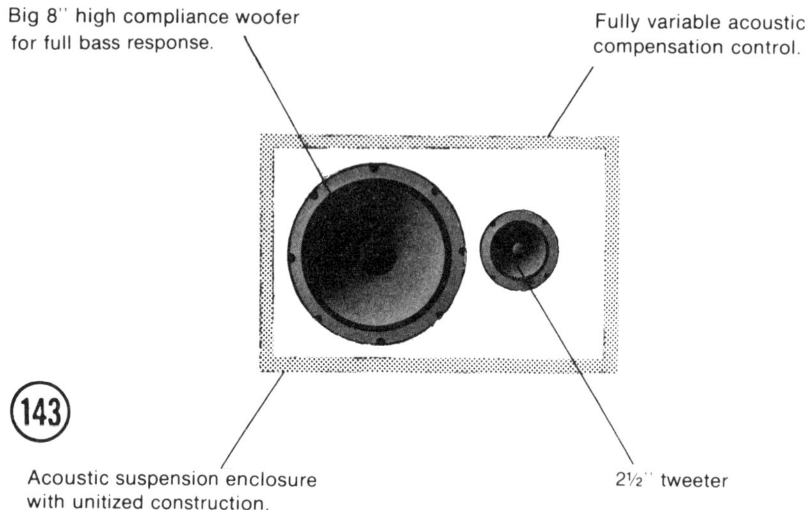

Make certain the speakers you buy can handle as many watts of power as your amplifier is rated to produce. In discussing your needs, explain room size with the retailer, height of ceiling, placement.

Coordinating power ratings and requirements of speakers to amplifiers can be both confusing and misleading. Momentary musical notes frequently demand a peak power reserve from the amplifier several times the rated average power to avoid distortion which will be translated in the speaker as an ugly noise. To avoid this, amplifiers with ratings somewhat higher than the speaker rating can be used, provided the volume control is not turned up to a point where the average amount of sound level is obviously beyond the normal capability of the speakers. The distorted sound of the speakers will surely signify when the condition has occurred.

A hard-surfaced 10" universal-joint-mounted disc, Illus. 144, helps this speaker achieve exceptional tonal qualities. The best of these units has a frequency response rated 20 Hz to inaudibility. Input Power minimum 30 watts (IHF per channel); Input Power maximum 100 watts (IHF per channel). System Impedance 8 ohms. Each speaker, without 1" bumpers, measures 28" high, 17¼" wide, 17" deep.

114

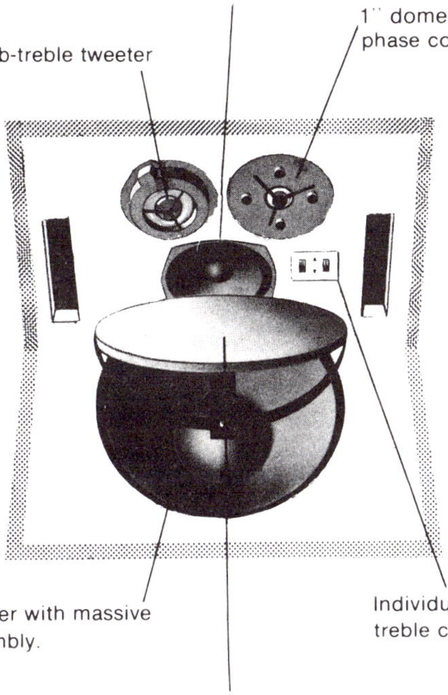

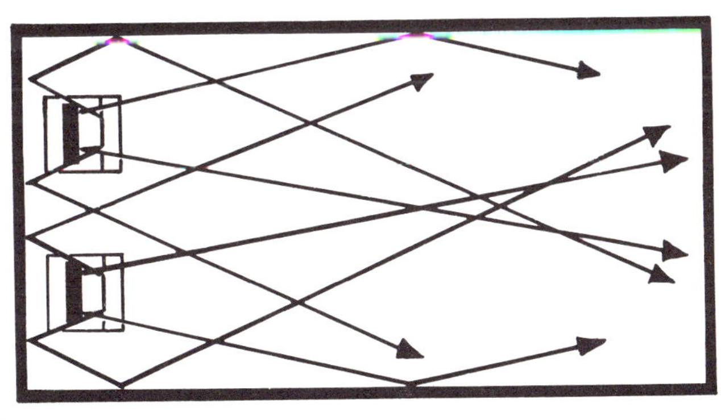

Illus. 145 shows two of these units spaced 6 to 8' apart. The disc can be set to tilt back toward the wall by an amount determined by the distance from the wall. The manufacturer provides detailed operating directions that permit amateurs to create tonal effects unlike any other system.

Speakers spaced normally apart

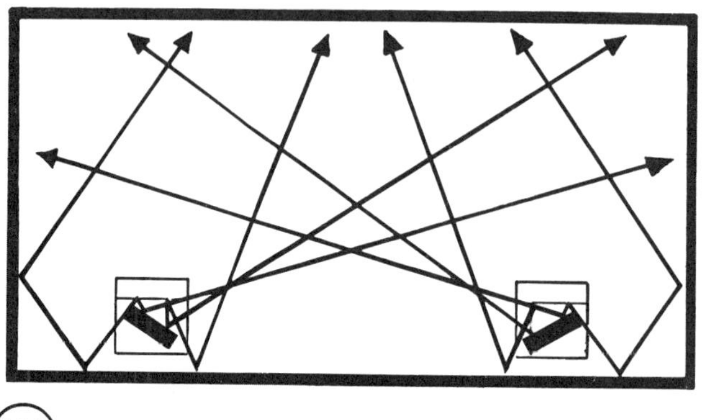

Speakers spaced far apart

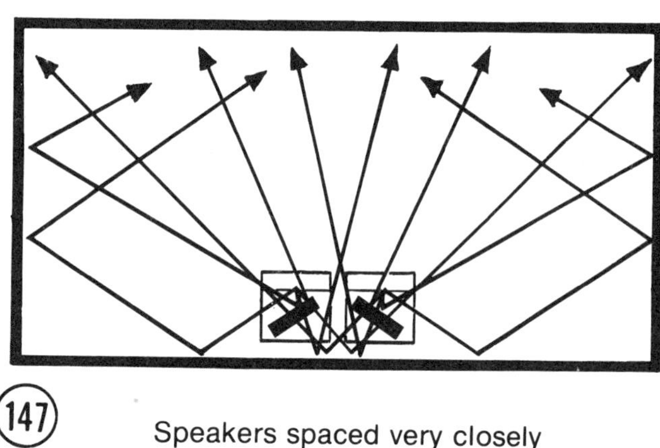

Speakers spaced very closely

Illus. 146 shows the reflected sound waves that can be achieved when speakers are placed as much as 15' or more apart. Note how the center area is covered. In many speaker systems, this area would require a third speaker. Even when speakers are spaced less than 6' apart, Illus. 147, the room is thoroughly saturated with sound.

116

Important to the installation of all electronic units is the need for proper ventilation. If you follow directions outlined, and allot space specified, sufficient ventilation will be provided. To be effective, ventilation requires a flow of cool air to enter at bottom and leave at top. Clearance of 6'' above chassis of a stereophonic receiver is recommended. Today's most popular amplifier-tuner modules are solid state. These require much less ventilation than components sold a few years ago.

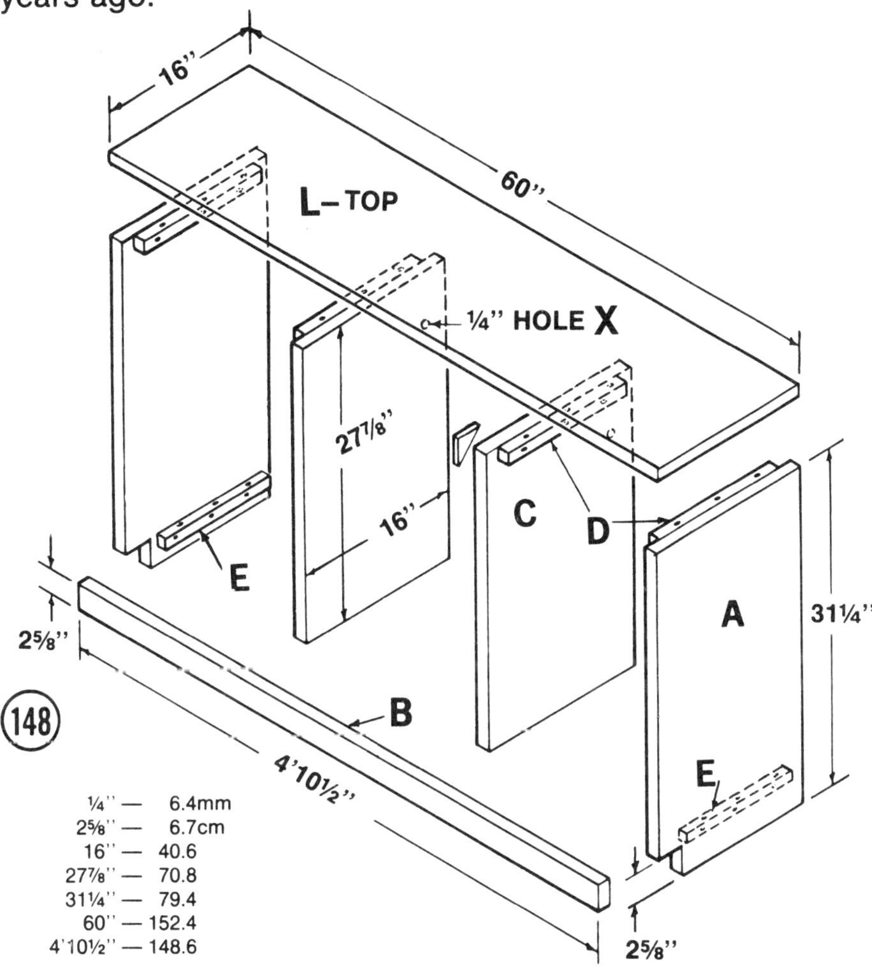

Illus. 148 shows construction of a 16 x 32 x 60'' cabinet; Illus. 149 shows an 80'' cabinet. An 80'' cabinet meets requirements of the stereo experts who recommend spacing speakers six feet apart.

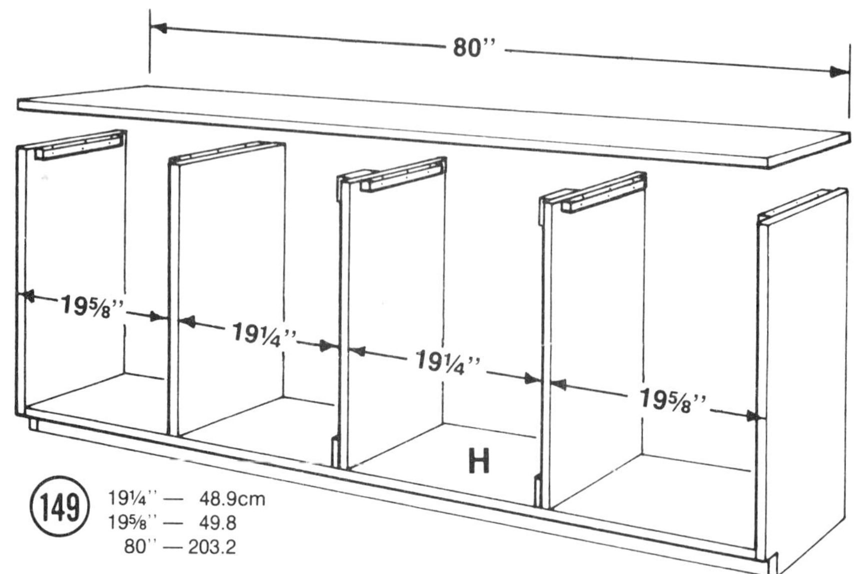

149

19¼'' — 48.9cm
19⅝'' — 49.8
80'' — 203.2

Spacing of partitions is optional. Allow 16⅝'' between C, if you want to install a slide out mounting base for the turntable shown in Illus. 150. The turntable can be mounted anywhere in the base cabinet you prefer, providing you allow 10'' clearance above.

150

118

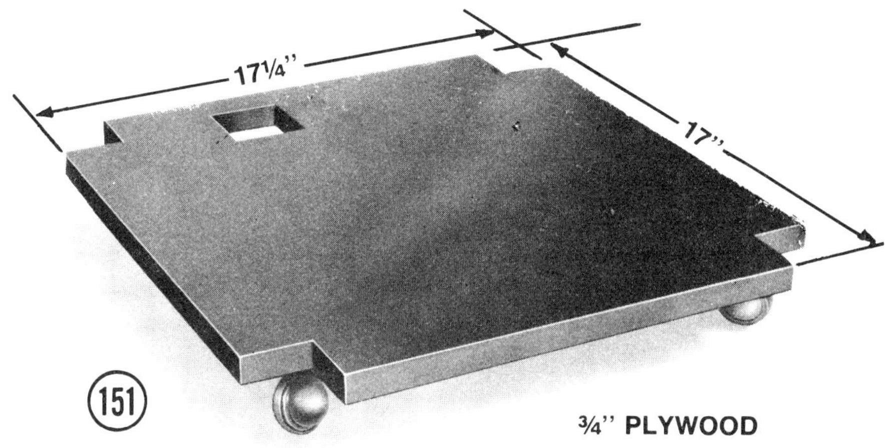

17" — 43.2cm
17¾" — 45.1

The turntable manufacturer offers a mounting base as optional equipment. These come with or without a plastic cover.

Those wishing to install a turntable on a slide out base, Illus. 155, should first assemble the base, then position partitions to accommodate same.

Use full size pattern manufacturer of turntable provides, Illus. 152. Smooth out folds in pattern, insert carbon paper, thumb tack, do not glue pattern in position. Trace outline of cutout, location of holes on ½" flakeboard M, Illus. 153. Drill a ½" hole inside area to be cut out. Use a saber or compass saw, cut opening to exact shape of pattern.

Locate speakers in a wall cabinet at distance retailer recommends. If you prefer placing speakers independent of wall cabinet, buy or make a roll out base, Illus. 151.

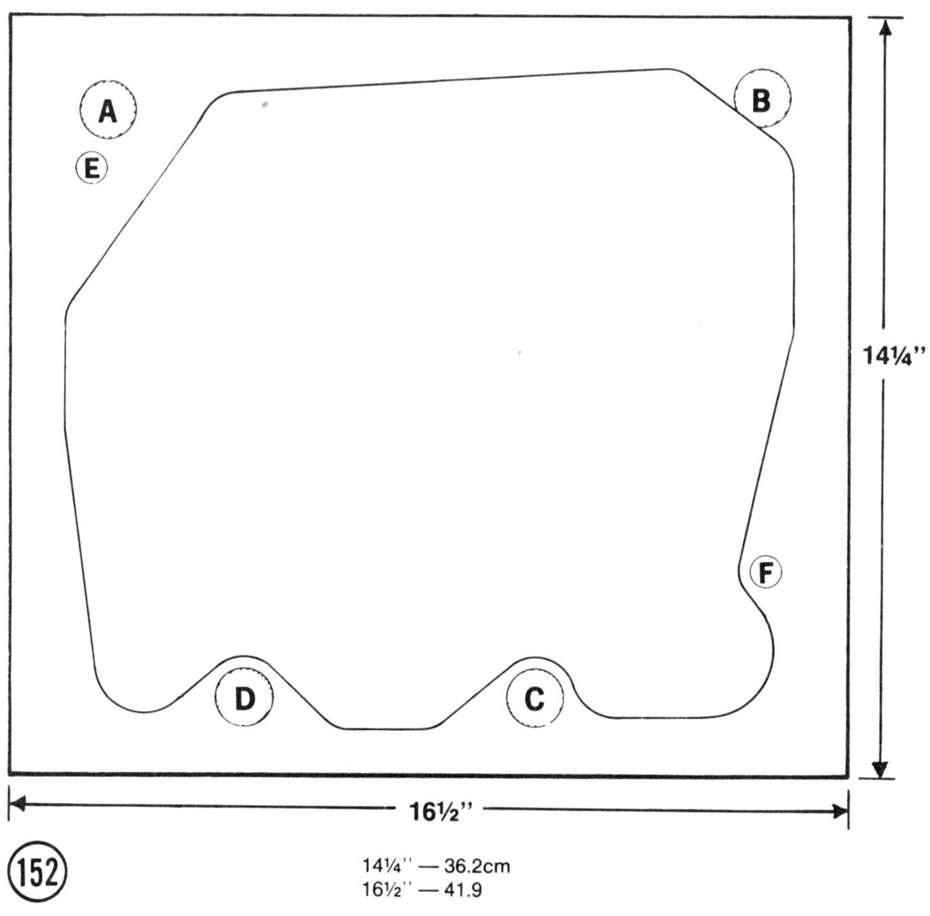

Drill four 1 1/16'' holes, ⅛'' deep in position pattern indicates for A,B,C,D, Illus. 152. Drill two 19/32'' holes E,F, clear through for transit screws, Illus. 153,154.

Cut parts for turntable base to following size:

M - ½ x 14¼ x 16½''
N - ¾ x 2⅝ x 16½''
O - ¾ x 4⅝ x 16⅝''
P - ¾ x 2⅝ x 13½''
PP - ⅜ x 1 x 14⅜''
RR - ⅜ x 3 x 13⅝''

120

M

153

TRANSIT SCREW AND CLIP
IN PLAYING POSITION
DAMPING
PAD
SPRING MOUNTING
FLAKEBOARD

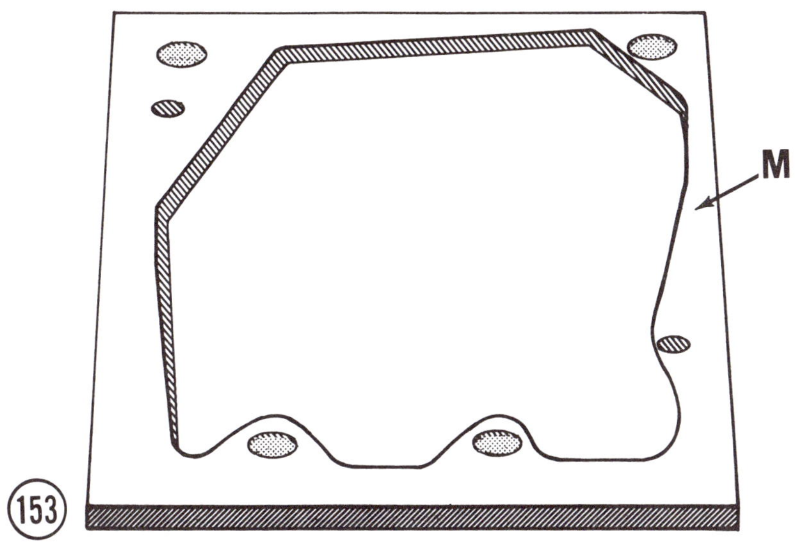

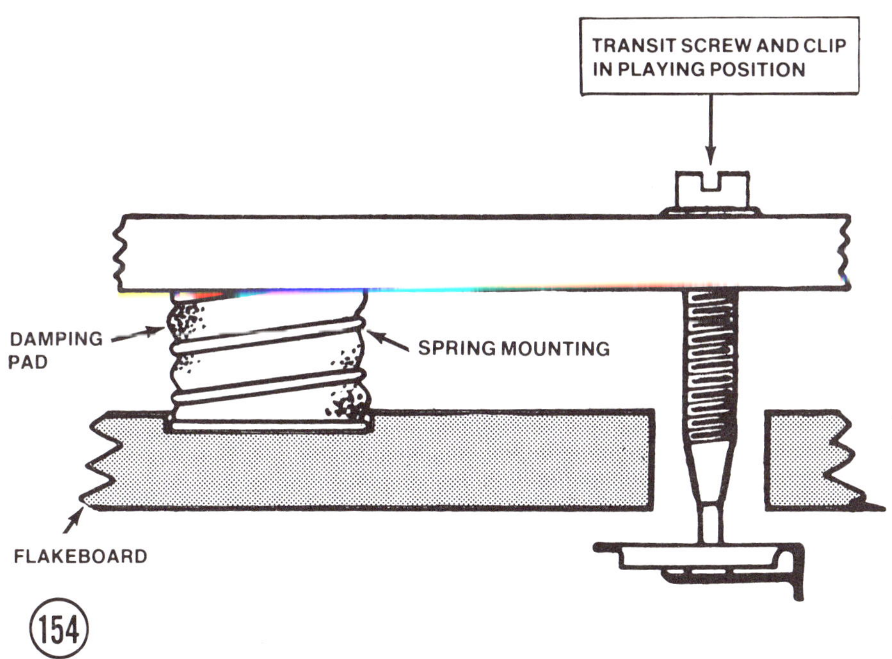

154

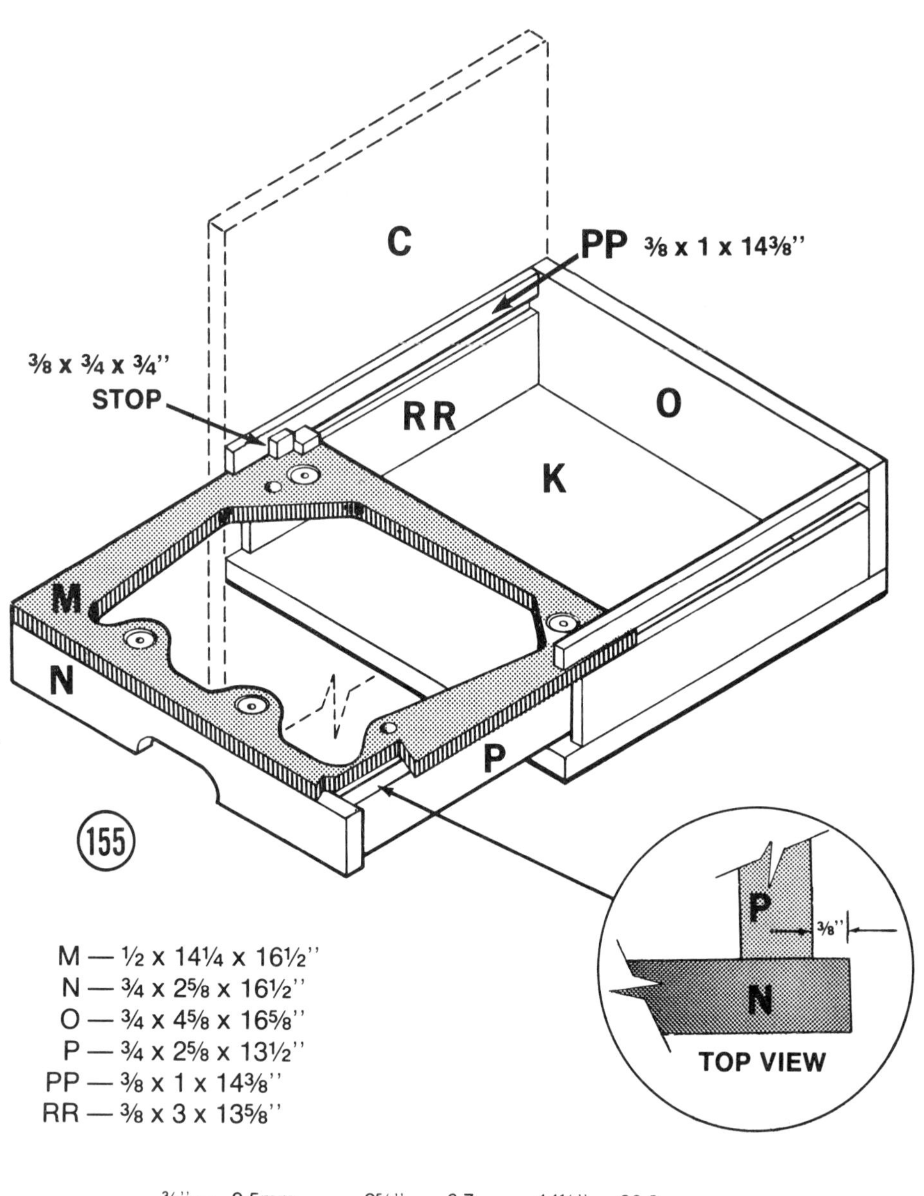

M — ½ x 14¼ x 16½''
N — ¾ x 2⅝ x 16½''
O — ¾ x 4⅝ x 16⅝''
P — ¾ x 2⅝ x 13½''
PP — ⅜ x 1 x 14⅜''
RR — ⅜ x 3 x 13⅝''

⅜'' — 9.5mm	2⅝'' — 6.7	14¼'' — 36.2
½'' — 1.27cm	3'' — 7.6	14⅜'' — 36.5
¾'' — 1.91	4⅝'' — 11.7	16½'' — 41.9
1'' — 2.54	13½'' — 34.3	16⅝'' — 42.2
	13⅝'' — 34.6	

Cut two P - ¾ x 2⅝ x 13½''. Cut one N - ¾ x 2⅝ x 16½''. Cut one M - ½ x 14¼ x 16½''. Do not use any material thicker than ½'' for M. Cut two RR - ⅜ x 3 x 13⅝''. Cut two PP - ⅜ x 1 x 14⅜'', Illus. 155.

Apply glue to end of P. Nail N to P, ⅜'' from end, Illus. 155. Apply glue to top edge of P,N and nail M to NP.

Nail ⅜ x 1 x 14⅜'' PP in position to C. Allow 9/16'' slot and nail RR in position. M rides on RR. PP keeps M from tipping. To keep M from coming all the way out, glue and screw a ⅜ x ¾ x ¾'' stop to M, another to PP in position shown.

To use turntable while building cabinets, carefully unpack turntable following directions manufacturer prints on carton. Thread power line, ground and phono leads through cutout in board. Make sure leads are clear of turntable motor.

With locking clips in vertical position, screw transit screws down, Illus. 154. Place unit in position on M, making certain mounting springs are in their respective recess. When unit is positioned properly, press down on springs, then turn transit screw locking clips horizontal.

16 x 32 x 60" BASE CABINET

Step-by-step directions explain how to build a cabinet measuring 16" deep, 32" high, 60" long, Illus. 148. This accommodates a turntable, stereophonic receiver and one speaker. The same cabinet can be built 80" or longer. Spacing of partitions is optional. The 80" cabinet meets requirements of stereo experts who recommend spacing speakers six feet apart. We obtained superb reproduction from one speaker in the 60" cabinet, the other free standing.

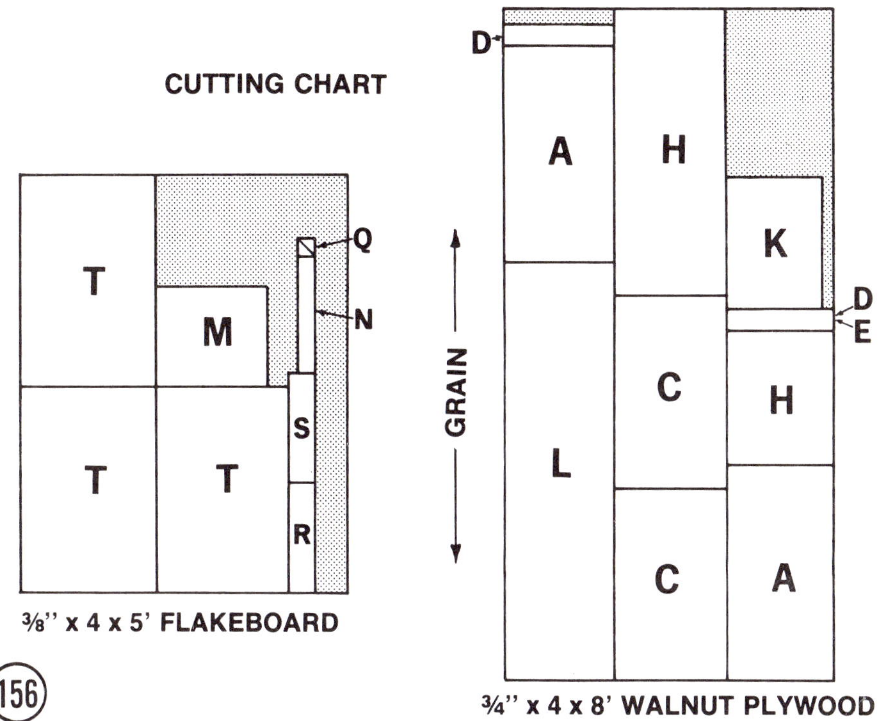

Use ¾" hardwood plywood for all parts unless other material is specified. Cut all parts with grain running in direction shown on cutting chart, Illus. 156. After starting to assemble a cabinet, cut all inner framing to size your construction requires.

NOTE: Lay out and cut parts according to cutting charts.

PARTS FOR CABINETS, BOOKCASE, ETC.

A — End
B — Base
C — Partition
D — Cleat
E — Cleat
F — Brace
G — Hinge Plate
H — Bottom
K — Shelf
L — Top

M — Platform
N — Platform
P — Platform
R — Cleat
S — Cleat
T — Door
U — Molding
V — Cleat
W — Sides
Y — Bookshelf

125

LIST OF MATERIAL

1 — ¾" x 4 x 8' walnut plywood for A,C,D,E,H,K,L
1 — 1 x 3 x 16' for B,F,P
1 — ⅛ x 20 x 32" perforated hardboard — back of
    component cabinet
1 — ⅜" x 4 x 5' flakeboard for G,M,N,R,S,T
25 lineal ft. walnut casing for U

HARDWARE & MISC.
3 tutch latches or equal
1 pr. drawer slides
3 prs. hinges
8 lineal ft. 18" wide acoustic fabric
glue
¼ lb. 6 penny finishing nails
1 box ¾" wire brads
3 doz. ¾" No. 6 roundhead screws
3 doz. 1¼" No. 9 flathead screws

NOTE:
If speaker enclosures are built, you will need:
1 — ¾" x 4 x 5' fir plywood
Approx. 26 sq.ft. of 1" fiberglass insulation
1 — 6" length, 3" diameter cardboard mailing tube

The cutting chart shows how to economically cut parts. If you cut on a table saw, or use a hand saw, keep good face up. Keep good face down if you use an electric hand, saber or radial arm saw.

Always check size of shelves, partitions and other inner framing members against assembled cabinet to insure cutting parts to size required.

To build a cabinet measuring 16 x 32 x 60", cut two ends A, Illus. 148, 16 x 31¼". Cut notch 2½ x 2½", if 1 x 3 measures 2½".

Cut two B, 2½" x 4'10½", use ¾" plywood or 1 x 3.

126

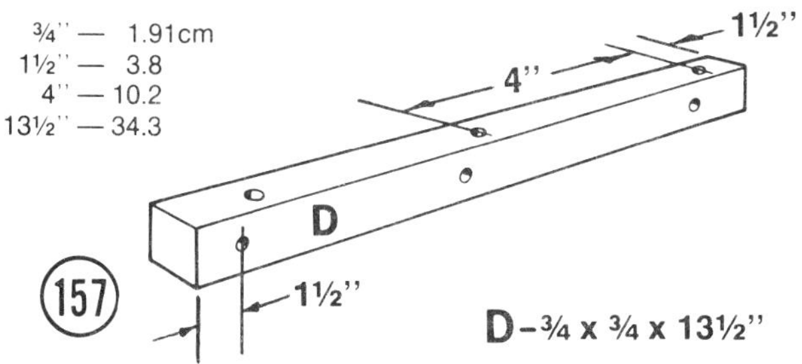

Cut two partitions C, 16 x 27⅞". Drill ¼" holes X, 5" down, 2" from back. Cut and drill 3/16" holes in cleats D,E in position shown, Illus. 157. Cut four D, ¾ x ¾ x 13½". Cut two E, ¾ x ¾ x 11⅞". Note position of X, Illus. 148.

When fastening cleats, etc., lay a smooth piece of corrugated board on your workbench or floor to protect the good face of plywood. Apply glue and screw cleats D and E ¾" from back edge of A and C, Illus. 148.

The top edge of E is on line with top of B, Illus. 161. Apply glue and nail A to B with 6 penny finishing nails.

Use care when driving nails so you don't mar face. Drive nails to within ¼" of A, then use a nailset. Countersink heads. Fill holes with matching wood filler.

Cut two F, 2½ x 11⅞", use 1 x 3, Illus. 158.

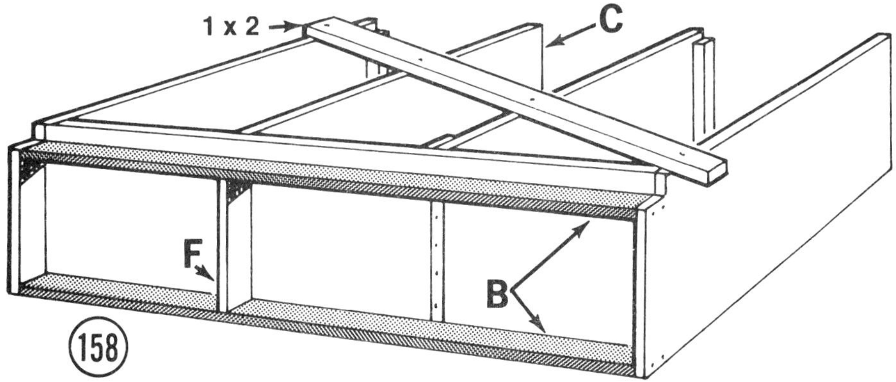

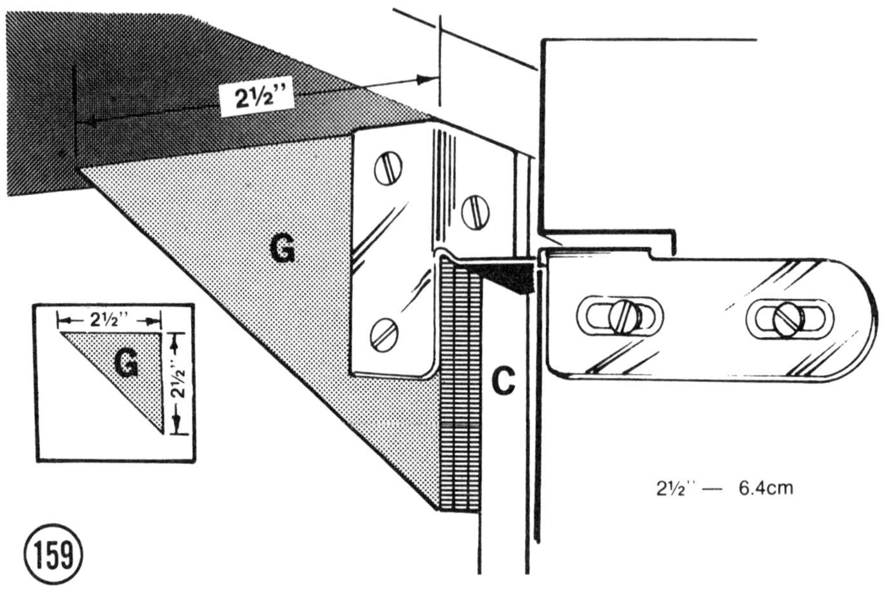

Cut one G, ⅜ x 2½ x 2½", Illus. 159.

Cut one R, ⅜ x 3½ x 16", Illus. 160.

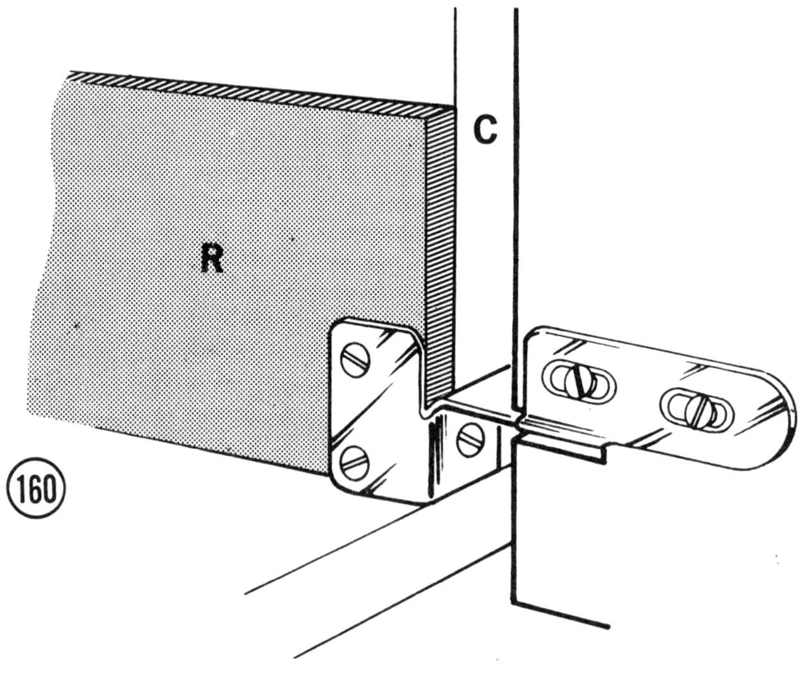

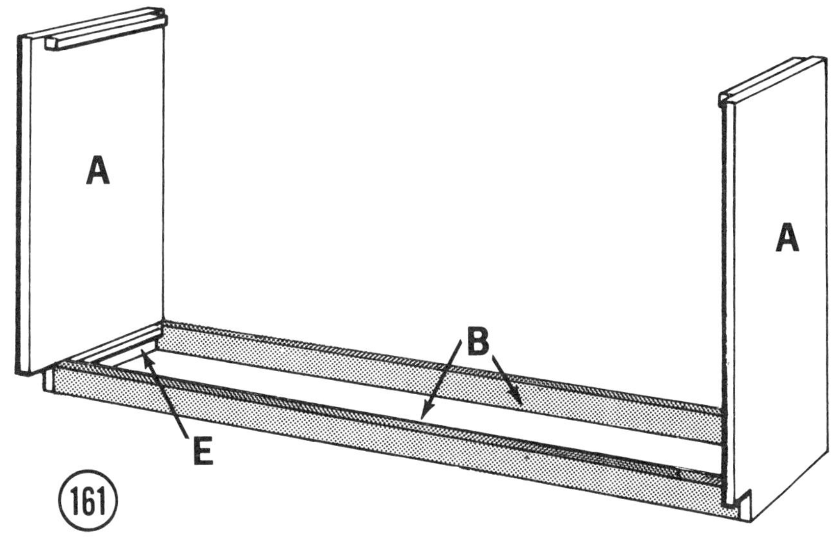

Since little except the front edge of H is exposed, you can use ¾'' fir plywood. Cut H, 16'' x 4'10½'', Illus. 162, or H can be cut from walnut. If walnut is used, it can be in two parts - 16 x 39¼'', 16 x 19¼'', as shown in cutting chart.

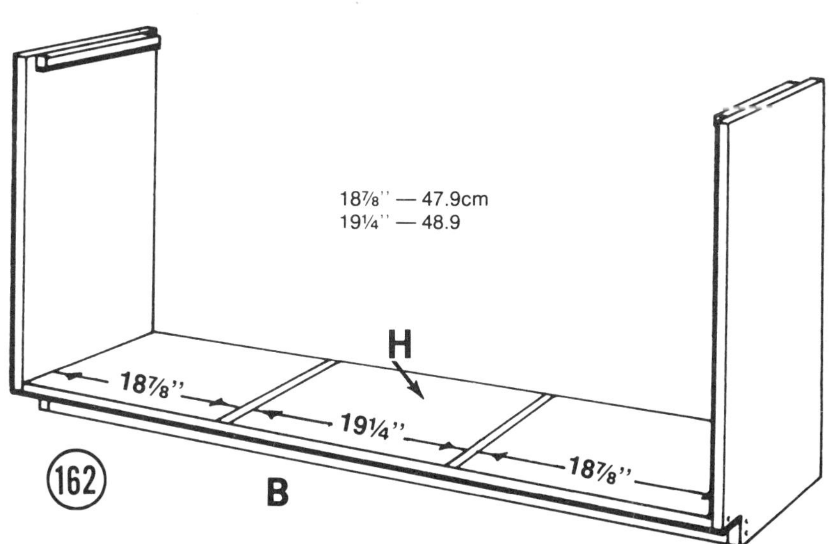

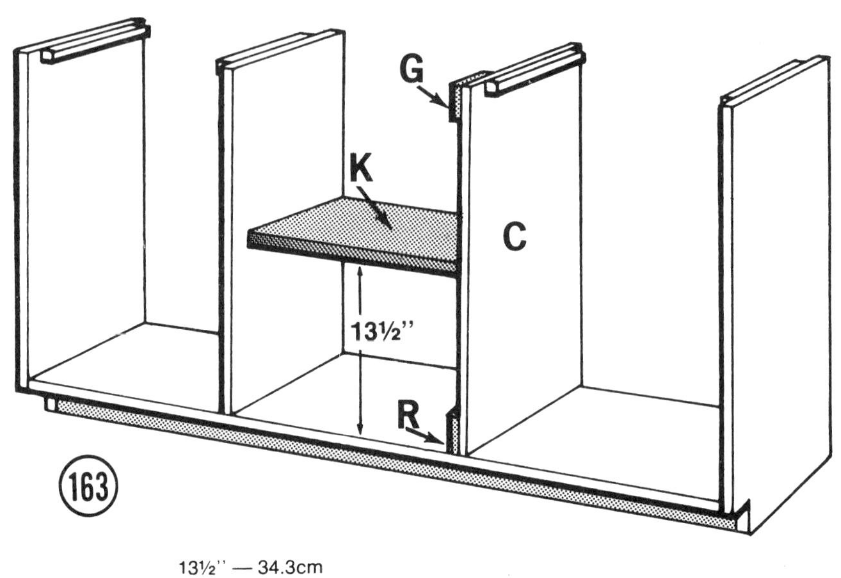

Nail H to B spacing nails approximately 12" apart. Draw lines to indicate position and width of partitions. Use a square. Run glue between lines. Turn cabinet on back, nail H to C, Illus. 158. Check C with a square and hold C plumb with a 1 x 2 temporary brace. Apply glue and nail B to F.

Glue and nail G and R to C in position shown, Illus. 159,160,163. Use ¾" wire brads.

Cut shelf K, 14½ x 19¼", or size required for turntable. Nail in position desired, Illus. 163. To dissipate heat, receiver should be placed above, or to one side of turntable.

Cut top L, 16 x 60", Illus. 164. Apply glue to top edge of A,C and D. Keeping good face up, place L in position. Fasten D to L with 1¼" No. 9 flathead wood screws.

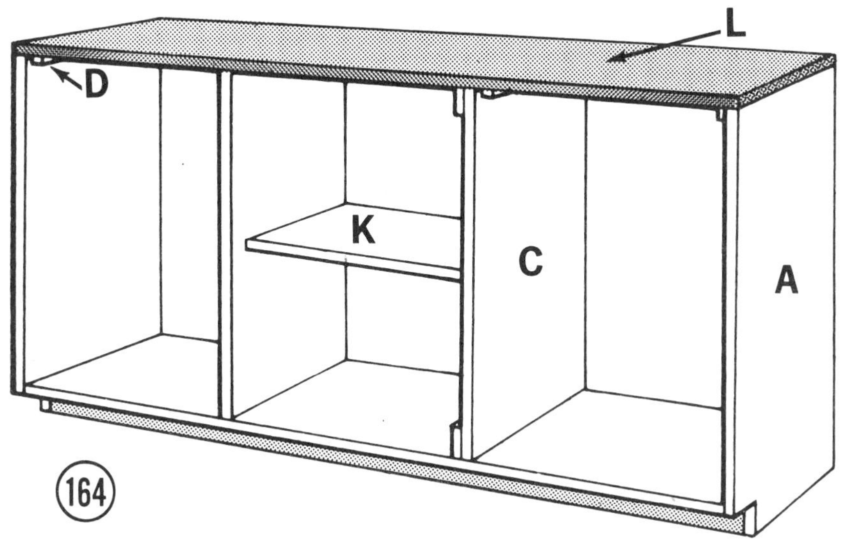

Cut ⅛'' hardboard pegboard to size back requires, Illus. 165. Screw in position with ½ or ¾'' roundhead screws after installing equipment. Hardboard or pegboard can be fastened to balance of back.

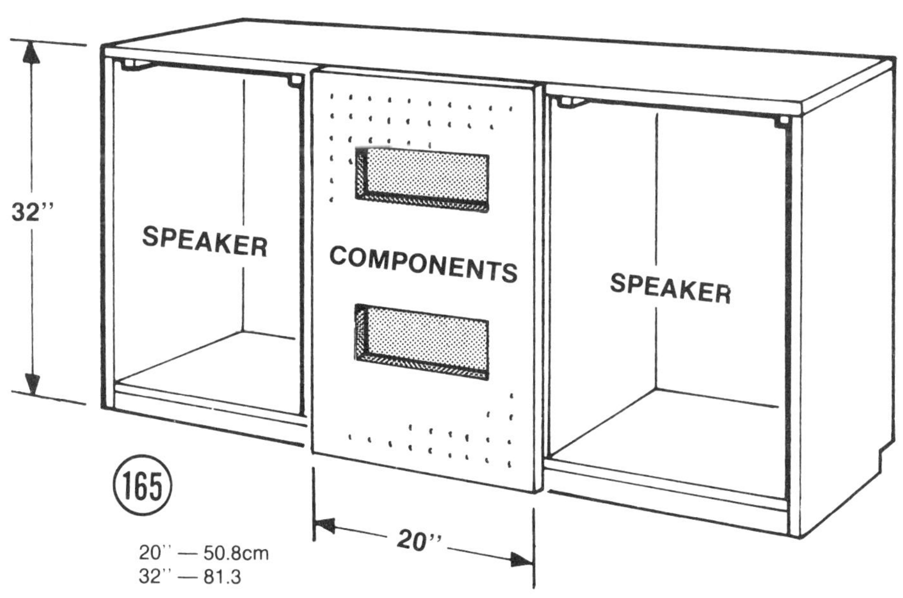

CABINET DOORS

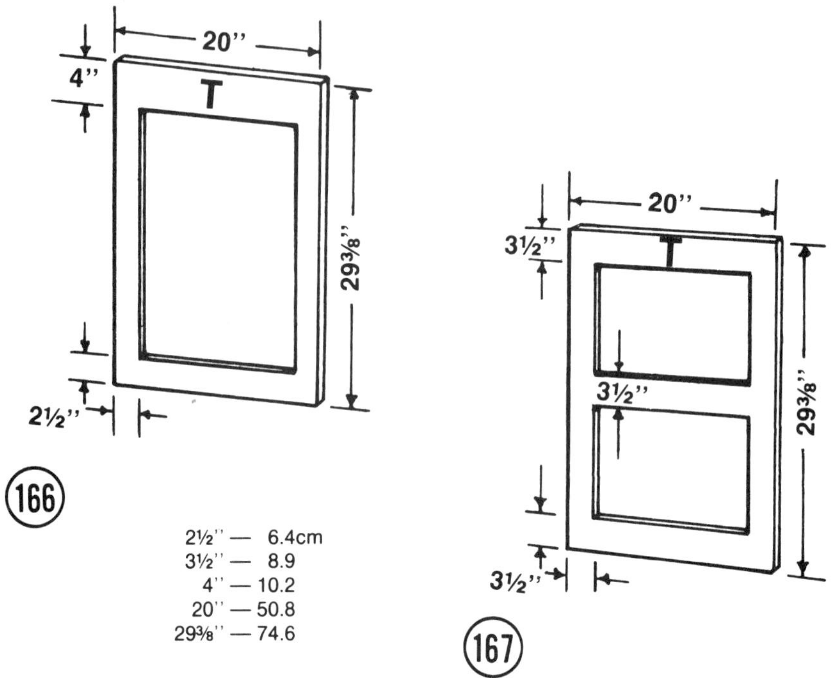

Illus. 166 shows door frame for a speaker cabinet.

Illus. 167 shows door frame for component compartment. Cut ⅜" flakeboard T to size indicated. Draw outline of opening. Drill ¼" hole in corner of opening. Insert a saber saw and cut along line.

Cut decorative acoustical fabric 18 x 27". With good face out, staple fabric to flakeboard with stapling gun.

Miter cut walnut casing U to length needed, Illus. 168. Apply glue to corners. Drill through T and fasten U in position with ¾" No. 6 roundhead screws.

Saw ¼" notch, ¼" deep on outside of door to ⅝" deep on inside, Illus. 169, 1½" down from top, 1¼" up from bottom of door.

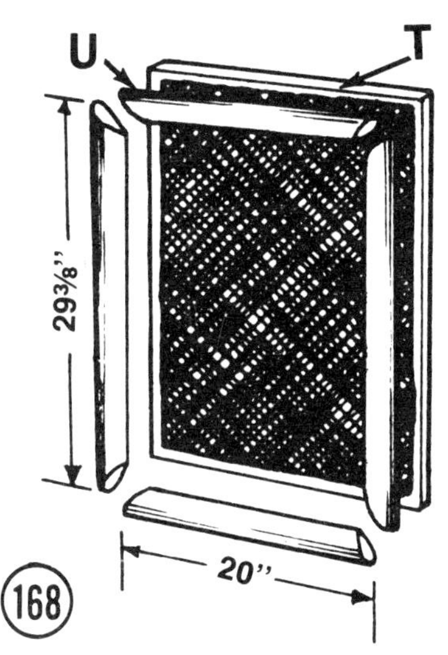

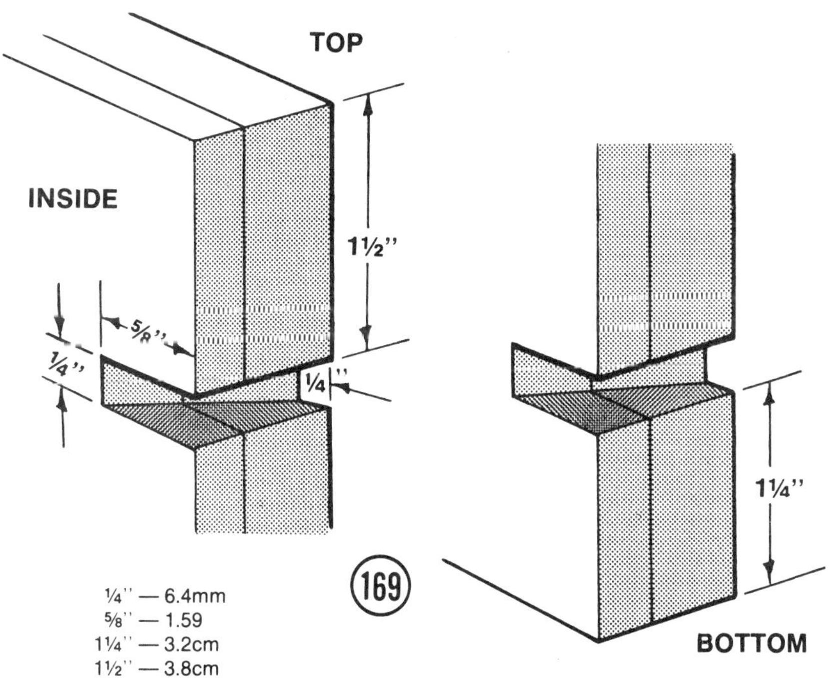

¼'' — 6.4mm
⁵⁄₈'' — 1.59
1¼'' — 3.2cm
1½'' — 3.8cm

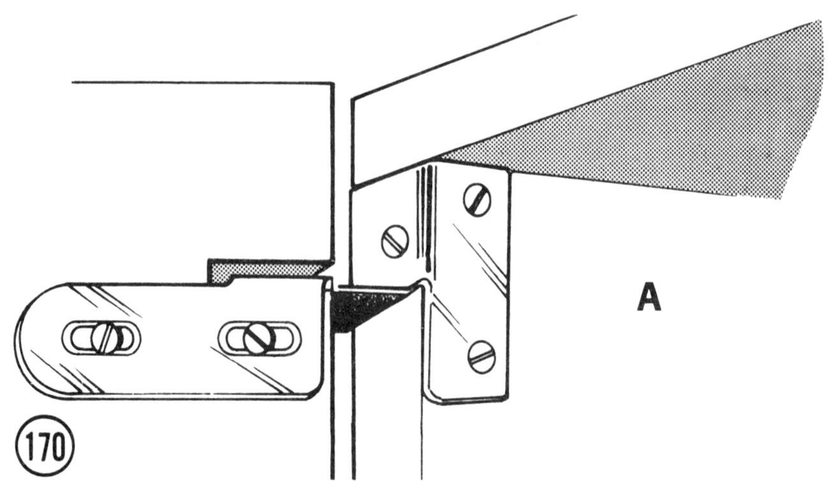

(170)

Fasten hinges to door and to A, Illus. 170, with screws hinge manufacturer provides.

Hinge on center cabinet door must be fastened to G and R, Illus. 159,160. (Use three hinges per door on top cabinet. Locate third hinge in center.) Fasten Tutch Latch in position shown, Illus. 171, following directions provided by manufacturer. Finish cabinet and door with good quality furniture wax. Stain or paint B to match.

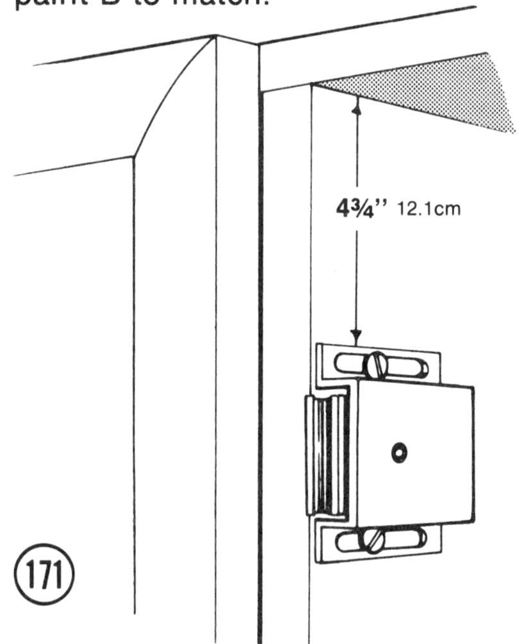

(171)

14 x 42 x 60" TOP CABINET

Build top cabinet following procedure outlined for base. Overall size is 14 x 42 x 60". The 14" depth will accommodate most components except a turntable.

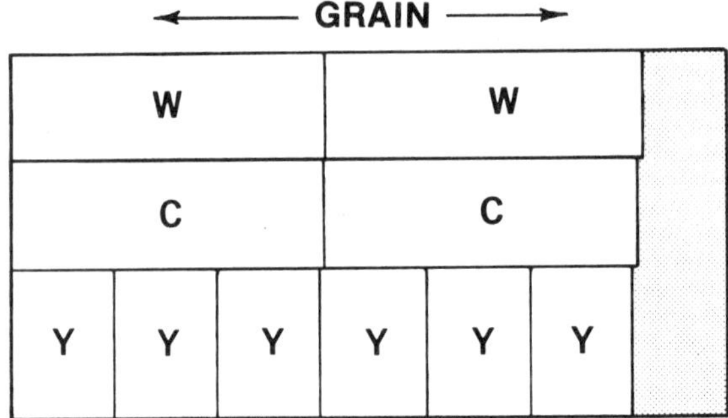

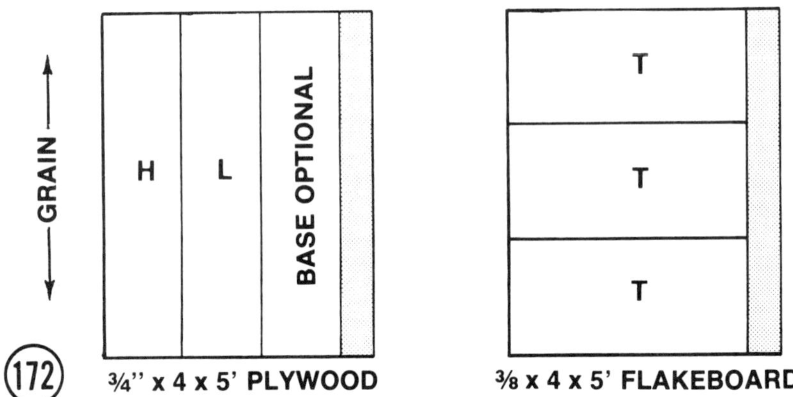

Illus. 172 shows cutting chart for a top cabinet.

LIST OF MATERIAL

1 — ¾'' x 4 x 8' walnut plywood for C,W,Y
1 — ¾'' x 4 x 5' walnut plywood for H,L and base*
1 x ⅜'' x 4 x 5' flakeboard for T
31 lineal ft. walnut casing for doors
1 — ⅛ x 42 x 60'' hardboard for back

HARDWARE & MISC.

3 tutch latches or equal
5 pr. hinges
10 lineal ft. 18'' wide acoustic fabric
¼ lb. 6 penny finishing nails
4 doz. ¾'' No. 7 roundhead screws
glue
shelf standards*

*Optional

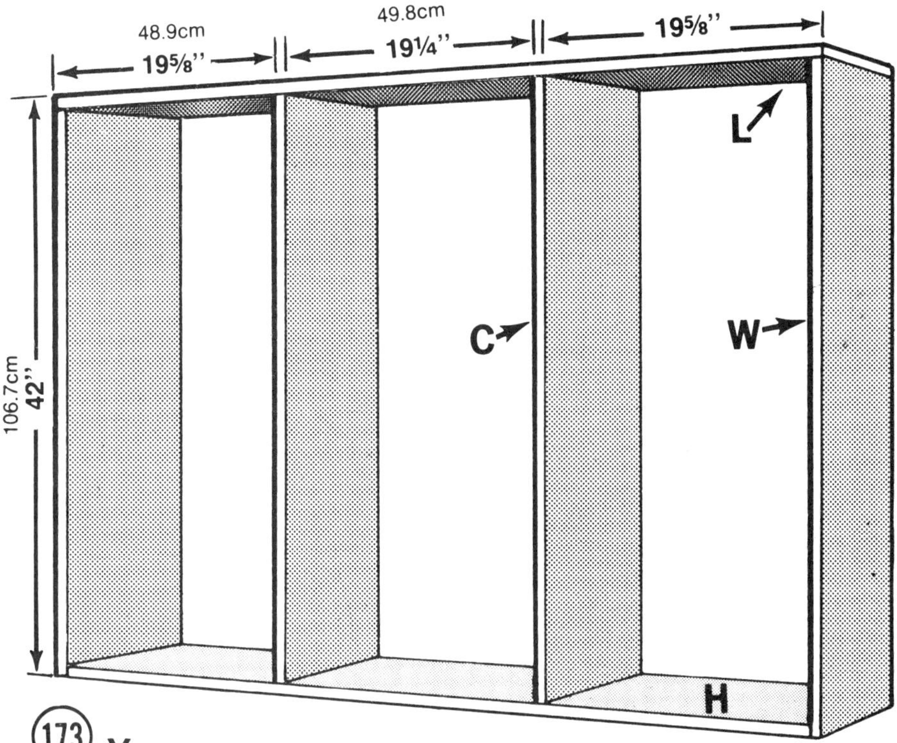

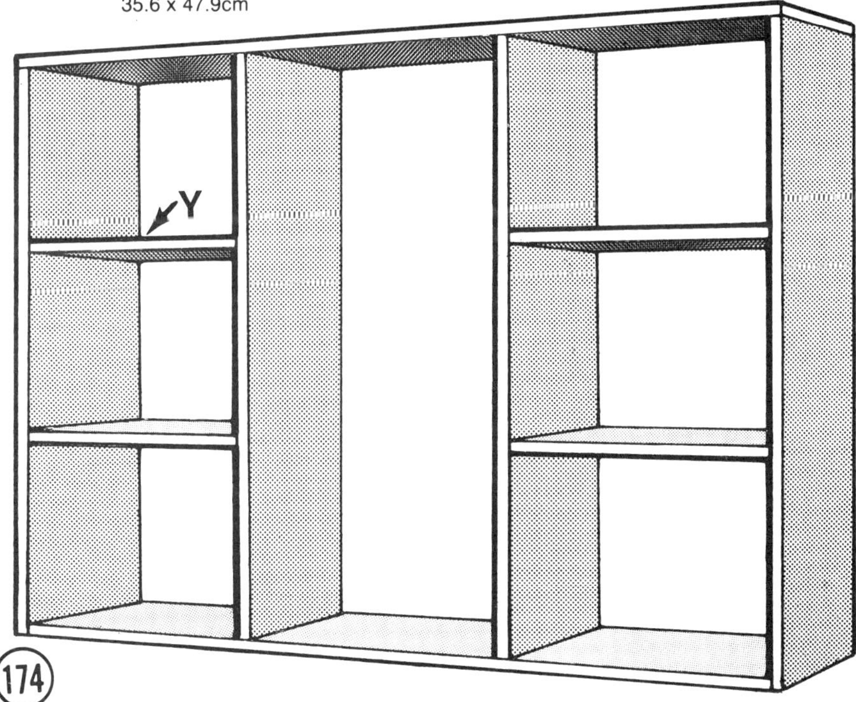

173) Y — 14 x 18⁷⁄₈"
35.6 x 47.9cm

(174)

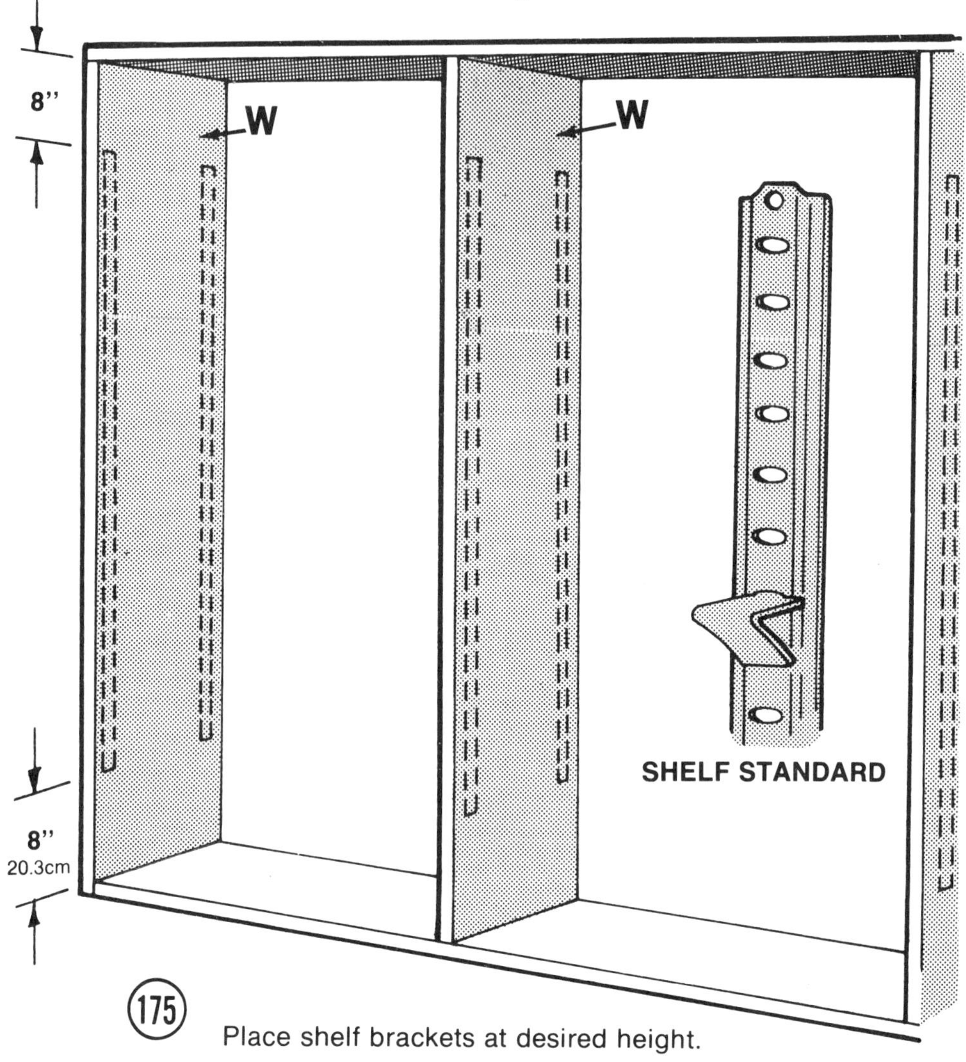

Illus. 173 shows placement of partitions.

Illus. 174 shows placement of shelves. Or you can install shelf standards, Illus. 46, 2" from edge of W, Illus. 175. Shelves can be positioned at height desired.

LO BOY CABINET

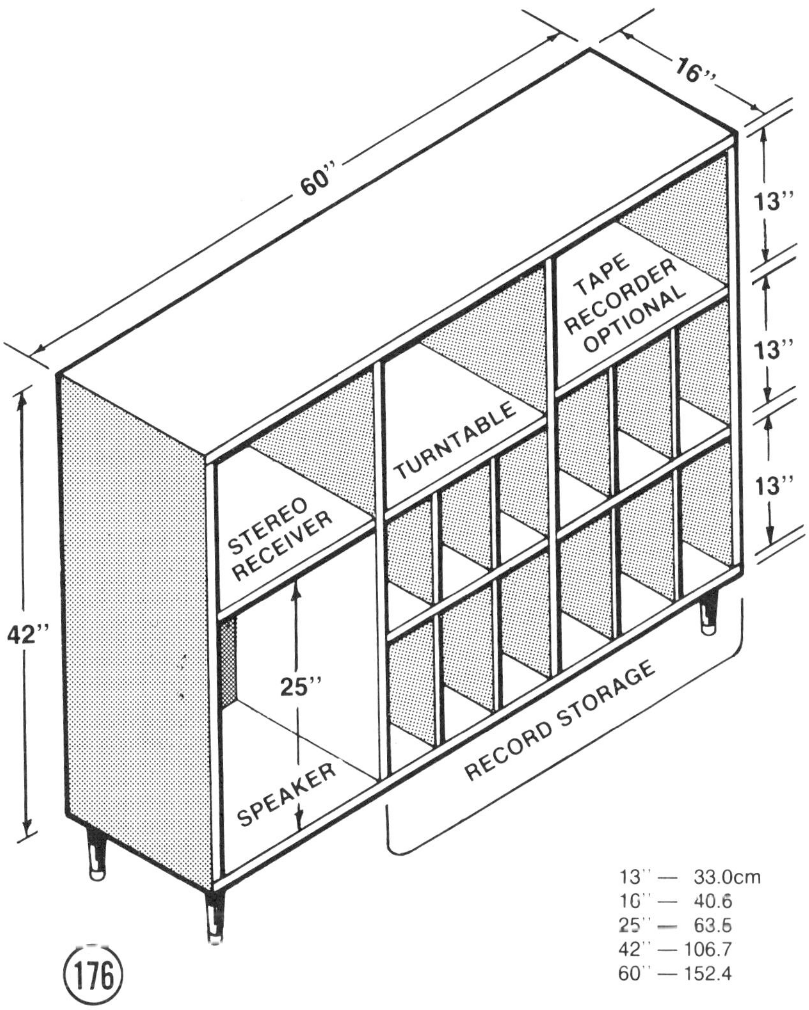

A 16 x 42 x 60'' cabinet will accommodate a receiver, turntable, tape recorder, one speaker and space for records, Illus. 176.

Fasten ⅜'' hinge blocks G and R, Illus. 159,160, when installing hinges for center door. Center third hinge on a 42'' door. Apply R when installing drawer slides for turntable.

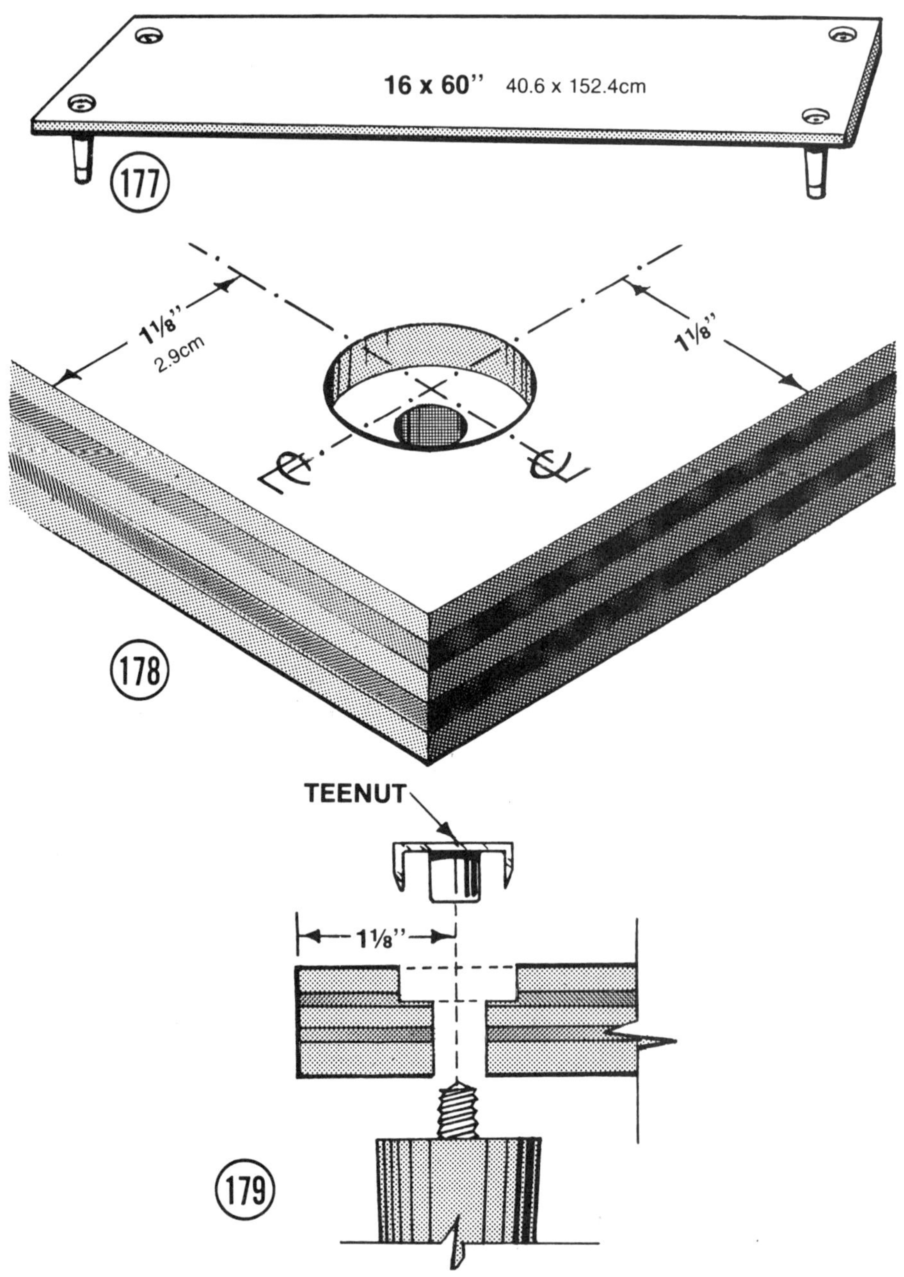

Cut ¾" fir plywood 16 x 60" for base, Illus. 177. Drill ⅞" holes ¼" deep, Illus. 178, in position indicated. Then drill ⅜" holes clear through, Illus. 179. Insert four 5/16-18 Teenuts. Fasten base to bottom with 1¼" No. 9 flathead screws. Screw 6" legs to Teenuts. Finish edges with walnut wood trim.

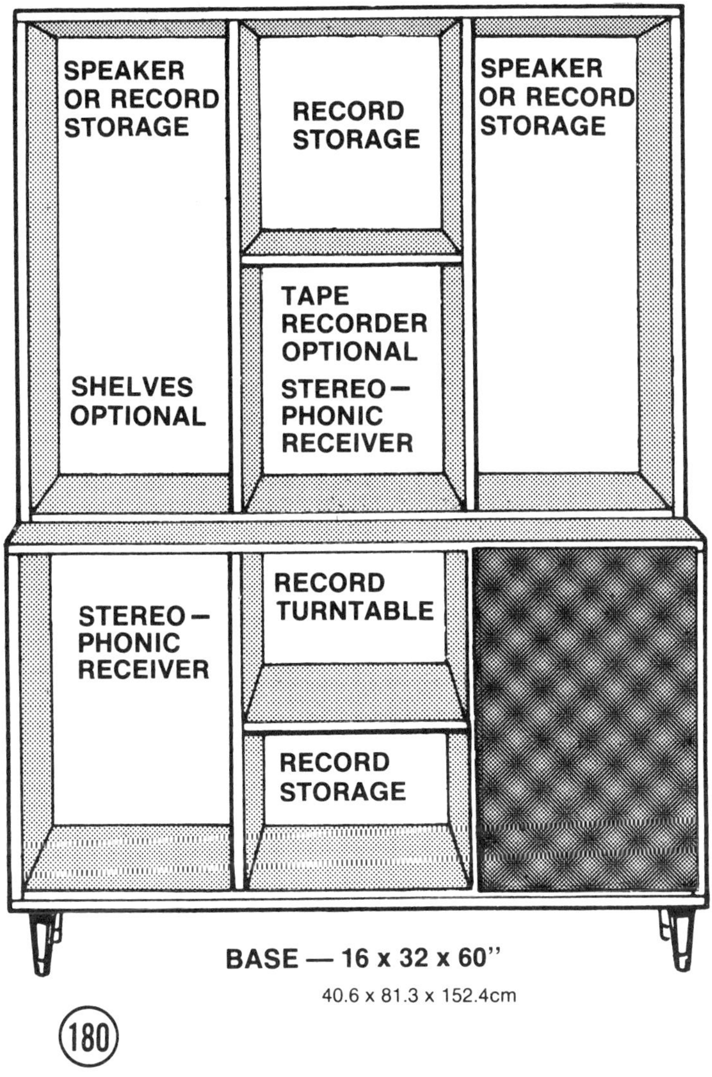

Illus. 180 shows the 14 x 42 x 60" top cabinet on a 16 x 32 x 60" base cabinet mounted on a 6" high base, Illus. 177.

SPEAKER ENCLOSURE

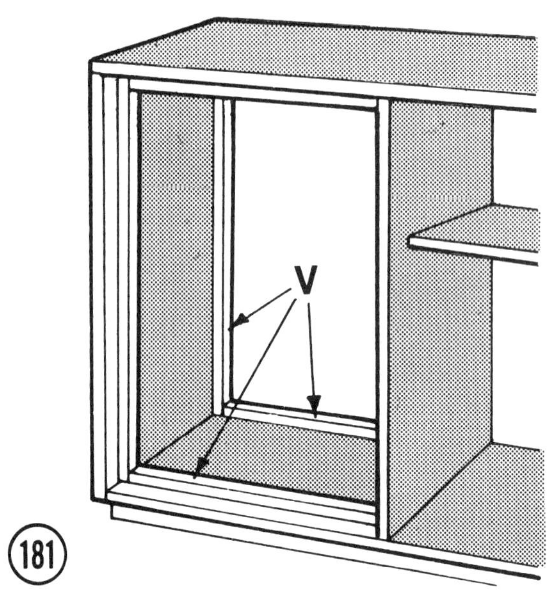

Speakers can be mounted in space allotted, or separate enclosures, mounted on casters, Illus. 151, can be used. Always build enclosure to overall size speaker manufacturer specifies.

Cut, glue and screw ¾ x ¾'' cleats V in position, Illus. 181. Install back cleats ¾'' from edge; front cleats 1¾'' from edge.

Insulate walls, floor and ceiling of enclosure with 1'' thick fiberglass blanket, or use thickness speaker manufacturer recommends, Illus. 182. Cut insulation to fit within area of V. Staple in position.

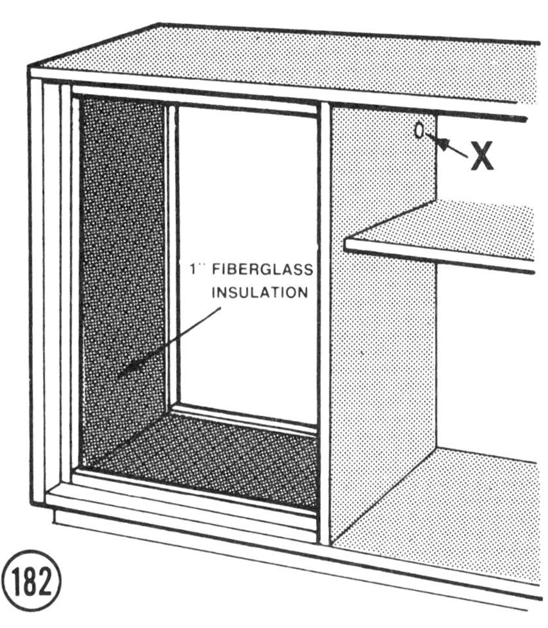

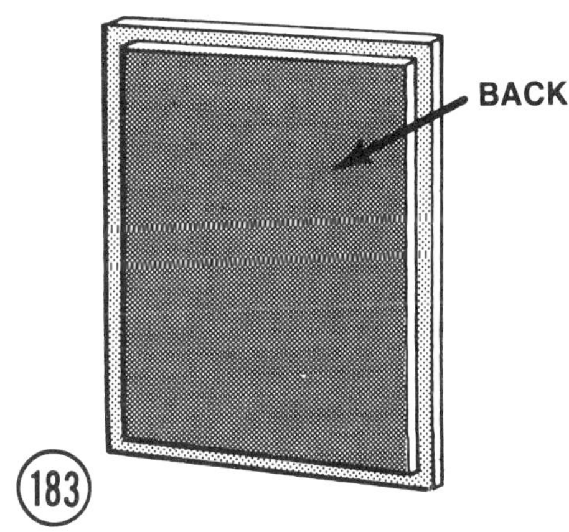

Cut two ¾ x 18⅞ x 27⅞" panels, or to exact size required. Place back panel in position against cleats V. Note size of area. Cut a piece of insulation to exact size. Staple or glue to inside face of back panel. Be sure no insulation interferes with fastening panel to V, Illus. 183.

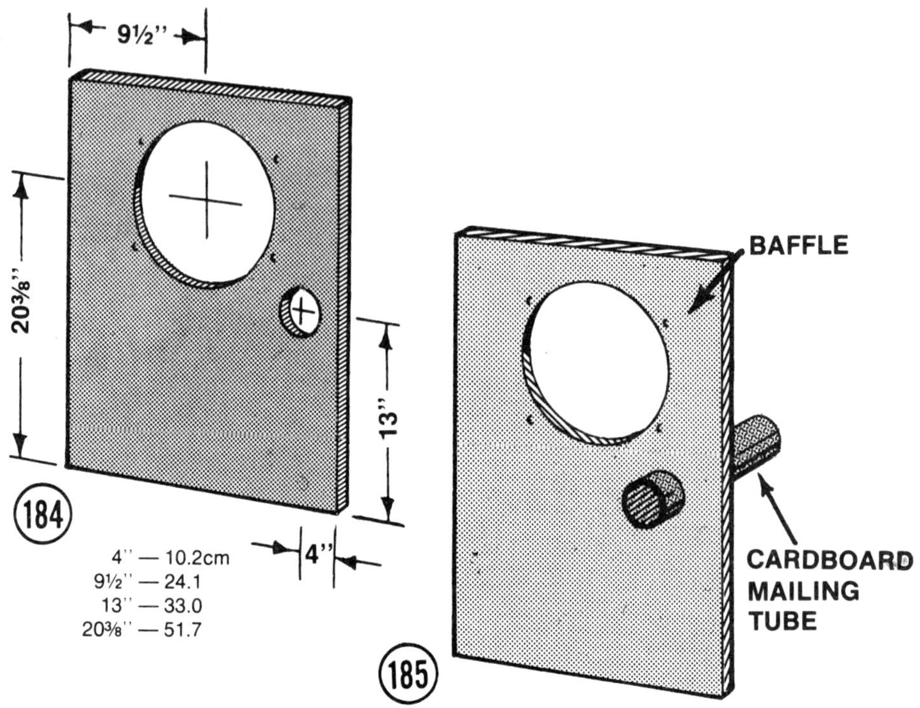

Cut an opening in front panel, Illus. 184, to size speaker manufacturer specifies. Cut a 3" or size hole speaker manufacturer specifies to receive a 3" inside diameter mailing tube. Cut tube to length specifications recommend.

Fasten tube in position so it projects 1 to 1½" from face of panel, Illus. 185.

Mount speaker to panel following speaker manufacturer's directions. Drill holes and mount panel in position using 1½" No. 7 flathead screws every 6". Insert speaker wire through hole X, Illus. 182. Screw back in position. Use care to cut both front and back panels to exact size required.

NOTE: If cabinet containing components is placed against a baseboard, the baseboard will position cabinet away from wall. If there is no baseboard or shoe molding, place cabinet ¾" away from wall with ¾" blocks to insure a free flow of air.

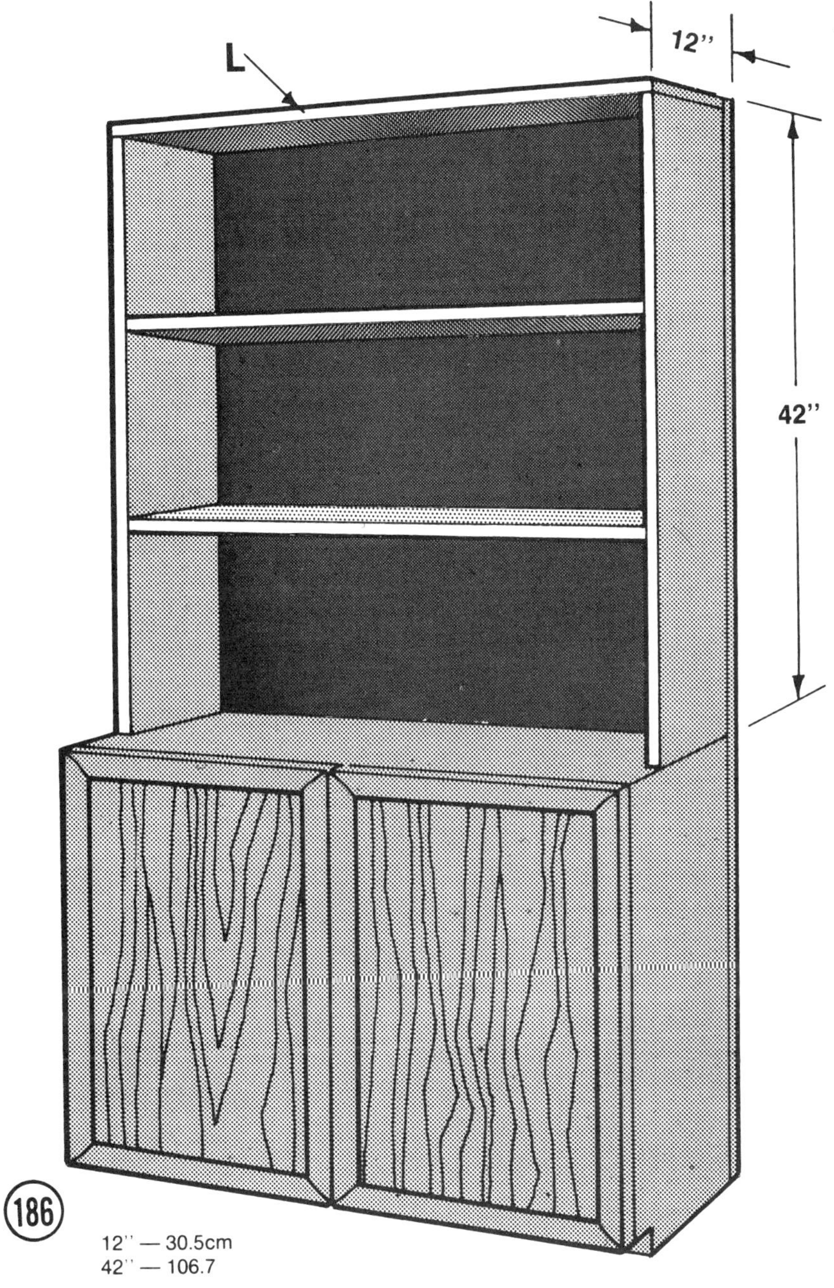

Bookcases can be built to size that matches base cabinet.
These can be 12" or depth desired, Illus. 186.

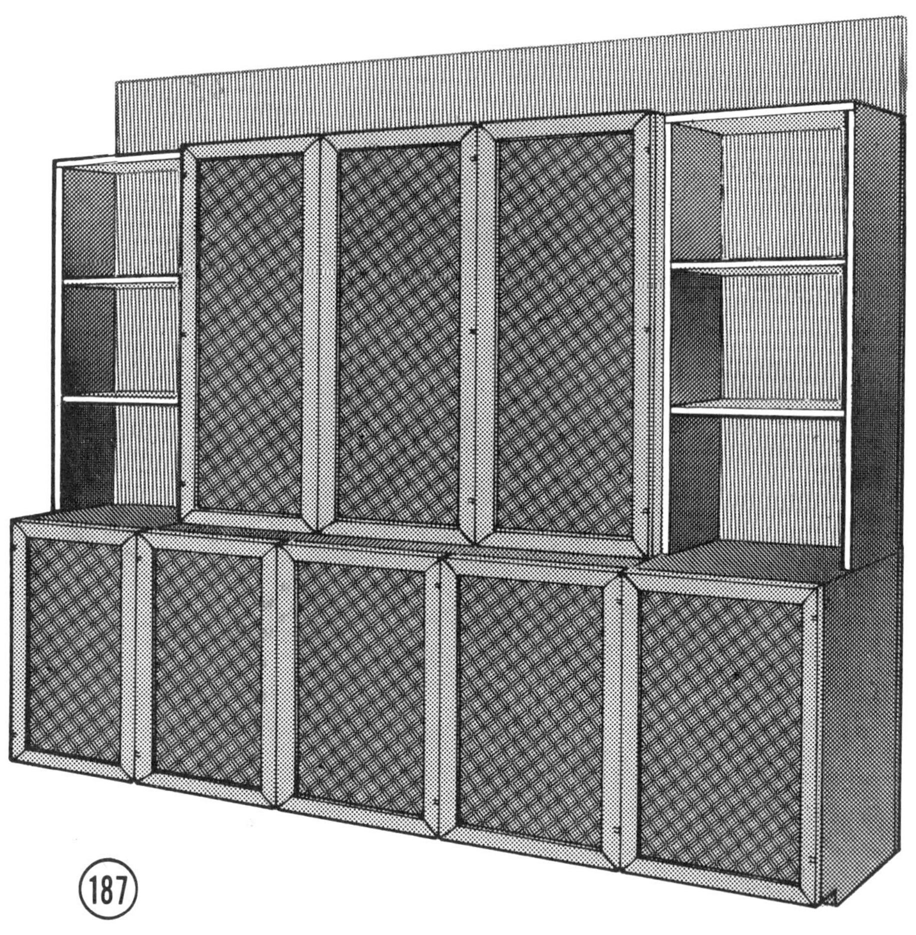

Those who decide to build cabinets for others should make up sample doors. Use ¾'' prefinished plywood, Illus. 186, or acoustic fabric, Illus. 187. Many customers will supply fabric, paneling or wallpaper for door inserts.

146

INDIRECT LIGHTING VALANCE

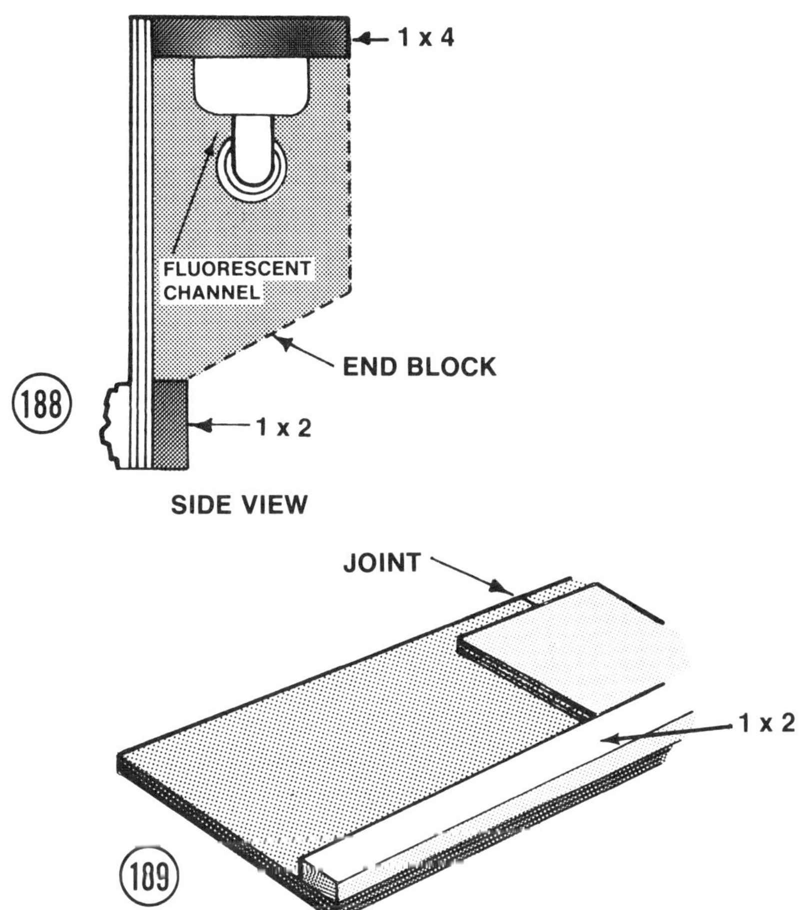

Illus. 188 shows how a matching plywood indirect lighting valance can be installed. Measure space available, i.e., width of cabinet or wall to wall. Apply matching paneling to wall above cabinet, or to back of cabinet if you live in an apartment, Illus. 187.

Cut ¼'' paneling 8'' wide by length required for valance, Illus. 189. Keep grain in direction shown on cutting diagram. When making a long valance, butt joints end to end over a stiffener.

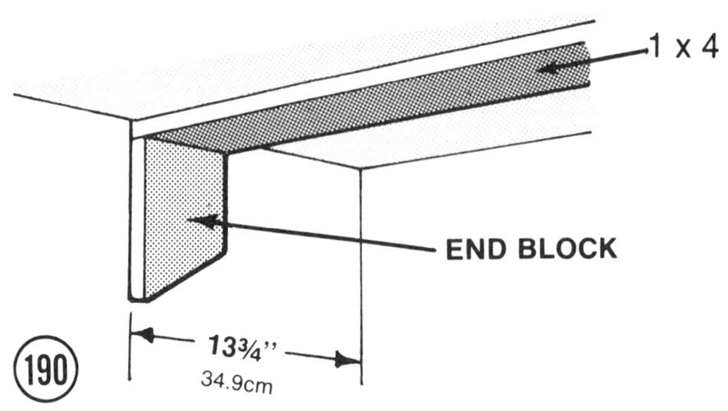

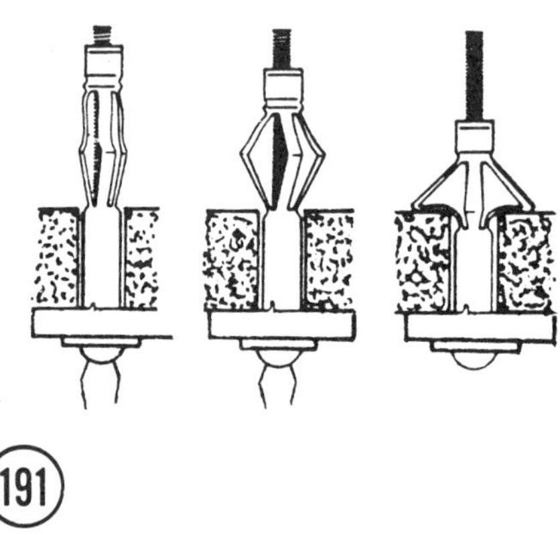

Cut a 1 x 2 to full length of valance. Glue and nail valance to 1 x 2.

Cut 1 x 4 to length required. Cut two 1 x 4 x 5½'' end blocks. Nail 1 x 4 to end blocks, Illus. 190.

Nail 1 x 4 to ceiling, 13¾'' from wall. Nail to ceiling joists. If ceiling joists run parallel to 1 x 4, drill holes through 1 x 4 and ceiling. Secure 1 x 4 in place with hollow wall fasteners, Illus. 191.

Apply glue and fasten carved wood trim across bottom edge of valance, Illus. 188. Hold with clamps until glue sets.

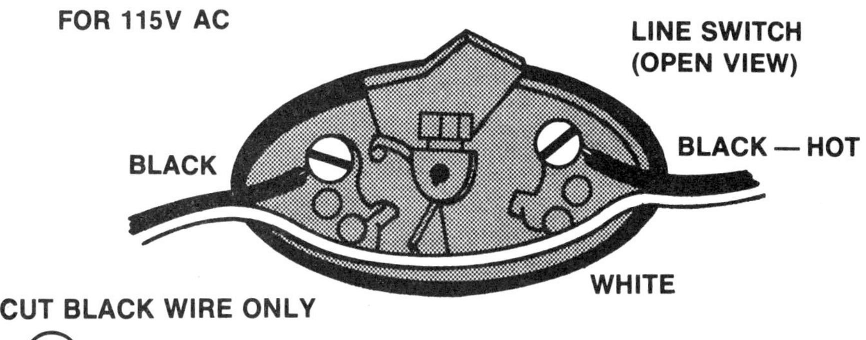

(192)

Fasten fluorescent channel to 1 x 4, ½'' from front edge, following channel manufacturer's directions. Connect to wall outlet. A line switch, Illus. 192, is connected as shown.

(193)

Apply glue, nail or screw valance in position. Cover bottom exposed edge of 1 x 2 with matching wood trim, paint or stain.

Those who go professional and build stereo cabinets for others should recommend installation of a line switch, Illus. 192, in the power line, or a toggle switch in a speaker line, Illus. 193. When an incoming call requires instant quiet, a conveniently located switch is greatly appreciated.

TO INSTALL AN EXTRA RECEPTACLE

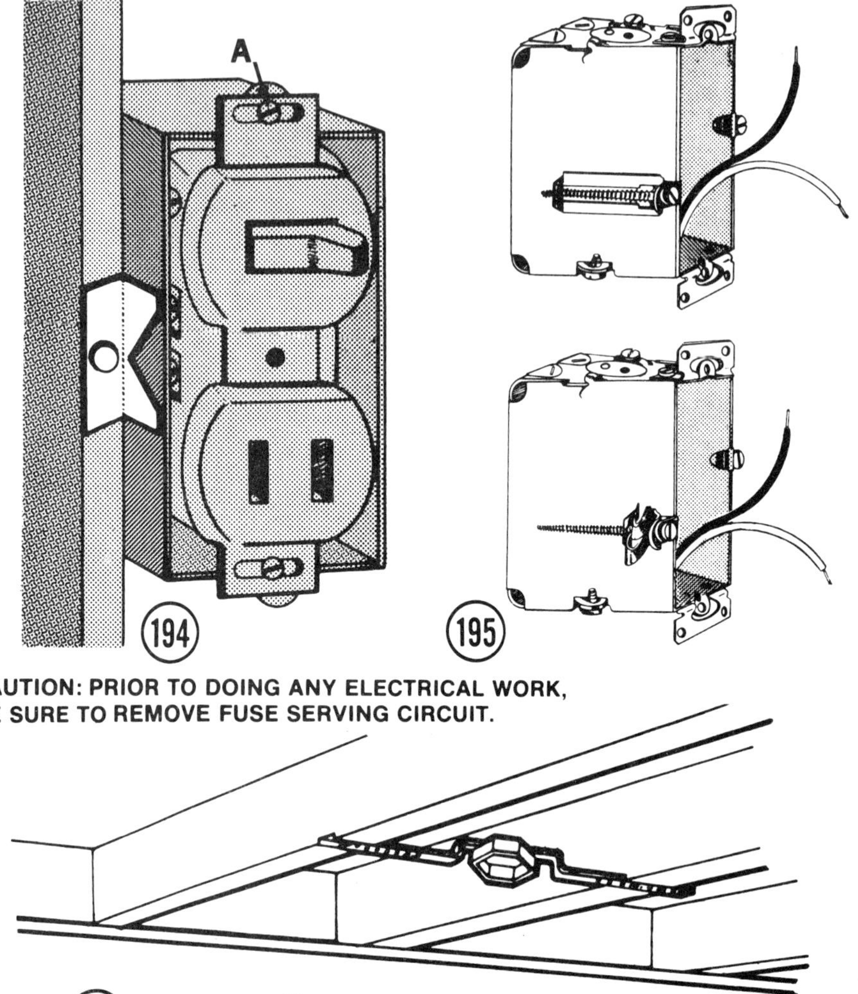

CAUTION: PRIOR TO DOING ANY ELECTRICAL WORK,
BE SURE TO REMOVE FUSE SERVING CIRCUIT.

Receptacle boxes come in different shapes and sizes. Each can be nailed to studs, Illus. 194, or fastened in position to plaster or wallboard with expansion ears, Illus. 195; mounting hangers, Illus. 196; or fastened to 1 x 2 or 2 x 4's nailed between studs, Illus. 213.

150

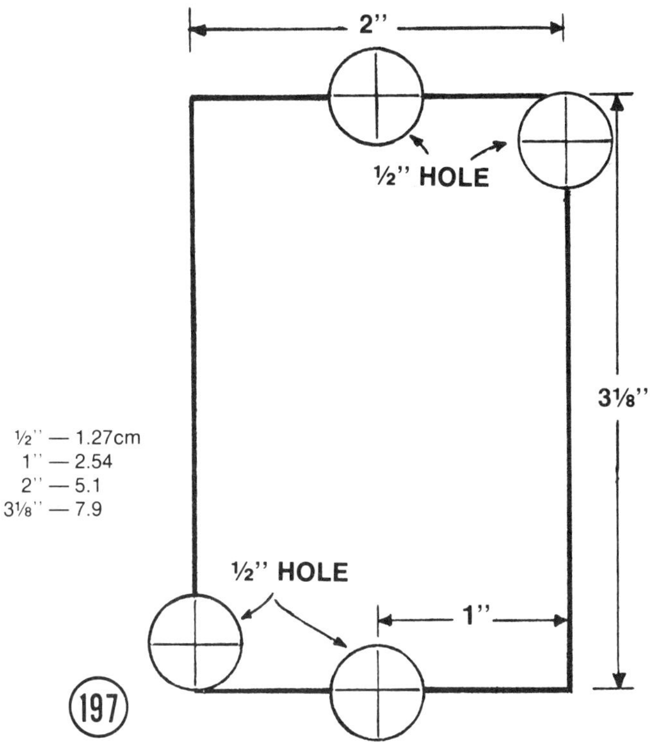

To install a box in a gypsum, paneled or plastered wall, saw hole to size and shape box requires, Illus. 197. Snake BX or armored cable through hole. Fasten connector to cable, Illus. 198; the connector to box. Place box in opening. Turn screw in ear, Illus. 195. This secures box in position.

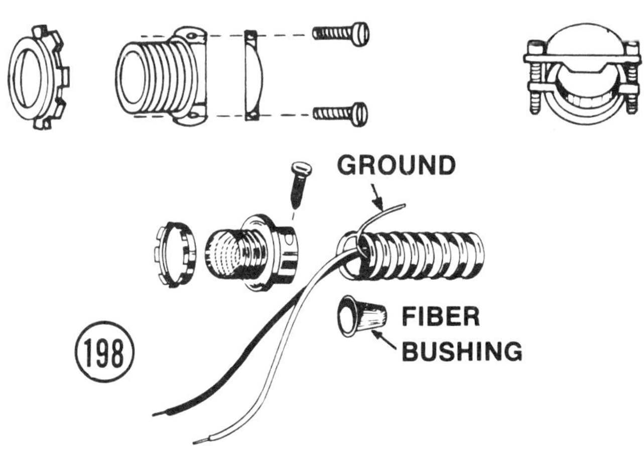

Receptacle, switch, fixture or junction boxes, all serve one purpose, to provide a safe housing and for mounting the switch, receptacle or fixture. The shape of the box is selected for its end use. Receptacle boxes can be taken apart. Two or more may be assembled together when you want to double up on switches or receptacles, Illus. 199. Loosen screw B, remove side and join another box.

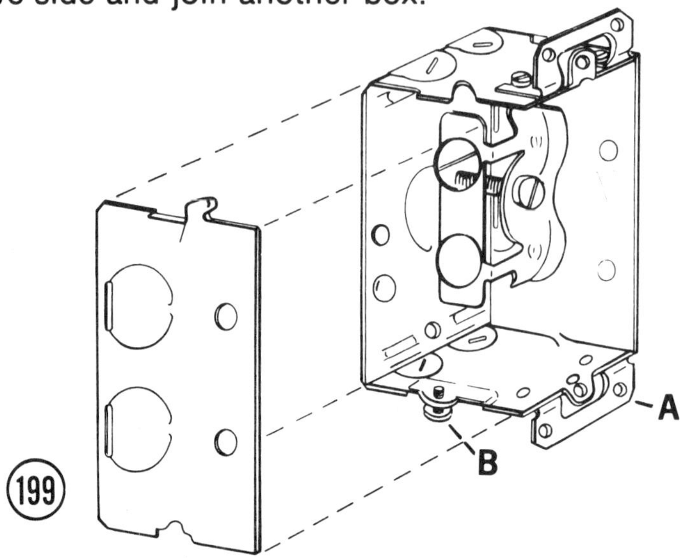

All receptacle boxes should be installed so they finish flush with plaster or wallboard. Where wall covering permits, ears A, Illus. 199, can be screwed to framing with No. 5 wood screws.

If you want to project box ½", for ½" gypsum board, reverse the ears, Illus. 200.

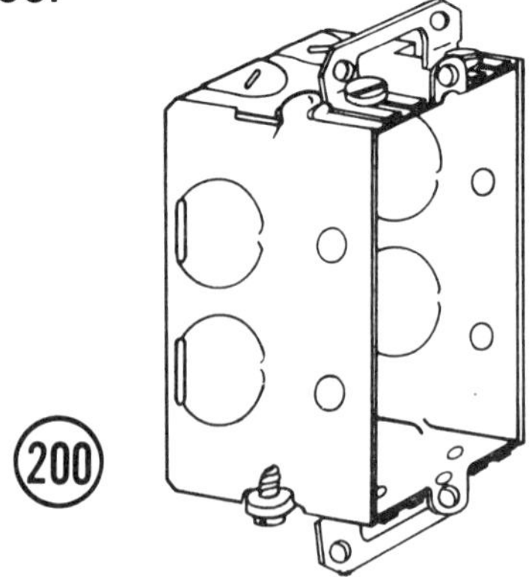

When paneling a wall, adjust screws A, Illus. 194. This permits switch to finish flush. If you need to apply furring strips, nail boxes to furring strips in position shown, Illus. 201. Boxes can also be fastened to side of stud.

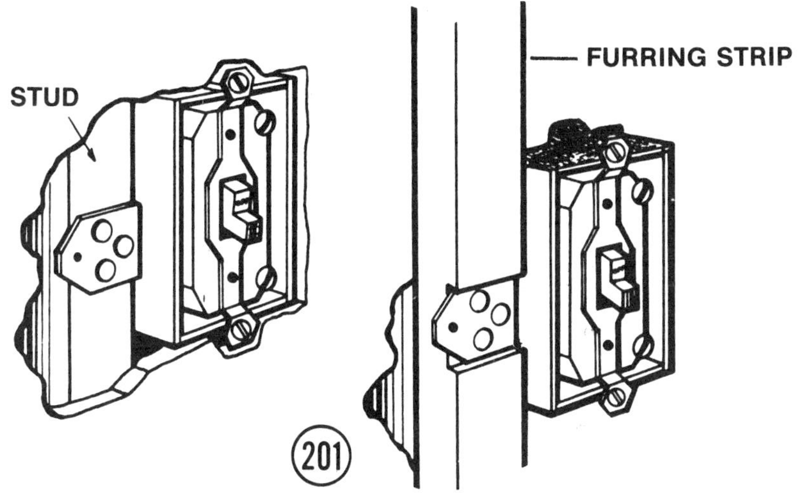

All cable must be connected to a receptacle box. Pre-punched knockouts in box, Illus. 202, permit installing cable where it's most convenient. While some knockouts can be pried out by inserting the tip of a screw driver in slot, others require knocking out.

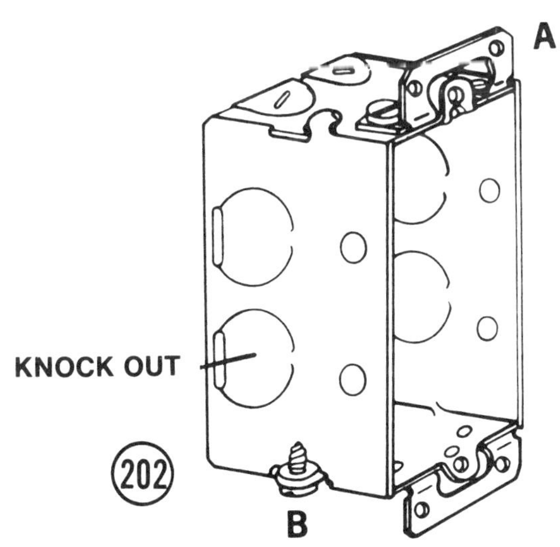

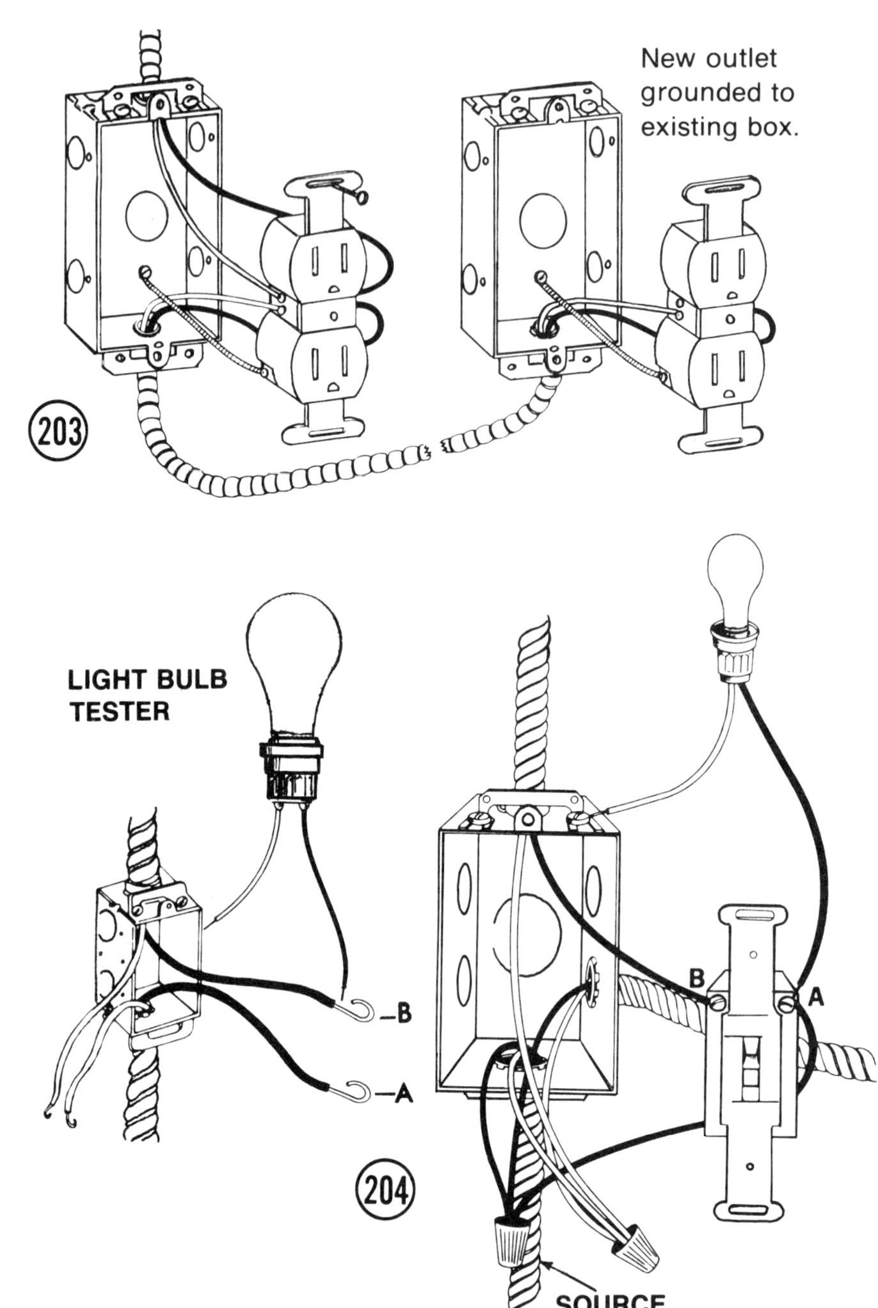

If you add a receptacle beyond one that's not controlled by a switch, Illus. 203, the new one will also be continually alive. If you install a receptacle beyond one that's controlled by a switch, the new one will be switch controlled.

154

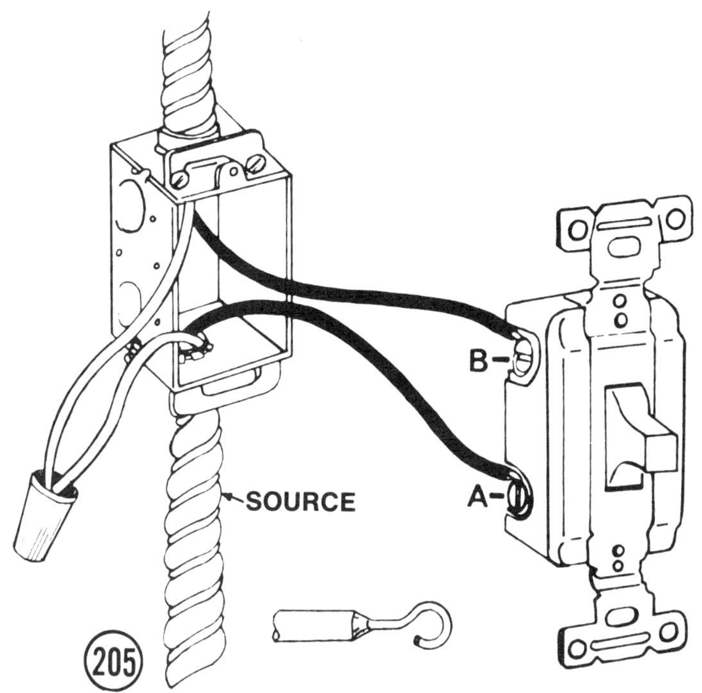

Any junction box that contains a white neutral, Illus. 203, 204, 205, can provide source of power.

If you need an extra receptacle, and want to make a quick installation by removing a single pole switch to install a combination switch and receptacle, Illus. 206, it can be done if you find a neutral wire in box, Illus. 204, 205.

1 — BLACK FROM SOURCE
2 — GROUND TO RECEPTACLE
3 — WHITE FROM SOURCE
WHITE TO OUTLET
4 — BLACK

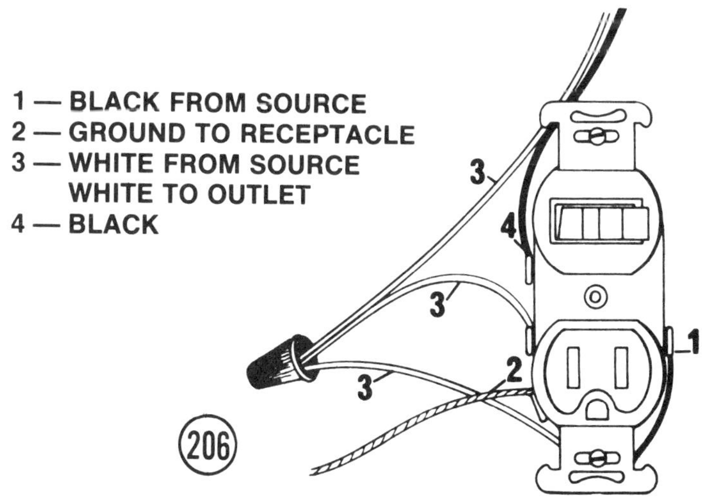

Remove plate and screws holding switch in receptacle. Pull out switch. If you find one or more white wires, fastened with a wire nut, you have a neutral line and can install a combination switch and receptacle.

If you find a white and black fastened to a switch, or the ends of the white painted black, Illus. 207, this is a switch loop. Both wires will test hot when switch is on. You should not, according to code, install receptacle.

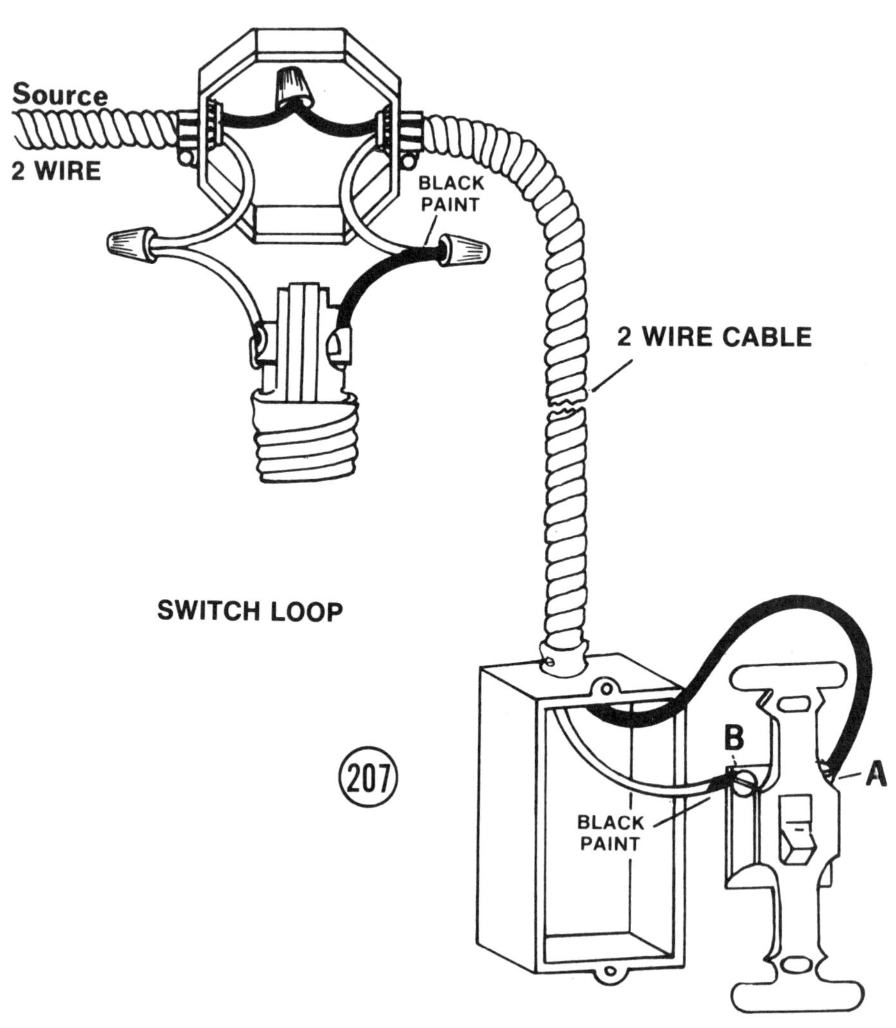

First floor receptacles can be connected to any junction box in basement, Illus. 208, or to an existing receptacle. Receptacles installed in second floor rooms can frequently be connected to a junction box in attic, Illus. 209.

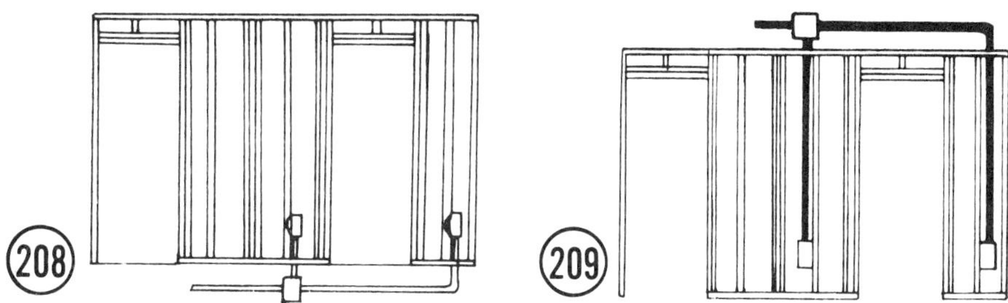

Always install a new receptacle or switch at same height from floor as existing ones. Install between studs in gypsum board, or plastered walls; to studs in new construction.

Follow this general procedure to install a receptacle, switch or fixture:

1. Disconnect fuse to power source.
2. Select location, in new construction, fasten box in position.
3. Locate a power source, another receptacle, junction box, etc.
4. Cut opening for box (when remodeling).
5. Drill holes required to run cable.
6. Remove knockout in position cable requires.
7. Strip cable to allow a 6" pigtail if BX or nonmetallic cable is used; 8" if wires are run through conduit.
8. Insert fiber bushing if BX is used.
9. Fasten connectors to cable.
10. Insert pigtails through hole in box.
11. When remodeling, fasten connectors to box, box in position.
12. Connect pigtails to switch, receptacle or fixture.
13. Connect pigtails to source.
14. Replace fuse.

Wall studs in older houses were frequently spaced 18 to 24" on centers. During the past 30 years, houses were built with studs 16" on centers.

An outside wall frame, Illus. 210, that contains a picture or a bow window will usually be framed with a double 2 x 4 plate, double 2 x 8, or larger headers over windows. Window sills will be a single or double 2 x 4. House framing varies with local codes, different builders, and the trend at time house was constructed.

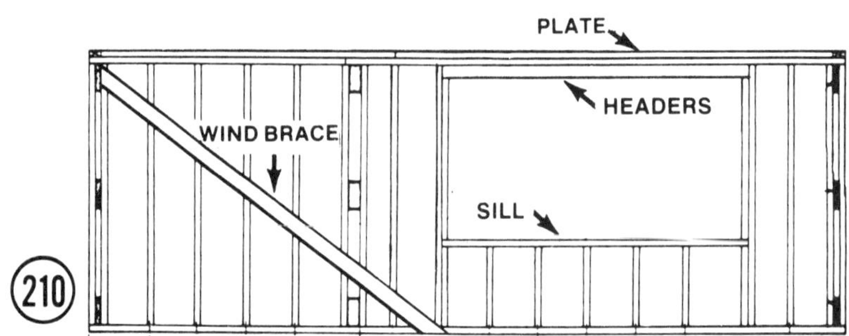

Interior doors were usually framed with a double 2 x 4 or 2 x 6 header on edge, Illus. 211. Whenever interior walls butt together, you invariably find 2 x 4 spacer blocks A. These will be 1½'' A, when edgewise, 3½'' when used flatwise. Lumber now used in house framing measures: 2 x 4 - 1½ x 3½''; 2 x 6 - 1½ x 5½''; 2 x 8 - 1½ x 7¼''.

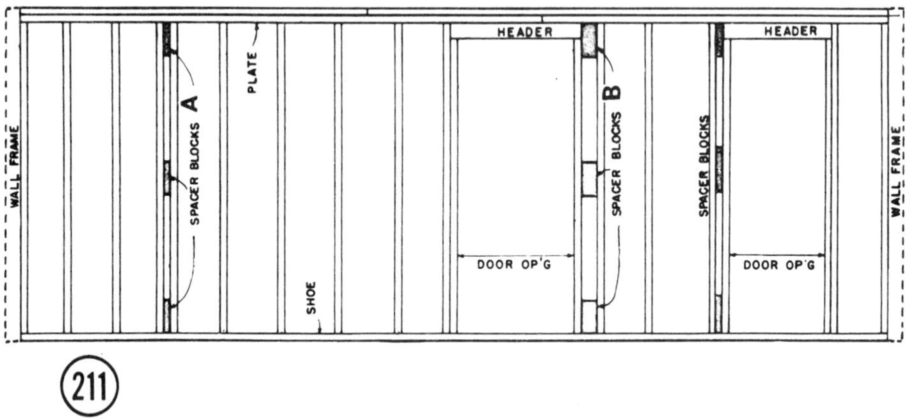

Partitions are frequently stiffened with 2 x 4 cats, Illus. 212. Nail 1 x 2 or 2 x 4's in position shown if you want to install a box between studs, Illus. 213.

158

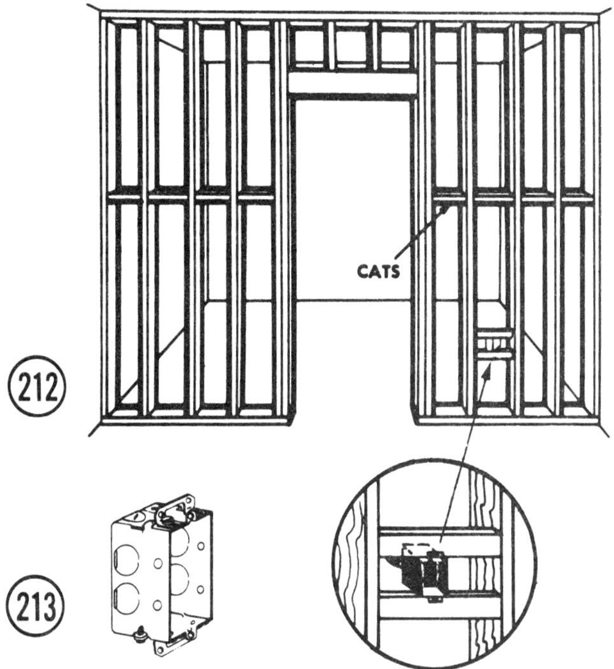

(212)

(213)

To simplify installing a new receptacle, always try to connect it to an existing one. This can be done in a number of different ways.

You can remove a shoe molding or cove, Illus. 214, bevel plane the edge, and bury the wire underneath, or under a baseboard, Illus. 215. Or notch the plaster or wallboard to receive nonmetallic cable. New patching cements simplify repairs.

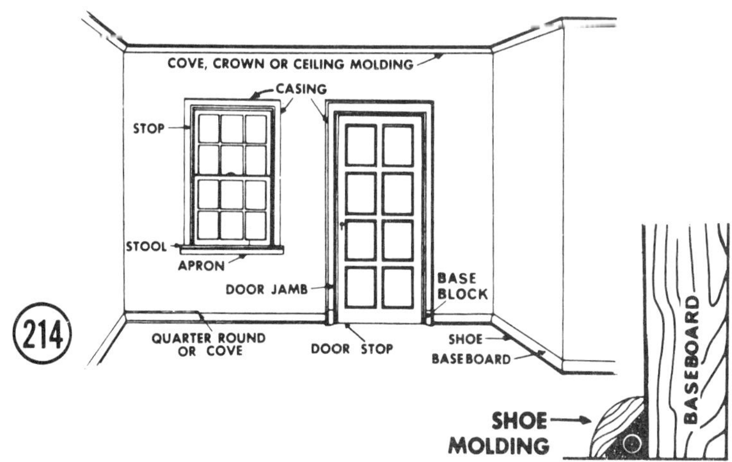

(214)

159

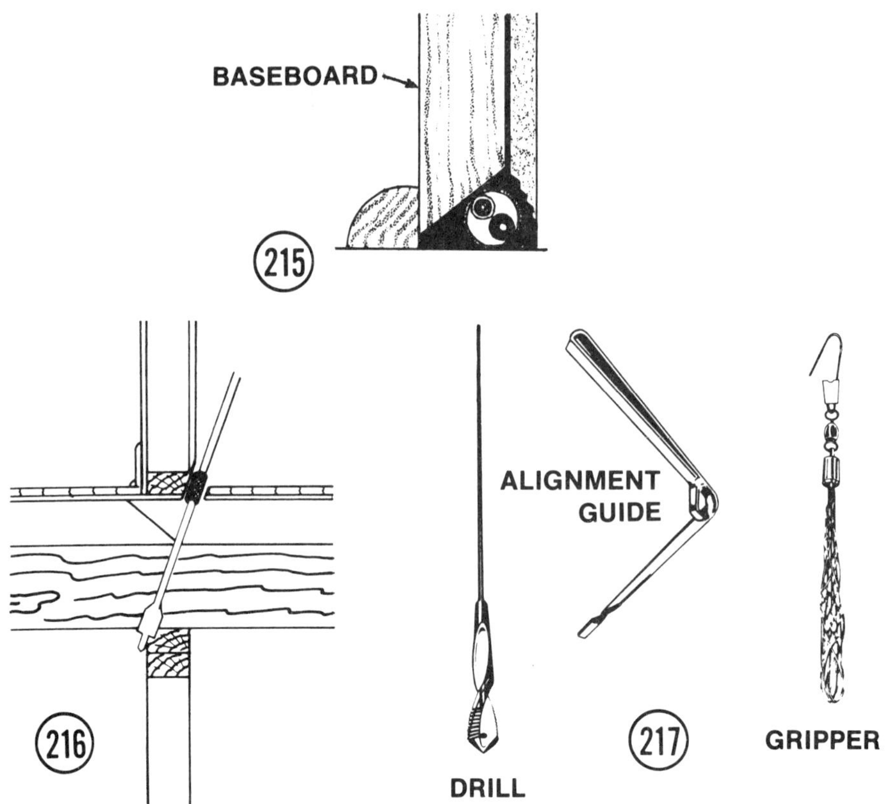

If you have to run a line into the basement, remove the shoe molding. Use a ⅝ or ¾'' spade bit, Illus. 216, fastened to an 18 or 24'' extension to drill through.

New tools now simplify running BX in the easiest possible manner. These consist of a ⅜ x 54'' long spring steel flexible shaft drill, Illus. 217, an alignment guide, plus a wire gripper. The gripper permits using the drill as a snake.

To fully appreciate how easily this can be done, note Illus. 218. After removing shoe or ceiling molding, or after selecting a location for a receptacle, drill a 1'' hole in position required for the alignment guide. The guide is inserted in the hole. The ⅜ x 54'' bit is inserted in a variable speed drill. The bit goes through hole in guide and is guided to arc through between joists into the basement or attic. The 54'' length permits drilling clear through.

160

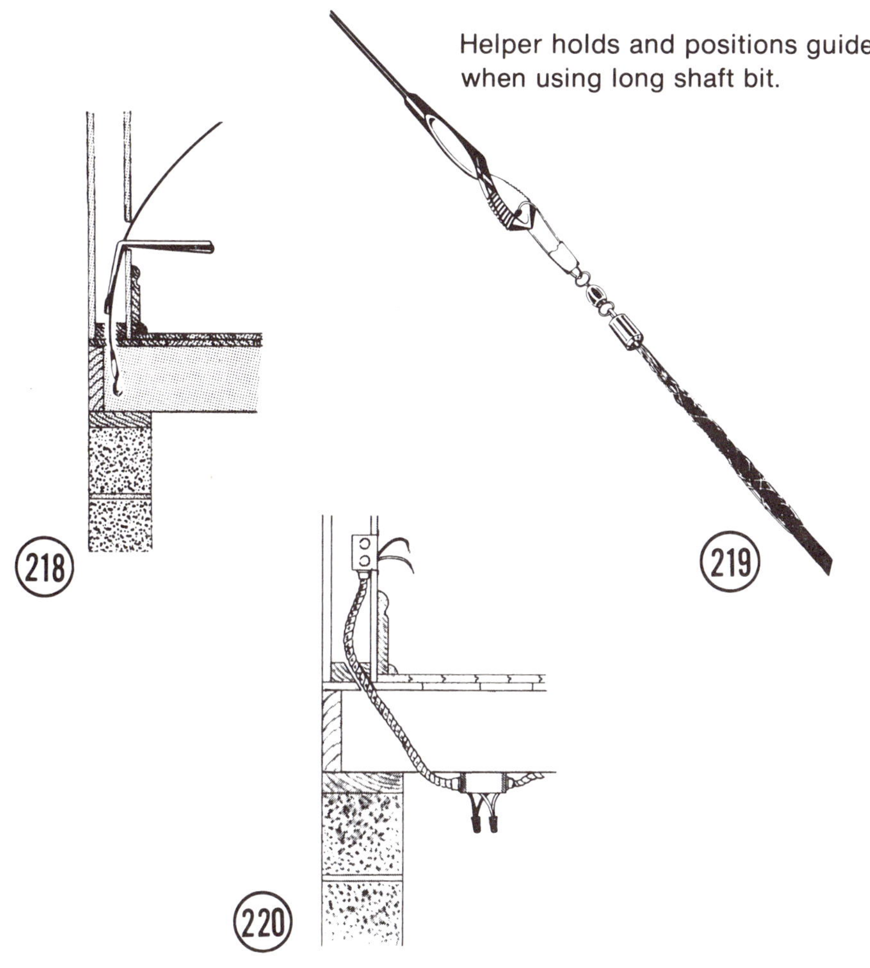

The spring steel permits keeping the arc while drilling. Since you drill at a slow speed, 850 rpm, you can maintain the position of the bit despite the arc.

When you have drilled clear through, merely fasten the safety pin on end of gripper onto the end of the bit, Illus. 219; insert cable into gripper, remove guide and draw bit and cable back up through the hole, Illus. 220.

Use a variable speed drill (850 to 1500 rpm) with a reverse gear. Consider obtaining these tools from a tool rental store if you don't wish to buy.

To run a cable through a wall from a room above, the long bit greatly simplifies the job. If you measure distance from an outside wall, you can usually cut opening for a box in direct line with hole. If you run into a cat halfway between, chip the plaster and recess the cable, Illus. 221. Cover notch with a steel plate, patch plaster.

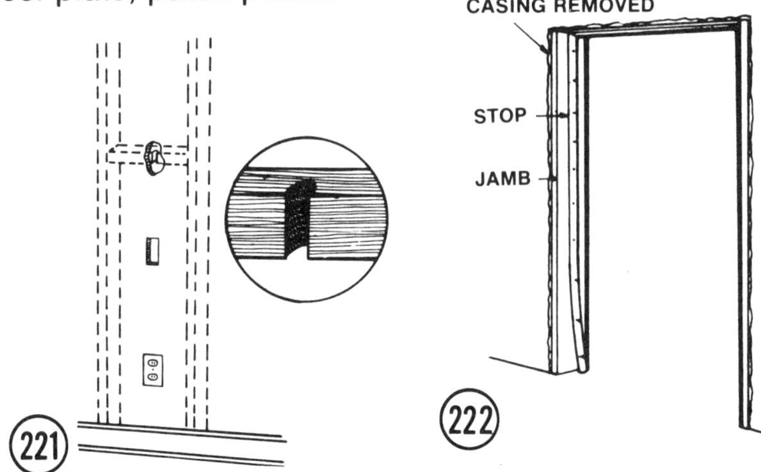

If you want to install a receptacle beyond a door, and you can't conveniently connect to a junction box in basement, you can plant cable under baseboard and under door casing. Illus. 222 shows casing removed from an interior door. This is usually nailed with 8 penny finishing nails.

To remove, start at base block, Illus. 214. Carefully pry it loose. Using a pry bar, placed under center of bottom end of casing, carefully pry up casing. When side casing is removed, pry up to top casing, then remaining side. Notch plaster or wallboard close to jamb to depth cable requires. Fasten cable in recess, then replace casing. Countersink nails, fill holes with putty or wood filler, then repaint casing.

When planning new receptacles, always make a survey. For example, if you install a receptacle below a picture window, or in a wall opposite an existing receptacle, consider whether it's easier to make a connection to a junction box in basement, or from an existing receptacle, rather than go around a door. Make certain junction box selected can take extra wires.

162

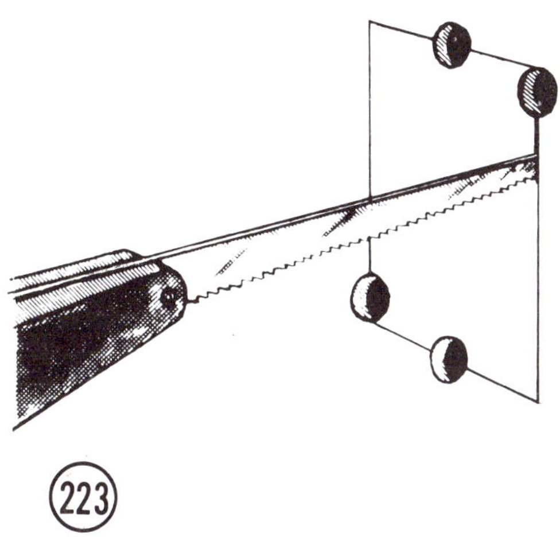

If you are installing a box in a lath and plaster wall, punch a small hole in position selected. Using a screw driver, chisel a narrow vertical slot to expose width of one lath. Use the full size template, Illus. 197, to draw outline of box. Position template so it's only necessary to saw and remove one piece of lath, and only notch the lath above and below.

While this may alter exact height of box, no one will know if you don't tell them. Drill ½" holes in position noted, Illus. 223. Saw plaster along line of template with a metal cutting keyhole saw, or use a hacksaw blade. Place a small block of wood alongside line of opening and hole saw blade so it only cuts when pulled toward you. If you press block when you pull blade, you can make a clean cut. If you tear plaster off wall, same can be repaired with patching plaster after box has been fastened in place.

A combination switch and outlet is available with screw terminals, Illus. 206.

Read and follow directions provided by manufacturer. Before you begin, turn the existing switch on and remove proper fuse in panel.

Remove screw and cover plate. Remove screws and pull existing switch out of box. Remove wires from existing switch. If you use a pressure lock outlet, straighten bare wire ½". Be sure to measure and cut it exactly ½".

Always strip insulation off ½" of wire.

If a splice is required, strip insulation wire as shown in Illus. 224, connect wire, and wrap wire in plastic tape, Illus. 225.

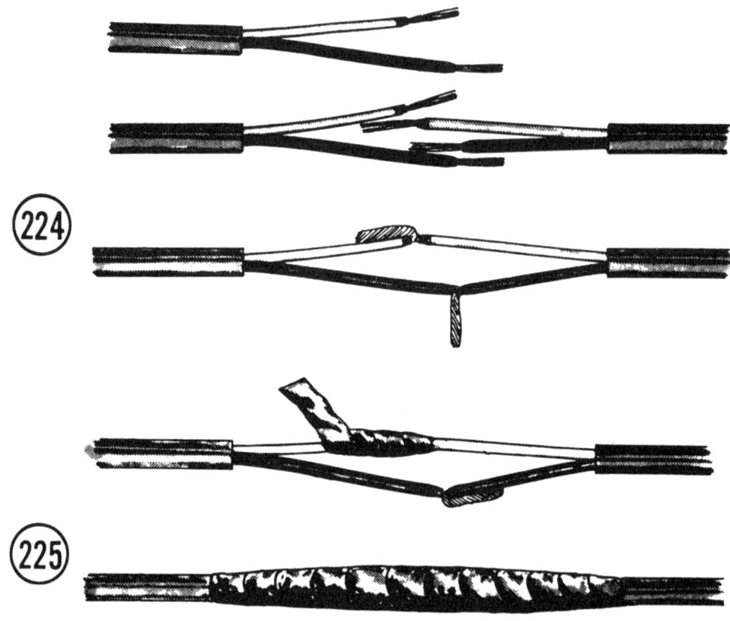

Insert receptacle in box and only start screws. Replace fuse and test switch and receptacle. If all is OK, fasten screws in place.

PLEASE NOTE:
As this book is based on the National Electrical Code (USA), modifications must be considered for use in Canada in order to ensure compliance with the Canadian Electrical Code. In Canada buy and use only those components and fittings that have been certified by CSA and that bear the CSA seal of approval. Easi-Bild Book #694 Electrical Repairs Simplified contains additional information.

how to
FIND A JOB
START A BUSINESS
Learn to Offer what Others want to Buy
No Capital Investment Required

(Excerpts from Book 850)

At a recent exhibit of high priced, custom built greenhouses, I was amazed to see the turnout consisted mainly of young people who were definitely "doing their own thing." As I visited each model, I overhead one couple discussing the economics of growing "their own." While the estimated cost of the greenhouses and equipment ran into the thousands, the price seemed to make little impression on their willingness to buy. The older couples inspecting the window and walk-in models were seriously interested in an activity, one that could consume free time the year round.

When we first introduced a build-it-yourself walk-in greenhouse pattern in 1965, and revised it each year to include a window greenhouse, and later an expandable greenhouse-sunhouse, we realized walk-in sunhouses provided motels with an income producing plus. As the book explains, sunbathing all winter has great appeal.

Today, building and selling greenhouses is a big business. Since Book #611 and the latest expanded edition #811 explain how to build from materials readily available at every home improvement center, those seeking to start a business of their own soon find customers for both the window greenhouses and the walk-ins that can be built to any length desired.

A sizeable market also exists for the easy to build toolhouse described in Book #811. As more and more people retire, finding a constructive use of time manufactures many customers. While the book simplifies building a 6'0'' x 7'9'' toolhouse, directions also explain how to lengthen it to size desired. This structure makes an ideal hobby shop, one that accommodates a workbench, photo darkroom, as well as provide instant relief to the storage of gardening tools which usually clutter most garages.

With living space for singles in short supply, and heating costs driving most homeowners up the wall, many are transforming basements into living space. Book #615 How to Modernize a Basement explains every step. It tells how to install a basement entry door if one isn't available. It also suggests building a walk through greenhouse as a vestibule for the entry. Every gardening enthusiast and plant lover flips when they see this combination. Since it provides a leisure time activity as well as shelter, it warrants a better than average rent. Modernizing a basement, with or without a greenhouse, not only produces rental income, but also a long term Capital Gains

come the day you decide to sell. This book, like others in the series, enables every reader to experience doing something they have never done before without leaving home. How each of us uses time determines how well we will live.

Losing a job may, in the long run, prove to be one of the luckiest things that happened, providing you transform the spare time into a constructive effort. Turning unused space into an income producing apartment, as explained in Books #603, 609, 615, 665 and 773, enables every reader to learn a profitable trade. Building a dormer, as explained in Books

#603 and 773, enables every reader to raise the roof to obtain additional headroom if same is needed. When you make this improvement, you gain experience. Neighbors see what you have done and many will want the same job done.

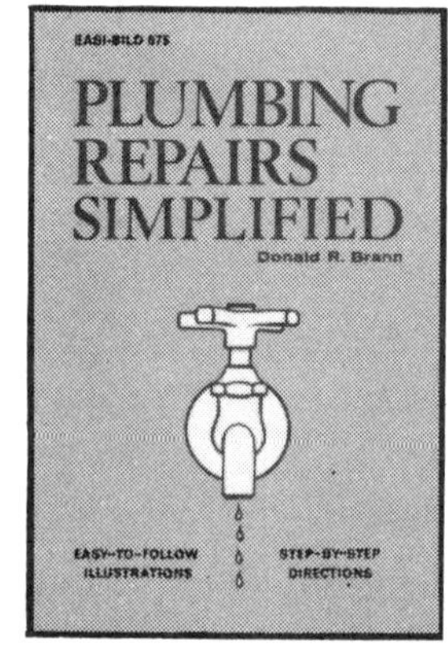

Besides explaining every step so everyone can transform an attic into highly acceptable space, Books #665 and 773 explain how to build inside stairs, while Book #763 explains how to build a second story deck and outside stairs.

Since a basement, attic or garage apartment needs a kitchenette and bathroom, read Books #675 Plumbing Repairs Simplified, #682 How to Add an Extra Bathroom and Book #758 or 608 How to Modernize a Kitchen.

Living requires doing. Unless we keep expanding our sphere of activity, we begin to die long before we have begun to live. The author believes everyone who can read can do everything he describes in each book. This is like having a second brain. All books were created to fill an important need. What you do in your home, you can do for others.

We live in a unique period. The American free enterprise system could go down the drain if the laws of the land allow the lawless to dictate terms of employment, who should be allowed to work, or go on welfare. The future of this nation depends on those who believe that everybody has the right to work wherever they want, for whatever wage they are willing to take.

For those who have little faith in their ability to go it alone, the first step is to rebuild self confidence. Getting to know The Real You, and your true potential, requires a continual appraisal of all plus and minus factors. Discovering who you are, and what you can accomplish, can prove to be one of life's most exciting adventures. Remember, the letters TRY, represent The Real You.

Everyone who wants a career in carpentry and cabinet making should read this book. When you know what needs to be done, make an installation. Note the savings achieved and how the completed unit makes you feel feet taller.

Learning to transform time into a way of life that satisfies one's physical, economic, marital and mental needs provides a lesson in living relatively few master. All too often a youthful attempt that failed creates loss of confidence, a no man's land that discourages trying again. Always remember, one's capabilities and confidence, like the ever changing hands on a clock, are in continual motion. What we couldn't do yesterday is frequently easy to do today.

Gaining experience is the first step. This was clearly illustrated many years ago when we received the first of three letters from an inmate in a state penetentiary. Signed only by the prisoner's number, the letter inquired whether we would mail a discarded copy of our bookcase book. He had begun to read a copy in the prison library, but due to time allowed, needed a copy to study in his cell. Having no funds, he asked for a free copy. Months later we received a second letter thanking us. He reported making scale models in the prison workshop. These gave him experience and confidence. It also strengthened his desire to do this work on release.

Several years later, we received a third letter, still signed by the same prisoner number. It stated he was out of prison and determined to stay that way. On release he had applied for a job in a home improvement center. During an interview, he showed the scale models and explained how he had gained experience. By an odd coincidence, the interviewer had also worked from an Easi-Bild book when making lawn furniture. When asked what wage he expected, he promptly answered, "Pay whatever you can afford." His frankness in revealing a prison record, his willingness to work, and to accept whatever sum the employer could pay, cinched the interview. The letter went on to say that after two of the best years of his life he left to start his own business. It closed with this statement, "Thanks to that Easi-Bild book you mailed me many years ago, I am now, at 48, beginning to live the kind of life I should have lived the past 30 years."

Your destiny is controlled entirely by one factor, i.e., how you use time. A teenager seeking work, a retiree climbing the walls with boredom, or an executive living under great stress soon discovers each book offers a magical use of time. Each provides Instant Escape without hitting a bottle. A case in point is Book #792. The nation is currently investing big money in purchasing collectibles of every kind, from china, dolls to you name it. The cases offered in

170

Book #792 shows every collector how to build museum quality display cases. It also shows everyone interested in going into a part or full time business how to turn acrylic into a fun way to earn a living. Due to high packing and shipping costs, any bulky item must be priced to include these excessive charges. When you buy acrylic locally, fabricate it into a cabinet, deliver to a gift, department, jewelry or silverware retailer, your price can be less than competition and still insure a profitable margin.

Almost everyone of every age develops a fondness for an animal. Encouraging this interest can help a 14 year old or retiree develop a business selling or renting pet shelters as explained in Book #751. This not only tells how to build a doghouse, dog kennel, cat entry, catpartment, parakeet cage, rabbit hutch, a duck inn, and much, much more, but also explains how everyone, regardless of age, can create income boarding cats in a catpartment, dogs in a kennel, or parakeets in an easy to build cage. The catpartment is easy to build. It contains three rooms, a sleeping, feeding and dropping area. No one but the owner need handle the cat. As everyone who has boarded a cat soon learns, the remuneration can be very profitable. Since cat lovers like to travel, finding a home for a pet while they are away is important to their peace of mind.

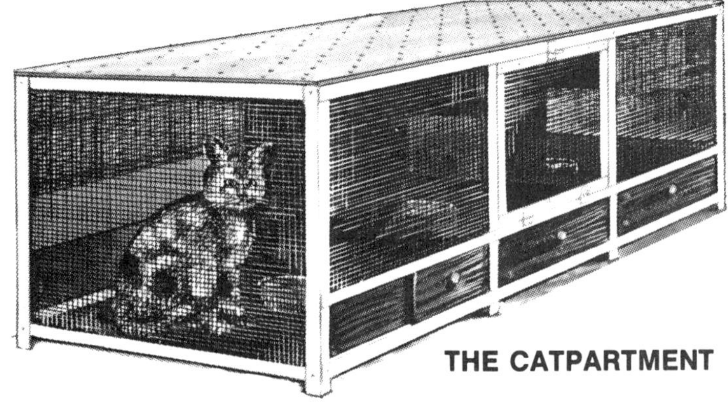

THE CATPARTMENT

172

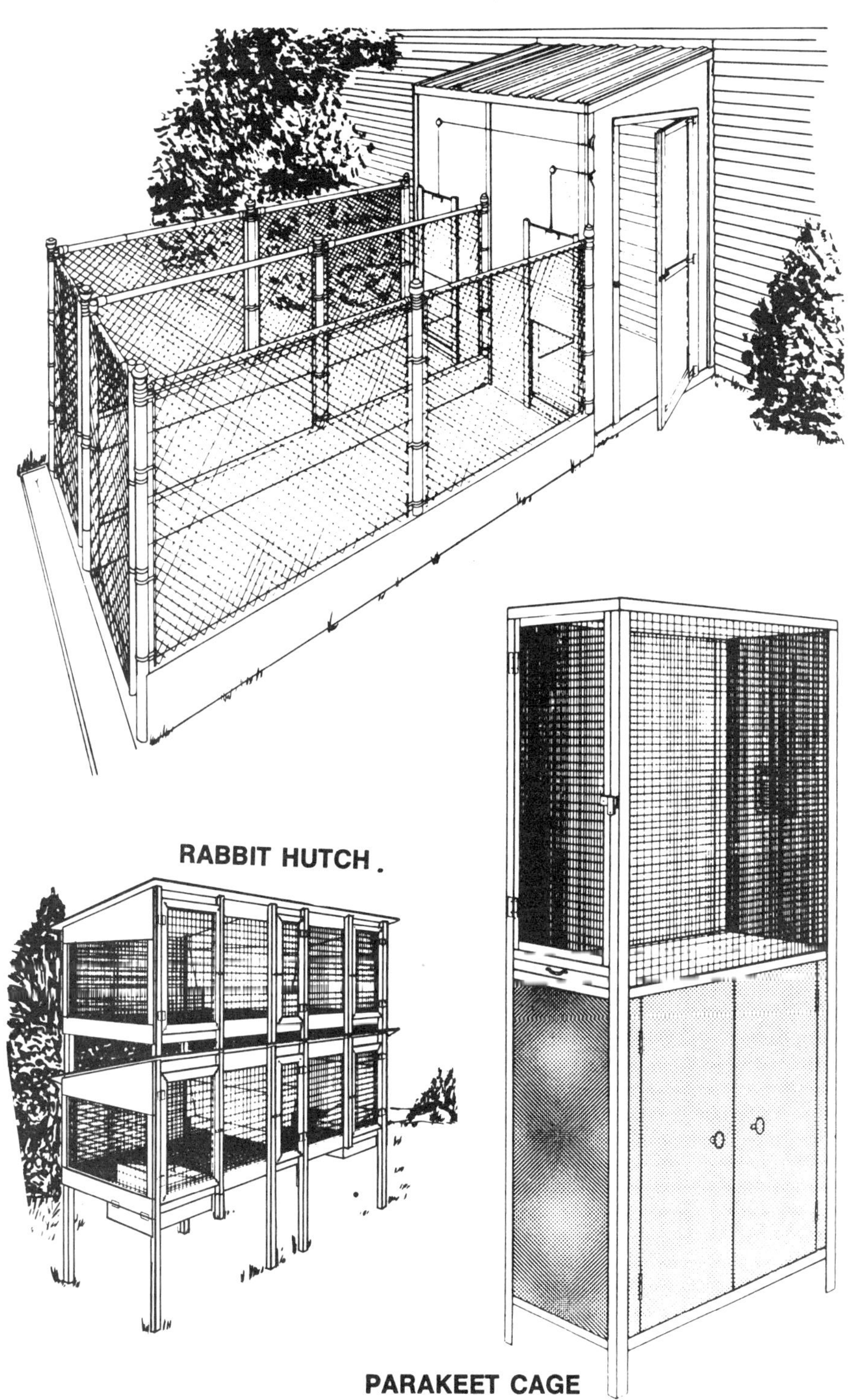

RABBIT HUTCH .
PARAKEET CAGE

Encouraging a youngster to watch while you build a shelter for his pet, allowing him to participate in its construction, can shape a lifetime interest in working with his hands. Every decision you make, every action you take, helps shape a child's future. In today's society, survival depends on turning the youngster into an individual, one who can withstand the pressures of his peers.

This book is an inanimate object that can generate positive vibrations. It explains how the Impulse Power, inherent in every problem, can be harnessed to create a better way of life. As this book goes to press, the nation is beginning to relive an economic period it witnessed many times in the past. As unemployment rises, finding work becomes increasingly more difficult for all who follow previous channels of thought. It is during these periods opportunity begins to knock on many doors.

This was clearly illustrated in a letter from a shop foreman. While a long time employee of a company making parts for the auto industry, he began getting "temporary layoffs" all too frequently. As his unemployment benefits began running out, he started climbing the walls with worry.

With time to think and observe, he realized the talk of a drug problem in the above average income school, attended by his two teenage daughters, was far more serious than he previously realized. Three of his closest neighbors' children were already hooked. His girls had one overwhelming interest — horses. To keep them occupied, interested and too busy to become joiners, he had encouraged them to ride regularly. Now, without income, it had to stop. This created a need to find other activities which he realized made them vulnerable to their peers.

Living on three acres, close to a state park that contained excellent trails, he read Book #679 How to Build a Stable. He

174

discussed the idea with his local bank to ascertain whether he could obtain a loan needed to buy material. His appraisal of the situation was unique and intelligent. Unless he could keep his daughters interested in a healthy, time consuming activity, they could easily become part of a growing group experimenting with drugs and sex. Since all material needed to build a stable costs less than a drug cure, it had much to offer. In addition, two other practical aspects entered his thinking. Good stable facilities were in short supply, and he needed something to do until he could go back to his job. Up to this point, his entire adult life had revolved around the kind of work he had followed since leaving school. Much to his surprise, the bank vice president in charge of mortgage loans also recognized the potential and approved a loan. Having daughters with the same hobby, he and his wife were also deeply concerned. While discussing the loan, the vice president inquired what board he would have to charge to make the investment feasible.

On finding a loan was possible, he discussed building a stable and boarding horses with his family. It created so much enthusiasm no one slept for the next three nights. Since finding boarders would be no problem, the question of chores, feeding, mucking out and grooming, was soon settled. From the moment the decision to build was made, the transformation in the girls' use of time was complete. No longer was either one dependent on a friend to do this or that. No longer was an invitation needed to have a good time. Each invested every spare hour helping in its construction, running errands for needed material. Each developed maturity and experience as they invested every spare hour making a dream come true. No work was too difficult. Even helping to mix cement, putting in footings, foundation and framing were fun ways to spend time. Building the barn absorbed all free time for almost eight months. Long before completion, six boarders wanted to rent three stalls.

The monthly income from boarders helped pay interest and principal on the loan, while the new building added a sizeable Capital Gains to the value of the property.

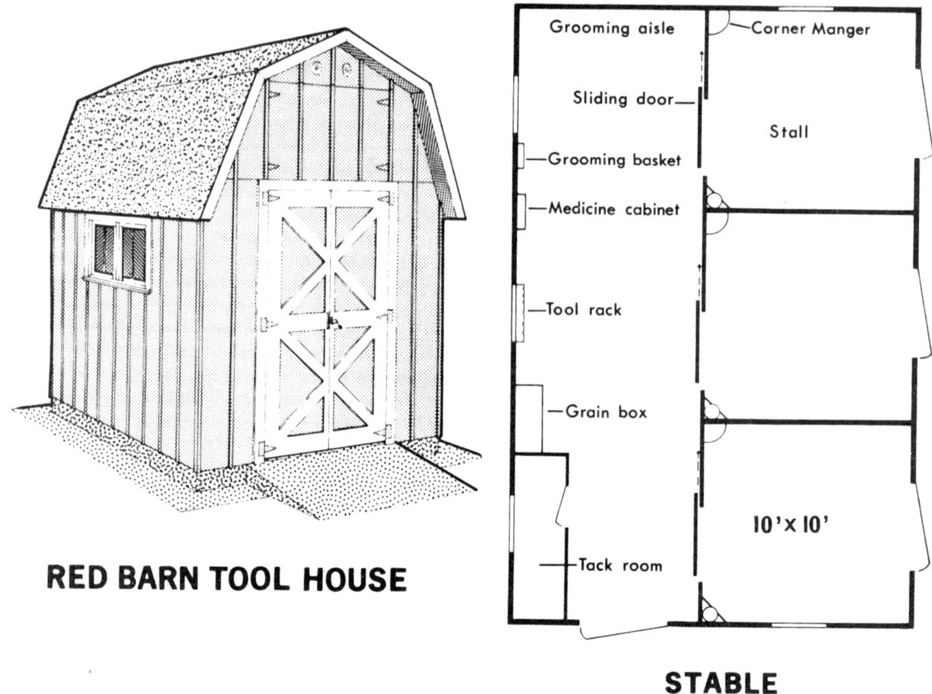

RED BARN TOOL HOUSE

STABLE

Both girls began to live a way of life they had only previously dreamed possible. Being permitted to exercise the horses whenever an owner couldn't ride, both soon turned into excellent riders and experienced horsewomen. Both only took time out for their studies. The father went back to the factory but was no longer satisfied doing what he had been doing for so many years. When word of the completed stable and the activity it created began to circulate, he was soon asked to build a barn for another family. One building led to another. Since being a carpenter and builder was far more satisfying, he gladly gave up the factory and decided to go it on his own. According to a recent letter, he has built a total of eight of the three box stall barns, and one stretched out version containing 12 stalls. In between, he built the red barn toolhouses. These he sold to garden supply and home improvement centers as well as homeowners.

If you find yourself resenting, rather than resolving problems, you have lots of comany. Most everyone considers a problem as something negative, when in no small sense it contains an equal or larger volume of positive vibrations. Every invention man has ever perfected started its life as a need — a problem someone did something about.

Book #758 explains how to modernize a kitchen, build base and wall cabinets and handsome pole type furniture.

There are many logical, financial and psychologically sound reasons that influence a homeowner to modernize a kitchen. If the cabinets, walls or floor need repair, if the place is ant infested, if the family has expanded, or a new owner likes to socialize or entertain business associates, a countrystyle kitchen, complete with fireplace or woodburning stove, adds convenience, prestige and a long term Capital Gains. Its overall cost can usually be recouped when the house is sold.

Shop local competition and read the latest magazines to keep abreast with current kitchen styles. If local firms use prefinished hardwood paneling, read Book #605 and offer same. If tile kitchen floors and countertops are the latest, read Book #606. If the customer wants a low cost floor, read Book #615 and install asphalt tile.

When you visit a prospect, analyze their needs and potential. If the family is looking for a quality installation, make inquiry to find out if there is a music lover in the family. Suggest installation of a ceiling speaker so it can be connected to a stereo system as explained in Book #612. Crime is on the rise, suggest installation of the wiring contacts and bells needed for a burglary alarm as detailed in Book #695. Book #674 explains how to install a prefabricated chimney needed for a woodburning stove or fireplace, while Book #668 explains how to build a masonry fireplace and chimney.

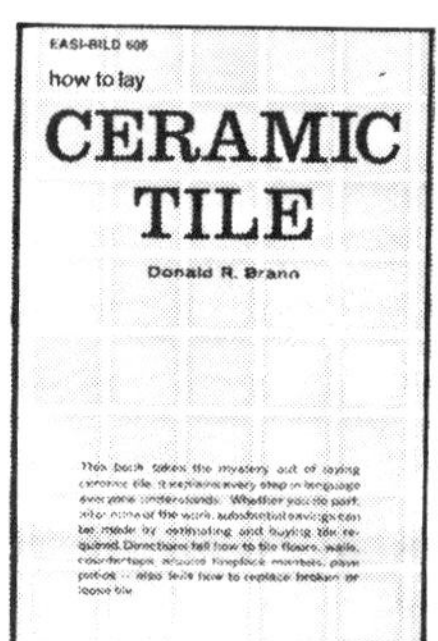

Note the complete list of Easi-Bild Books offered on pages 193, 194. Study the cross reference index and you find the answers to many problems. Always read directions before purchasing material and you soon discover THE REAL YOU.

179

Guides To Good Living

675 — Plumbing Repairs Simplified —194pp.,820 illus.

677 — How to Plan and Build a Home Workshop —98pp.,133 illus.

679 — How to Build a Stable and Red Barn Tool House —178pp.,197 illus.

680 — How to Build a One Car Garage, Carport,
  Convert a Garage to Stable —146pp.,181 illus.

682 — How to Add an Extra Bathroom —162pp.,200 illus.

683 — Carpeting Simplified —178pp.,223 illus.

684 — How to Transform a Garage into Living Space —130pp.,139 illus.

685 — How to Remodel Buildings —258pp.,345 illus.

690 — How to Build Bars —162pp.,195 illus.

694 — Electrical Repairs Simplified, Dollhouse Wiring —134pp.,218 illus.

695 — How to Install Protective Alarm Devices —130pp.,146 illus.

696 — Roofing Simplified —130pp.,168 illus.

697 — Forms, Footings, Foundations, Framing,
  Stair Building —210pp.,308 illus.

751 — How to Build Pet Housing —178pp.,252 illus.

753 — How to Build Dollhouses — Furniture —210pp.,316 illus.

754 —* How to Build Outdoor Furniture —130pp.,174 illus.

756 — Scroll Saw Projects —130pp.,146 illus.

757 —* How to Build a Kayak, 14'3'', 16'9'', 18'0'' —66pp.,plus pattern

758 — How to Modernize a Kitchen, Build Base and Wall Cabinets,
  Pole Type Furniture —210pp.,263 illus.

761 — How to Build Colonial Furniture —258pp.,342 illus.

763 —* How to Build a Two Car Garage
  with Apartment Above —194pp.,226 illus.

771 —* Toymaking and Children's Furniture Simplified —194pp.,330 illus.

773 — How to Create Room at the Top —162pp.,239 illus.

781 — How to Build a Patio, Porch and Sundeck —146pp.,220 illus.

792 — How to Build Collectors' Display Cases —194pp.,229 illus.

804 — How to Build Wall-to-Wall Bookcases
  and Stereo Cabinets —194pp.,232 illus.

811 — How to Build Greenhouses — Walk-In, Window, Sun House,
  Garden Tool House —210pp.,229 illus.

850 — How to Find a Job, Start a Business

600 — Complete Catalog — illustrates Patterns and Books —130pp.,300 illus.

Write to Easi-Bild Directions Simplified, Inc., P.O. Box 215, Briarcliff Manor, NY 10510, for complete information concerning Easi-Bild Patterns and Home Improvement Books.